THE CONSTRUCTION MANAGER

1991

Andrew M. Civitello, Jr.

PRENTICE HALL
Englewood Cliffs, New Jersey 07632

Prentice-Hall International, (U.K.) Limited, *London*
Prentice-Hall of Australia, Pty. Ltd., *Sydney*
Prentice-Hall Canada, Inc., *Toronto*
Prentice-Hall Hispanoamericana, S.A., *Mexico*
Prentice-Hall of India Private Ltd., *New Delhi*
Prentice-Hall of Japan, Inc., *Tokyo*
Prentice-Hall of Southeast Asia Pte. Ltd., *Singapore*
Editora Prentice-Hall do Brasil Ltda., *Rio de Janeiro*

© 1991 by

PRENTICE-HALL, INC.

Englewood Cliffs, N.J.

PRINTED IN THE UNITED STATES OF AMERICA

10   9   8   7   6   5   4   3   2   1

ISBN 0-13-173535-7

PRENTICE HALL
BUSINESS & PROFESSIONAL DIVISION
A division of Simon & Schuster
Englewood Cliffs, New Jersey 07632

PERSONAL DATA

Name: _____

Address:

    (Home)   Street _____

                 City _____

                 State _____ ZIP _____

    (Business)

                 Company _____

                 Street _____

                 City _____

                 State _____ ZIP _____

Telephone:

    (Home)   (   ) _____

    (Business) (   ) _____

    (Fax)   (   ) _____

In case of emergency, please notify:

                 Name _____

                 Street _____

                 City _____ State _____ ZIP _____

                 Telephone (   ) _____

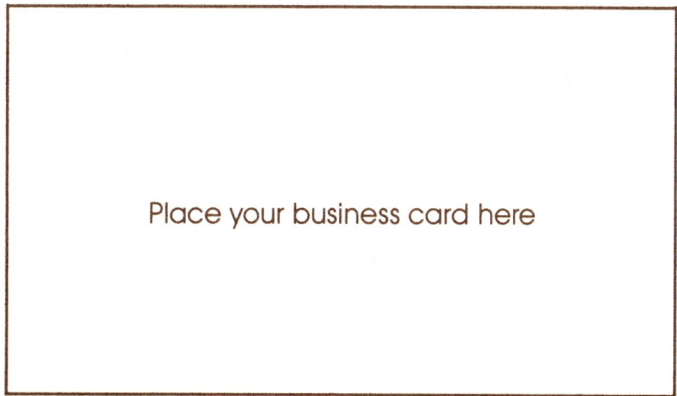

Place your business card here

ABOUT THE AUTHOR

ANDREW M. CIVITELLO, JR. is President of Civitello Building Company, a construction management, general contracting, and management consulting firm in Hamden, Connecticut. He has managed construction projects of nearly every size and type since 1976. His clients include local and federal government agencies and departments, municipalities, banks, service organizations, health maintenance organizations, and private developers on assignments ranging to $36 million. His experience includes project management responsibilities in many forms of general contracting, design-build, and construction management contract arrangements.

He was project manager for the Gilbane Building Co., and is an independent scheduling and project management consultant to contractors, subcontractors, and lawyers. He is an arbitrator for the American Arbitration Association, university instructor to senior engineers for project planning and scheduling, and an expert witness in scheduling, estimating, and claims. He is the author of *Construction Operations Manual of Policies and Procedures* (Prentice-Hall, 1982), co-author of *Construction Scheduling Simplified* (Prentice-Hall, 1985), *Contractor's Guide to Change Orders* (Prentice-Hall, 1987), and *The Builder's and Contractor's Yearbook, 1987* (Prentice-Hall). He has led and participated in seminars presenting various topics related to the construction field. Mr. Civitello studied civil engineering and received his Bachelor of Science degree in business administration from Syracuse University.

ACKNOWLEDGMENTS

Special thanks goes to:

Deere and Company, Moline, IL, for the source information used to prepare the *Equipment Safety, Prestart, and Maintenance Checklist*

HOW TO USE
THE CONSTRUCTION MANAGER

The Construction Manager is designed specifically for contracting professionals. It's the only project management tool of its kind. You'll find daily, weekly, and monthly pages geared to organize your busy workday in the most efficient and timely manner. (All non-working days are indicated by bold type.) In addition, there's a handy reference section at the back of the *Planner* packed with construction checklists, references, personal telephone directories, and much more!

Here's what the *Planner* features:

DAILY PAGES: Each daily page provides a day-to-day diary for maintaining the most complete records possible with a minimum of effort. You'll find

- *Working day/calendar day schedule* for easy reference. The calculation subtracts Saturdays, Sundays, New Year's Day, Good Friday, Memorial Day (observed), Independence Day, Labor Day, Thanksgiving, and Christmas. (If you have additional non-working days specific to your area, you need only to subtract them from the working day information as provided.)
- *Daily minder* section with time-sensitive reminders to make sure these important, recurring items don't get overlooked.
- *7 A.M. to 6 P.M. appointment* section with a job number column to help organize responsibilities by project and save time when researching previous jobs.
- *Key events* section that pinpoints such common contracting situations as meetings, change order proposals, and material deliveries.
- *A daily diary* section to record information that's important to you.
- *Daily expense* section for isolating expenses that can be recapitulated later in your own expense forms.
- *Weather* section to record temperature 8 A.M., noon and 4 P.M.
- *Construction vocabulary builders* with terms found in all areas of the business.

WEEKLY PAGES: Each week begins with a "head start" page that includes

- *Weekly events checklist* highlighting the most common items likely to be scheduled that week
- *To do* list to organize important items and events
- *Weekly milestone checklist* to keep track of all immediately critical project activities and their status

MONTHLY RECAP PAGES: Each month features a two-page summary form that includes

- *Months at a glance* with current, previous, and next month displays
- *Monthly working day/calendar day schedules*
- *Key activity* and *schedule update summaries*
- *Monthly event checklist*
- *Critical item cost report* and *change order summaries*

REFERENCE SECTION: The back of the *Planner* features six different sections on reference, construction checklists, construction forms, travel, general services, and personal information. In all, you'll find *The Construction Manager* a timely and useful tool to help you in your daily, weekly, and monthly planning throughout the year.

If you have any suggestions, ideas, or remarks about *The Construction Manager* that would improve its usefulness to contracting professionals, please send them to

The Construction Manager
P.O. Box 190
Bethany, CT 06525

CONTENTS

JANUARY

22 Working Days

31 Calendar Days

DECEMBER

S	M	T	W	T	F	S
						1
2	3	4	5	6	7	8
9	10	11	12	13	14	15
16	17	18	19	20	21	22
23	24	25	26	27	28	29
30	31					

JANUARY

S	M	T	W	T	F	S
		1	2	3	4	5
6	7	8	9	10	11	12
13	14	15	16	17	18	19
20	21	22	23	24	25	26
27	28	29	30	31		

FEBRUARY

S	M	T	W	T	F	S
					1	2
3	4	5	6	7	8	9
10	11	12	13	14	15	16
17	18	19	20	21	22	23
24	25	26	27	28		

MONTHLY KEY ACTIVITY UPDATE

Job/C.O. No.	Description	Planned Date	Actual Date	Variance	Remarks

MONTHLY SCHEDULE UPDATE SUMMARY

Job/C.O. No.	Activities	Original Duration	Days Spent	Days Remaining	Status/Remarks

MONTHLY RECAP

S	M	T	W	T	F	S
		1	2	3	4	5
6	7	8	9	10	11	12
13	14	15	16	17	18	19
20	21	22	23	24	25	26
27	28	29	30	31		

JANUARY

MONTHLY EVENT CHECKLIST

- Schedule updates complete
- Requests out for all required info.
- Outstanding sub/supplier responses rec'd
- Outstanding owner responses rec'd
- Outstanding arch./eng. responses rec'd
- Critical material deliveries confirmed
- Shop drawings for ongoing work in/appr
- Submittals for pending work in/appr
- All other submittals in/approved

- All sub change proposals in
- All change proposals to owner prepared
- Submitted change proposals approved
- Guarantees/warrantees rec'd
- Inspection certificates rec'd
- As-built drawings rec'd
- Safety inspections performed
- Safety reports complete
- Narratives complete

- Sub/supplier contract(s) rec'd
- Requisition(s) submitted to owner(s)
- Sub/supplier adjustments complete
- Progress photos taken
- Job cost report info. assembled
- Job cost reports complete
- Other:
- _____
- _____

CRITICAL ITEM COST REPORT SUMMARY

Job/CO No.	Description	(A) Budget $ Amount	(B) Cost To Date	(C) Cost Remaining	(D) Total Commitment (B + C)	(E) +/− (A − D)

CHANGE ORDER SUMMARY

Job No.	C.O. No.	Description	Submission Date Required	Submission Date Actual	Approval Date Required	Approval Date Actual	Remarks

WEEK Beginning 31 DECEMBER
Ending 6 JANUARY

WEEKLY EVENT CHECKLIST

Job meetings and preparation	☐ Submittals for pending work in/appr	☐ All permits in place ☐
Special meetings	☐ All other submittals in/approved	☐ Req testing/inspections arranged ☐
Dinners and seminars	☐ Shop drawing log up to date	☐ Inspection certificates received ☐
Assemble schedule information	☐ All sub change proposals in	☐ Safety inspections performed ☐
Complete schedule updates	☐ All change proposals to owner prep'd	☐ Safety recommendations acted on ☐
Requests out for all required information ☐	☐ Submitted change proposals appr	☐ Field reports complete ☐
Outstanding sub/supplier responses	☐ Change order logs up to date	☐ Special photos taken ☐
Outstanding owner responses	☐ Required bonds received for all subs ☐	☐_____ ☐
Outstanding architect/engineer responses ☐	☐ Certificates of insurance rec'd for all	☐_____ ☐
Critical material deliveries confirmed ☐	subs (proper amounts) ☐	☐_____ ☐
Shop drawings for ongoing work in/appr	☐ Equipment/scaffolding release forms in ☐	☐_____ ☐

TO DO

Item	Job No.	Item	Job No.

WEEKLY MILESTONE UPDATE

	Planned Date	Actual Date	Variance

31

DECEMBER
New Year's
Eve
MONDAY

	WORK	CAL
MONTH TO DATE	21	30
MONTH REMAINING	0	0
YEAR TO DATE	??	365
YEAR REMAINING	0	0

DAILY MINDER

JOB NO. APPOINTMENTS/EVENTS/CALLS

7 A.M.

8 A.M.

9 A.M.

10 A.M.

11 A.M.

12 NOON

1 P.M.

2 P.M.

3 P.M.

4 P.M.

5 P.M.

6 P.M.

KEY EVENTS

Meetings

Schedule Updates

Cost Report Updates

Change Proposals

Material Deliveries

Special Information/Instructions

Arch./Owner Direction Received

DAILY DIARY

WEATHER/TEMP.   8 A.M.   12 NOON   4 P.M.

EXPENSES

Wood Fiber Plaster: A gypsum plaster containing the fine particles of wood fiber resulting in lighter weight plaster with increased fire resistance.

DAILY MINDER

✓ Any good New Year's resolutions?

WORK	CAL
MONTH TO DATE	0	1
MONTH REMAINING	22	30
YEAR TO DATE	0	1
YEAR REMAINING	254	364

JANUARY
New Year's Day
TUESDAY

1

KEY EVENTS

Meetings

Schedule Updates

Cost Report Updates

Change Proposals

Material Deliveries

Special Information/Instructions

Arch./Owner Direction Received

DAILY DIARY

JOB NO. APPOINTMENTS/EVENTS/CALLS

7 A.M.

8 A.M.

9 A.M.

10 A.M.

11 A.M.

12 NOON

1 P.M.

2 P.M.

3 P.M.

4 P.M.

5 P.M.

6 P.M.

WEATHER/TEMP.   8 A.M.   12 NOON   4 P.M.

EXPENSES

DECEMBER								JANUARY							FEBRUARY						
S	M	T	W	T	F	S		S	M	T	W	T	F	S	S	M	T	W	T	F	S
						1				1	2	3	4	5						1	2
2	3	4	5	6	7	8		6	7	8	9	10	11	12	3	4	5	6	7	8	9
9	10	11	12	13	14	15		13	14	15	16	17	18	19	10	11	12	13	14	15	16
16	17	18	19	20	21	22		20	21	22	23	24	25	26	17	18	19	20	21	22	23
23	24	25	26	27	28	29		27	28	29	30	31			24	25	26	27	28		
30	31																				

2 JANUARY
WEDNESDAY

WORK CAL		
MONTH TO DATE	1	2
MONTH REMAINING	21	29
YEAR TO DATE	1	2
YEAR REMAINING	253	363

JOB NO. APPOINTMENTS/EVENTS/CALLS

7 A.M.

8 A.M.

9 A.M.

10 A.M.

11 A.M.

12 NOON

1 P.M.

2 P.M.

3 P.M.

4 P.M.

5 P.M.

6 P.M.

KEY EVENTS
Meetings

Schedule Updates

Cost Report Updates

Change Proposals

Material Deliveries

Special Information/Instructions

Arch./Owner Direction Received

DAILY DIARY

WEATHER/TEMP.   8 A.M.   12 NOON   4 P.M.

EXPENSES

Overturning Moment: Structual design term meaning horizontal force times vertical distance, which tends to overturn a structural element.

DAILY MINDER

√ Job meeting minutes and reports complete?
√ Key material deliveries confirmed?
√ December invoices submitted?
√ Schedule updates complete?

KEY EVENTS

Meetings

Schedule Updates

Cost Report Updates

Change Proposals

Material Deliveries

Special Information/Instructions

Arch./Owner Direction Received

DAILY DIARY

WEATHER/TEMP.   8A.M.   12NOON   4P.M.

EXPENSES

WORK	CAL		
MONTH TO DATE	2	3
MONTH REMAINING	20	28
YEAR TO DATE	2	3
YEAR REMAINING	252	362

JANUARY

3

THURSDAY

JOB NO. APPOINTMENTS/EVENTS/CALLS

7 A.M.

8 A.M.

9 A.M.

10 A.M.

11 A.M.

12 NOON

1 P.M.

2 P.M.

3 P.M.

4 P.M.

5 P.M.

6 P.M.

	DECEMBER							JANUARY							FEBRUARY					
S	M	T	W	T	F	S	S	M	T	W	T	F	S	S	M	T	W	T	F	S
						1			1	2	3	4	5						1	2
2	3	4	5	6	7	8	6	7	8	9	10	11	12	3	4	5	6	7	8	9
9	10	11	12	13	14	15	13	14	15	16	17	18	19	10	11	12	13	14	15	16
16	17	18	19	20	21	22	20	21	22	23	24	25	26	17	18	19	20	21	22	23
23	24	25	26	27	28	29	27	28	29	30	31			24	25	26	27	28		
30	31																			

4 JANUARY
FRIDAY

	WORK	CAL
MONTH TO DATE	3	4
MONTH REMAINING	19	27
YEAR TO DATE	3	4
YEAR REMAINING	251	361

JOB NO. APPOINTMENTS/EVENTS/CALLS

7 A.M.

8 A.M.

9 A.M.

10 A.M.

11 A.M.

12 NOON

1 P.M.

2 P.M.

3 P.M.

4 P.M.

5 P.M.

6 P.M.

DAILY MINDER

√ Job meeting minutes and reports complete?

√ Winter precautions taken at jobsites?

√ December narratives complete?

√ Schedule updates complete?

KEY EVENTS

Meetings

Schedule Updates

Cost Report Updates

Change Proposals

Material Deliveries

Special Information/Instructions

Arch./Owner Direction Received

DAILY DIARY

WEATHER/TEMP.   8A.M.   12NOON   4P.M.

EXPENSES

Intumesce: To expand with heat to provide a low-density film; used in reference to certain fire retardant coatings.

5

JANUARY

SATURDAY

WORK CAL		
MONTH TO DATE	3	6
MONTH REMAINING	19	25
YEAR TO DATE	3	6
YEAR REMAINING	251	359

JANUARY

SUNDAY

6

JOB NO. APPOINTMENTS/EVENTS/CALLS

DAILY DIARY

JOB NO. APPOINTMENTS/EVENTS/CALLS

DAILY DIARY

WEEK Beginning 7 JANUARY
Ending 13 JANUARY

WEEKLY EVENT CHECKLIST

Job meetings and preparation	Submittals for pending work in/appr	All permits in place
Special meetings	All other submittals in/approved	Req testing/inspections arranged
Dinners and seminars	Shop drawing log up to date	Inspection certificates received
Assemble schedule information	All sub change proposals in	Safety inspections performed
Complete schedule updates	All change proposals to owner prep'd	Safety recommendations acted on
Requests out for all required information	Submitted change proposals appr	Field reports complete
Outstanding sub/supplier responses	Change order logs up to date	Special photos taken
Outstanding owner responses	Required bonds received for all subs	
Outstanding architect/engineer responses	Certificates of insurance rec'd for all	
Critical material deliveries confirmed	subs (proper amounts)	
Shop drawings for ongoing work in/appr	Equipment/scaffolding release forms in	

TO DO

Item	Job No.	Item	Job No.

WEEKLY MILESTONE UPDATE

	Planned Date	Actual Date	Variance

DAILY MINDER

√ Job meeting minutes and reports complete?

√ Key material deliveries confirmed?

√ Attending any professional improvement seminars?

	WORK	CAL
MONTH TO DATE	4	7
MONTH REMAINING	18	24
YEAR TO DATE	4	7
YEAR REMAINING	250	358

JANUARY

7

MONDAY

KEY EVENTS

Meetings

Schedule Updates

Cost Report Updates

Change Proposals

Material Deliveries

Special Information/Instructions

Arch./Owner Direction Received

DAILY DIARY

WEATHER/TEMP.   8A.M.   12NOON   4P.M.

EXPENSES

JOB NO. APPOINTMENTS/EVENTS/CALLS

7 A.M.

8 A.M.

9 A.M.

10 A.M.

11 A.M.

12 NOON

1 P.M.

2 P.M.

3 P.M.

4 P.M.

5 P.M.

6 P.M.

	DECEMBER							JANUARY							FEBRUARY					
S	M	T	W	T	F	S	S	M	T	W	T	F	S	S	M	T	W	T	F	S
						1			1	2	3	4	5						1	2
2	3	4	5	6	7	8	6	7	8	9	10	11	12	3	4	5	6	7	8	9
9	10	11	12	13	14	15	13	14	15	16	17	18	19	10	11	12	13	14	15	16
16	17	18	19	20	21	22	20	21	22	23	24	25	26	17	18	19	20	21	22	23
23	24	25	26	27	28	29	27	28	29	30	31			24	25	26	27	28		
30	31																			

8 JANUARY

TUESDAY

DAILY MINDER

√ Verify outstanding change orders.

√ Jobsite safety reviews performed?

JOB NO. APPOINTMENTS/EVENTS/CALLS

7 A.M.

8 A.M.

9 A.M.

10 A.M.

11 A.M.

12 NOON

1 P.M.

2 P.M.

3 P.M.

4 P.M.

5 P.M.

6 P.M.

KEY EVENTS

Meetings

Schedule Updates

Cost Report Updates

Change Proposals

Material Deliveries

Special Information/Instructions

Arch./Owner Direction Received

DAILY DIARY

WEATHER/TEMP.   8 A.M.   12 NOON   4 P.M.

EXPENSES

Pozzolan: A concrete mix additive that will reduce heat generation and thermal volume change.

DAILY MINDER

√ Key material deliveries confirmed?

√ Scheduled a complete physical examination this year?

√ Winter precautions being maintained at sites?

KEY EVENTS

Meetings

Schedule Updates

Cost Report Updates

Change Proposals

Material Deliveries

Special Information/Instructions

Arch./Owner Direction Received

DAILY DIARY

WEATHER/TEMP.   8A.M.   12NOON   4P.M.

EXPENSES

JOB NO. APPOINTMENTS/EVENTS/CALLS

7 A.M.

8 A.M.

9 A.M.

10 A.M.

11 A.M.

12 NOON

1 P.M.

2 P.M.

3 P.M.

4 P.M.

5 P.M.

6 P.M.

	DECEMBER							JANUARY							FEBRUARY					
S	M	T	W	T	F	S	S	M	T	W	T	F	S	S	M	T	W	T	F	S
						1			1	2	3	4	5					1	2
2	3	4	5	6	7	8	6	7	8	9	10	11	12	3	4	5	6	7	8	9
9	10	11	12	13	14	15	13	14	15	16	17	18	19	10	11	12	13	14	15	16
16	17	18	19	20	21	22	20	21	22	23	24	25	26	17	18	19	20	21	22	23
23	24	25	26	27	28	29	27	28	29	30	31			24	25	26	27	28
30	31																			

10 JANUARY
THURSDAY

	WORK	CAL
MONTH TO DATE	7	10
MONTH REMAINING	15	21
YEAR TO DATE	7	10
YEAR REMAINING	247	355

DAILY MINDER

√ Job meeting minutes and reports complete?
√ Personal tax records assembled?

JOB NO. APPOINTMENTS/EVENTS/CALLS

7 A.M.

8 A.M.

9 A.M.

10 A.M.

11 A.M.

12 NOON

1 P.M.

2 P.M.

3 P.M.

4 P.M.

5 P.M.

6 P.M.

KEY EVENTS

Meetings

Schedule Updates

Cost Report Updates

Change Proposals

Material Deliveries

Special Information/Instructions

Arch./Owner Direction Received

DAILY DIARY

WEATHER/TEMP.   8 A.M.   12 NOON   4 P.M.

EXPENSES

Refractory: Any material that will withstand high heat, such as lining of kiln or furnace.

DAILY MINDER

√Job meeting minutes and reports complete?
√Field reports up-to-date?
√Submitted change orders approved?

WORK CAL		
MONTH TO DATE	8	11
MONTH REMAINING	14	20
YEAR TO DATE	8	11
YEAR REMAINING	246	354

JANUARY

11

FRIDAY

KEY EVENTS

Meetings
Schedule Updates
Cost Report Updates
Change Proposals
Material Deliveries
Special Information/Instructions
Arch./Owner Direction Received

DAILY DIARY

WEATHER/TEMP.   8A.M.   12NOON   4P.M.

EXPENSES

JOB NO. APPOINTMENTS/EVENTS/CALLS

7A.M.

8A.M.

9A.M.

10A.M.

11A.M.

12NOON

1P.M.

2P.M.

3P.M.

4P.M.

5P.M.

6P.M.

	DECEMBER							JANUARY							FEBRUARY					
S	M	T	W	T	F	S	S	M	T	W	T	F	S	S	M	T	W	T	F	S
						1			1	2	3	4	5						1	2
2	3	4	5	6	7	8	6	7	8	9	10	11	12	3	4	5	6	7	8	9
9	10	11	12	13	14	15	13	14	15	16	17	18	19	10	11	12	13	14	15	16
16	17	18	19	20	21	22	20	21	22	23	24	25	26	17	18	19	20	21	22	23
23	24	25	26	27	28	29	27	28	29	30	31			24	25	26	27	28		
30	31																			

12 JANUARY

SATURDAY

	WORK	CAL
MONTH TO DATE	8	12
MONTH REMAINING	14	19
YEAR TO DATE	8	12
YEAR REMAINING	246	353

WORK	CAL	
MONTH TO DATE	8	13
MONTH REMAINING	14	18
YEAR TO DATE	8	13
YEAR REMAINING	246	352

JANUARY 13

SUNDAY

JOB NO. APPOINTMENTS/EVENTS/CALLS

JOB NO. APPOINTMENTS/EVENTS/CALLS

DAILY DIARY

DAILY DIARY

WEEK Beginning 14 JANUARY
Ending 20 JANUARY

WEEKLY EVENT CHECKLIST

Job meetings and preparation	Submittals for pending work in/appr	All permits in place
Special meetings	All other submittals in/approved	Req testing/inspections arranged
Dinners and seminars	Shop drawing log up to date	Inspection certificates received
Assemble schedule information	All sub change proposals in	Safety inspections performed
Complete schedule updates	All change proposals to owner prep'd	Safety recommendations acted on
Requests out for all required information	Submitted change proposals appr	Field reports complete
Outstanding sub/supplier responses	Change order logs up to date	Special photos taken
Outstanding owner responses	Required bonds received for all subs	
Outstanding architect/engineer responses	Certificates of insurance rec'd for all	
Critical material deliveries confirmed	subs (proper amounts)	
Shop drawings for ongoing work in/appr	Equipment/scaffolding release forms in	

TO DO

Item	Job No.	Item	Job No.

WEEKLY MILESTONE UPDATE

	Planned Date	Actual Date	Variance

14

JANUARY
MONDAY

DAILY MINDER

√ Verify approval of outstanding change orders.

√ Personal tax records assembled?

JOB NO. APPOINTMENTS/EVENTS/CALLS

7 A.M.

8 A.M.

9 A.M.

10 A.M.

11 A.M.

12 NOON

1 P.M.

2 P.M.

3 P.M.

4 P.M.

5 P.M.

6 P.M.

KEY EVENTS

Meetings

Schedule Updates

Cost Report Updates

Change Proposals

Material Deliveries

Special Information/Instructions

Arch./Owner Direction Received

DAILY DIARY

WEATHER/TEMP.   8 A.M.   12 NOON   4 P.M.

EXPENSES

Transverse: Crosswise; at right angles to a long axis.

DAILY MINDER

✓ Assemble all schedule update information.
✓ Key material deliveries confirmed?

WORK	CAL
MONTH TO DATE	10	15
MONTH REMAINING	12	16
YEAR TO DATE	10	15
YEAR REMAINING	244	350

JANUARY

15

TUESDAY

KEY EVENTS

Meetings

Schedule Updates

Cost Report Updates

Change Proposals

Material Deliveries

Special Information/Instructions

Arch./Owner Direction Received

DAILY DIARY

WEATHER/TEMP.   8 A.M.   12 NOON   4 P.M.

EXPENSES

JOB NO.   APPOINTMENTS/EVENTS/CALLS

7 A.M.

8 A.M.

9 A.M.

10 A.M.

11 A.M.

12 NOON

1 P.M.

2 P.M.

3 P.M.

4 P.M.

5 P.M.

6 P.M.

	DECEMBER							JANUARY							FEBRUARY					
S	M	T	W	T	F	S	S	M	T	W	T	F	S	S	M	T	W	T	F	S
										1	2	3	4						1	2
2	3	4	5	6	7	8	6	7	8	9	10	11	12	3	4	5	6	7	8	9
9	10	11	12	13	14	15	13	14	15	16	17	18	19	10	11	12	13	14	15	16
16	17	18	19	20	21	22	20	21	22	23	24	25	26	17	18	19	20	21	22	23
23	24	25	26	27	28	29	27	28	29	30	31			24	25	26	27	28		
30	31																			

16 JANUARY
WEDNESDAY

WORK	CAL
MONTH TO DATE	11	16
MONTH REMAINING	11	15
YEAR TO DATE	11	16
YEAR REMAINING	243	349

DAILY MINDER

√ Verify receipt of all sub and supplier payment requisitions.

√ Meeting minutes prepared or received?

√ Last week's schedule commitments in-process?

JOB NO. APPOINTMENTS/EVENTS/CALLS

7 A.M.

8 A.M.

9 A.M.

10 A.M.

11 A.M.

12 NOON

1 P.M.

2 P.M.

3 P.M.

4 P.M.

5 P.M.

6 P.M.

KEY EVENTS

Meetings

Schedule Updates

Cost Report Updates

Change Proposals

Material Deliveries

Special Information/Instructions

Arch./Owner Direction Received

DAILY DIARY

WEATHER/TEMP.   8 A.M.   12 NOON   4 P.M.

EXPENSES

Water Hammer: A term applied to the noise made by a fast moving liquid inside a pipe when its flow is abruptly shut off.

DAILY MINDER

√ Assemble all schedule update information.

√ Job meeting minutes and reports complete?

√ Key material deliveries confirmed?

WORK	CAL
MONTH TO DATE	12	17
MONTH REMAINING	10	14
YEAR TO DATE	12	17
YEAR REMAINING	242	348

JANUARY

THURSDAY

17

KEY EVENTS

Meetings

Schedule Updates

Cost Report Updates

Change Proposals

Material Deliveries

Special Information/Instructions

Arch./Owner Direction Received

DAILY DIARY

WEATHER/TEMP.   8A.M.   12NOON   4P.M.

EXPENSES

JOB NO.   APPOINTMENTS/EVENTS/CALLS

7A.M.

8A.M.

9A.M.

10A.M.

11A.M.

12NOON

1P.M.

2P.M.

3P.M.

4P.M.

5P.M.

6P.M.

DECEMBER							JANUARY							FEBRUARY						
S	M	T	W	T	F	S	S	M	T	W	T	F	S	S	M	T	W	T	F	S
						1			1	2	3	4	5						1	2
2	3	4	5	6	7	8	6	7	8	9	10	11	12	3	4	5	6	7	8	9
9	10	11	12	13	14	15	13	14	15	16	17	18	19	10	11	12	13	14	15	16
16	17	18	19	20	21	22	20	21	22	23	24	25	26	17	18	19	20	21	22	23
23	24	25	26	27	28	29	27	28	29	30	31			24	25	26	27	28		
30	31																			

18

JANUARY
FRIDAY

DAILY MINDER

√ Verify approval of outstanding change orders.
√ Verify receipt of all sub and supplier payment requisitions.
√ Schedule update info assembled?
√ Job meeting minutes and reports complete?

JOB NO. APPOINTMENTS/EVENTS/CALLS

7 A.M.

8 A.M.

9 A.M.

10 A.M.

11 A.M.

12 NOON

1 P.M.

2 P.M.

3 P.M.

4 P.M.

5 P.M.

6 P.M.

KEY EVENTS

Meetings

Schedule Updates

Cost Report Updates

Change Proposals

Material Deliveries

Special Information/Instructions

Arch./Owner Direction Received

DAILY DIARY

WEATHER/TEMP.   8 A.M.   12 NOON   4 P.M.

EXPENSES

Photogrammetry: The use of aerial photography to measure land distances and elevations.

19 JANUARY

SATURDAY

JOB NO. APPOINTMENTS/EVENTS/CALLS

DAILY DIARY

JANUARY 20

SUNDAY

JOB NO. APPOINTMENTS/EVENTS/CALLS

DAILY DIARY

WEEK Beginning 21 JANUARY
Ending 27 JANUARY

WEEKLY EVENT CHECKLIST

Job meetings and preparation ___
Special meetings ___
Dinners and seminars ___
Assemble schedule information ___
Complete schedule updates ___
Requests out for all required information ___
Outstanding sub/supplier responses ___
Outstanding owner responses ___
Outstanding architect/engineer responses ___
Critical material deliveries confirmed ___
Shop drawings for ongoing work in/appr ___

Submittals for pending work in/appr ___
All other submittals in/approved ___
Shop drawing log up to date ___
All sub change proposals in ___
All change proposals to owner prep'd ___
Submitted change proposals appr ___
Change order logs up to date ___
Required bonds received for all subs ___
Certificates of insurance rec'd for all subs (proper amounts) ___
Equipment/scaffolding release forms in ___

All permits in place ___
Req testing/inspections arranged ___
Inspection certificates received ___
Safety inspections performed ___
Safety recommendations acted on ___
Field reports complete ___
Special photos taken ___
_____ ___
_____ ___
_____ ___
_____ ___

TO DO

Item	Job No.	Item	Job No.

WEEKLY MILESTONE UPDATE

	Planned Date	Actual Date	Variance

DAILY MINDER

√ Verify approval of outstanding change orders.

√ Submit requisition(s) to owner(s).

√ Authorize sub and supplier payments.

√ All cost report information assembled?

WORK CAL		
MONTH TO DATE	14	21
MONTH REMAINING	8	10
YEAR TO DATE	14	21
YEAR REMAINING	240	344

JANUARY
Martin Luther
King, Jr. Day
MONDAY

21

KEY EVENTS

Meetings

Schedule Updates

Cost Report Updates

Change Proposals

Material Deliveries

Special Information/Instructions

Arch./Owner Direction Received

DAILY DIARY

WEATHER/TEMP.   8 A.M.   12 NOON   4 P.M.

EXPENSES

JOB NO.   APPOINTMENTS/EVENTS/CALLS

7 A.M.

8 A.M.

9 A.M.

10 A.M.

11 A.M.

12 NOON

1 P.M.

2 P.M.

3 P.M.

4 P.M.

5 P.M.

6 P.M.

DECEMBER								JANUARY								FEBRUARY						
S	M	T	W	T	F	S		S	M	T	W	T	F	S		S	M	T	W	T	F	S
						1				1	2	3	4	5							1	2
2	3	4	5	6	7	8		6	7	8	9	10	11	12		3	4	5	6	7	8	9
9	10	11	12	13	14	15		13	14	15	16	17	18	19		10	11	12	13	14	15	16
16	17	18	19	20	21	22		20	21	22	23	24	25	26		17	18	19	20	21	22	23
23	24	25	26	27	28	29		27	28	29	30	31				24	25	26	27	28		
30	31																					

22

JANUARY

TUESDAY

DAILY MINDER

√ Authorize/approve sub and supplier payments.
√ Assemble all schedule update information.
√ All monthly reports and narratives complete?
√ Key material deliveries confirmed?

JOB NO. APPOINTMENTS/EVENTS/CALLS

7 A.M.

8 A.M.

9 A.M.

10 A.M.

11 A.M.

12 NOON

1 P.M.

2 P.M.

3 P.M.

4 P.M.

5 P.M.

6 P.M.

KEY EVENTS

Meetings

Schedule Updates

Cost Report Updates

Change Proposals

Material Deliveries

Special Information/Instructions

Arch./Owner Direction Received

DAILY DIARY

WEATHER/TEMP.   8 A.M.   12 NOON   4 P.M.

EXPENSES

Vitreous: Descriptive of a glass-like appearance.

DAILY MINDER

√ Verify approval of outstanding change orders.

√ Submit requisition(s) to owner(s).

√ Authorize/approve sub and supplier payments.

√ Personal tax records assembled?

	WORK	CAL
MONTH TO DATE	16	23
MONTH REMAINING	6	8
YEAR TO DATE	16	23
YEAR REMAINING	238	342

JANUARY 23
WEDNESDAY

KEY EVENTS

Meetings

Schedule Updates

Cost Report Updates

Change Proposals

Material Deliveries

Special Information/Instructions

Arch./Owner Direction Received

DAILY DIARY

WEATHER/TEMP.   8A.M.   12NOON   4P.M.

EXPENSES

JOB NO.   APPOINTMENTS/EVENTS/CALLS

7 A.M.

8 A.M.

9 A.M.

10 A.M.

11 A.M.

12 NOON

1 P.M.

2 P.M.

3 P.M.

4 P.M.

5 P.M.

6 P.M.

DECEMBER						
S	M	T	W	T	F	S
						1
2	3	4	5	6	7	8
9	10	11	12	13	14	15
16	17	18	19	20	21	22
23	24	25	26	27	28	29
30	31					

JANUARY						
S	M	T	W	T	F	S
		1	2	3	4	5
6	7	8	9	10	11	12
13	14	15	16	17	18	19
20	21	22	23	24	25	26
27	28	29	30	31		

FEBRUARY						
S	M	T	W	T	F	S
					1	2
3	4	5	6	7	8	9
10	11	12	13	14	15	16
17	18	19	20	21	22	23
24	25	26	27	28		

24 JANUARY
THURSDAY

WORK		CAL
MONTH TO DATE	17	24
MONTH REMAINING	5	7
YEAR TO DATE	17	24
YEAR REMAINING	237	341

JOB NO. APPOINTMENTS/EVENTS/CALLS

7 A.M.

8 A.M.

9 A.M.

10 A.M.

11 A.M.

12 NOON

1 P.M.

2 P.M.

3 P.M.

4 P.M.

5 P.M.

6 P.M.

DAILY MINDER

√ Authorize/approve sub and supplier payments.

√ Schedule update complete?

√ All monthly reports and narratives complete?

√ Cost report complete?

KEY EVENTS

Meetings

Schedule Updates

Cost Report Updates

Change Proposals

Material Deliveries

Special Information/Instructions

Arch./Owner Direction Received

DAILY DIARY

WEATHER/TEMP.   8 A.M.   12 NOON   4 P.M.

EXPENSES

Penetrometer: Device that measures relative density and/or bearing capacity of soil.

DAILY MINDER

√ Verify approval of outstanding change orders.
√ Submit requisition(s) to owner(s).
√ Authorize/approve sub and supplier payments.
√ Cost report complete?

KEY EVENTS

Meetings

Schedule Updates

Cost Report Updates

Change Proposals

Material Deliveries

Special Information/Instructions

Arch./Owner Direction Received

DAILY DIARY

WEATHER/TEMP.   8A.M.   12NOON   4P.M.

EXPENSES

	WORK	CAL
MONTH TO DATE	18	25
MONTH REMAINING	4	6
YEAR TO DATE	18	25
YEAR REMAINING	236	340

JANUARY
25
FRIDAY

JOB NO.   APPOINTMENTS/EVENTS/CALLS

7A.M.

8A.M.

9A.M.

10A.M.

11A.M.

12NOON

1P.M.

2P.M.

3P.M.

4P.M.

5P.M.

6P.M.

	DECEMBER							JANUARY							FEBRUARY					
S	M	T	W	T	F	S	S	M	T	W	T	F	S	S	M	T	W	T	F	S
						1			1	2	3	4	5						1	2
2	3	4	5	6	7	8	6	7	8	9	10	11	12	3	4	5	6	7	8	9
9	10	11	12	13	14	15	13	14	15	16	17	18	19	10	11	12	13	14	15	16
16	17	18	19	20	21	22	20	21	22	23	24	25	26	17	18	19	20	21	22	23
23	24	25	26	27	28	29	27	28	29	30	31			24	25	26	27	28		
30	31																			

26

JANUARY

SATURDAY

	WORK	CAL
MONTH TO DATE	18	26
MONTH REMAINING	4	5
YEAR TO DATE	18	26
YEAR REMAINING	236	339

	WORK	CAL
MONTH TO DATE	18	27
MONTH REMAINING	4	4
YEAR TO DATE	18	27
YEAR REMAINING	236	338

27

JANUARY

SUNDAY

JOB NO. APPOINTMENTS/EVENTS/CALLS

JOB NO. APPOINTMENTS/EVENTS/CALLS

DAILY DIARY

DAILY DIARY

WEEK Beginning 28 JANUARY
Ending 3 FEBRUARY

WEEKLY EVENT CHECKLIST

Job meetings and preparation	☐ Submittals for pending work in/appr	☐ All permits in place
Special meetings	☐ All other submittals in/approved	☐ Req testing/inspections arranged
Dinners and seminars	☐ Shop drawing log up to date	☐ Inspection certificates received
Assemble schedule information	☐ All sub change proposals in	☐ Safety inspections performed
Complete schedule updates	☐ All change proposals to owner prep'd	☐ Safety recommendations acted on
Requests out for all required information	☐ Submitted change proposals appr	☐ Field reports complete
Outstanding sub/supplier responses	☐ Change order logs up to date	☐ Special photos taken
Outstanding owner responses	☐ Required bonds received for all subs	☐ _____
Outstanding architect/engineer responses	☐ Certificates of insurance rec'd for all	☐ _____
Critical material deliveries confirmed	subs (proper amounts)	☐ _____
Shop drawings for ongoing work in/appr	☐ Equipment/scaffolding release forms in	☐ _____

TO DO

Item	Job No.	Item	Job No.

WEEKLY MILESTONE UPDATE

	Planned Date	Actual Date	Variance

28 JANUARY
MONDAY

DAILY MINDER

√General requisitions submitted?
√Schedule update complete?
√Reports and narratives complete?
√Key material deliveries confirmed?

JOB NO. APPOINTMENTS/EVENTS/CALLS

7 A.M.

8 A.M.

9 A.M.

10 A.M.

11 A.M.

12 NOON

1 P.M.

2 P.M.

3 P.M.

4 P.M.

5 P.M.

6 P.M.

KEY EVENTS

Meetings

Schedule Updates

Cost Report Updates

Change Proposals

Material Deliveries

Special Information/Instructions

Arch./Owner Direction Received

DAILY DIARY

WEATHER/TEMP.   8 A.M.   12 NOON   4 P.M.

EXPENSES

Igneous Rock: Formed by solidification of a molten mixture of minerals.

DAILY MINDER

√Schedule updates complete?
√Reports and narratives complete?
√Progress photos taken?
√Personal income tax prepared?

KEY EVENTS

Meetings

Schedule Updates

Cost Report Updates

Change Proposals

Material Deliveries

Special Information/Instructions

Arch./Owner Direction Received

DAILY DIARY

WEATHER/TEMP.   8A.M.   12NOON   4P.M.

EXPENSES

	WORK	CAL
MONTH TO DATE	20	29
MONTH REMAINING	2	2
YEAR TO DATE	20	29
YEAR REMAINING	234	336

JANUARY
TUESDAY
29

JOB NO.   APPOINTMENTS/EVENTS/CALLS

7A.M.

8A.M.

9A.M.

10A.M.

11A.M.

12NOON

1P.M.

2P.M.

3P.M.

4P.M.

5P.M.

6P.M.

		DECEMBER								JANUARY								FEBRUARY				
S	M	T	W	T	F	S	S	M	T	W	T	F	S	S	M	T	W	T	F	S
						1			1	2	3	4	5						1	2
2	3	4	5	6	7	8	6	7	8	9	10	11	12	3	4	5	6	7	8	9
9	10	11	12	13	14	15	13	14	15	16	17	18	19	10	11	12	13	14	15	16
16	17	18	19	20	21	22	20	21	22	23	24	25	26	17	18	19	20	21	22	23
23	24	25	26	27	28	29	27	28	29	30	31			24	25	26	27	28		
30	31																			

30 JANUARY
WEDNESDAY

WORK	CAL
MONTH TO DATE	21	30
MONTH REMAINING	1	1
YEAR TO DATE	21	30
YEAR REMAINING	233	335

JOB NO. APPOINTMENTS/EVENTS/CALLS

7 A.M.

8 A.M.

9 A.M.

10 A.M.

11 A.M.

12 NOON

1 P.M.

2 P.M.

3 P.M.

4 P.M.

5 P.M.

6 P.M.

DAILY MINDER

√ Schedule updates complete?
√ Reports and narratives complete?
√ Progress photos taken?
√ Personal income tax prepared?

KEY EVENTS

Meetings

Schedule Updates

Cost Report Updates

Change Proposals

Material Deliveries

Special Information/Instructions

Arch./Owner Direction Received

DAILY DIARY

WEATHER/TEMP.   8 A.M.   12 NOON   4 P.M.

EXPENSES

Hyperbolic Paraboloid: Saddle-shaped structural surface usually of thin-shelled concrete, for architecturally dramatic roofs.

DAILY MINDER

√Schedule updates complete?

√Reports and narratives complete?

√Key material deliveries confirmed?

√Progress photos taken?

	WORK	CAL
MONTH TO DATE	22	31
MONTH REMAINING	0	0
YEAR TO DATE	22	31
YEAR REMAINING	232	334

JANUARY

31

THURSDAY

KEY EVENTS

Meetings

Schedule Updates

Cost Report Updates

Change Proposals

Material Deliveries

Special Information/Instructions

Arch./Owner Direction Received

DAILY DIARY

WEATHER/TEMP.   8A.M.   12NOON   4P.M.

EXPENSES

JOB NO. APPOINTMENTS/EVENTS/CALLS

7A.M.

8A.M.

9A.M.

10A.M.

11A.M.

12NOON

1P.M.

2P.M.

3P.M.

4P.M.

5P.M.

6P.M.

	DECEMBER							JANUARY							FEBRUARY					
S	M	T	W	T	F	S	S	M	T	W	T	F	S	S	M	T	W	T	F	S
						1			1	2	3	4	5						1	2
2	3	4	5	6	7	8	6	7	8	9	10	11	12	3	4	5	6	7	8	9
9	10	11	12	13	14	15	13	14	15	16	17	18	19	10	11	12	13	14	15	16
16	17	18	19	20	21	22	20	21	22	23	24	25	26	17	18	19	20	21	22	23
23	24	25	26	27	28	29	27	28	29	30	31			24	25	26	27	28		
30	31																			

FEBRUARY

20 Working Days

28 Calendar Days

JANUARY						
S	M	T	W	T	F	S
			1	2	3	4	5
6	7	8	9	10	11	12
13	14	15	16	17	18	19
20	21	22	23	24	25	26
27	28	29	30	31		

FEBRUARY						
S	M	T	W	T	F	S
					1	2
3	4	5	6	7	8	9
10	11	12	13	14	15	16
17	18	19	20	21	22	23
24	25	26	27	28		

MARCH						
S	M	T	W	T	F	S
					1	2
3	4	5	6	7	8	9
10	11	12	13	14	15	16
17	18	19	20	21	22	23
24	25	26	27	28	29	30
31						

MONTHLY KEY ACTIVITY UPDATE

Job/C.O. No.	Description	Planned Date	Actual Date	Variance	Remarks

MONTHLY SCHEDULE UPDATE SUMMARY

Job/C.O. No.	Activities	Original Duration	Days Spent	Days Remaining	Status/Remarks

MONTHLY RECAP

FEBRUARY

MONTHLY EVENT CHECKLIST

Schedule updates complete ☐
Requests out for all required info. ☐
Outstanding sub/supplier responses rec'd ☐
Outstanding owner responses rec'd ☐
Outstanding arch./eng. responses rec'd ☐
Critical material deliveries confirmed ☐
Shop drawings for ongoing work in/appr ☐
Submittals for pending work in/appr ☐
All other submittals in/approved ☐

All sub change proposals in ☐
All change proposals to owner prepared ☐
Submitted change proposals approved ☐
Guarantees/warrantees rec'd ☐
Inspection certificates rec'd ☐
As-built drawings rec'd ☐
Safety inspections performed ☐
Safety reports complete ☐
Narratives complete ☐

Sub/supplier contract(s) rec'd ☐
Requisition(s) submitted to owner(s) ☐
Sub/supplier adjustments complete ☐
Progress photos taken ☐
Job cost report info. assembled ☐
Job cost reports complete ☐
Other: ☐
_____ ☐
_____ ☐

CRITICAL ITEM COST REPORT SUMMARY

Job/CO No.	Description	(A) Budget $ Amount	(B) Cost To Date	(C) Cost Remaining	(D) Total Commitment (B + C)	(E) +/− (A − D)

CHANGE ORDER SUMMARY

Job No.	C.O. No.	Description	Submission Date Required	Submission Date Actual	Approval Date Required	Approval Date Actual	Remarks

1 FEBRUARY
FRIDAY

WORK	CAL
MONTH TO DATE	1	1
MONTH REMAINING	19	30
YEAR TO DATE	23	32
YEAR REMAINING	231	333

DAILY MINDER

√ Job meeting minutes and reports complete?

√ Scheduled a physical examination?

√ Attend any professional improvement seminars?

√ Last month's requisitions submitted?

JOB NO. APPOINTMENTS/EVENTS/CALLS

7 A.M.

8 A.M.

9 A.M.

10 A.M.

11 A.M.

12 NOON

1 P.M.

2 P.M.

3 P.M.

4 P.M.

5 P.M.

6 P.M.

KEY EVENTS

Meetings

Schedule Updates

Cost Report Updates

Change Proposals

Material Deliveries

Special Information/Instructions

Arch./Owner Direction Received

DAILY DIARY

WEATHER/TEMP.	8 A.M.	12 NOON	4 P.M.

EXPENSES

Annealing: Heat treating process producing a softening of metals and alloys.

2

FEBRUARY

SATURDAY

JOB NO. APPOINTMENTS/EVENTS/CALLS

DAILY DIARY

FEBRUARY

SUNDAY

3

JOB NO. APPOINTMENTS/EVENTS/CALLS

DAILY DIARY

WEEK Beginning 4 FEBRUARY
Ending 10 FEBRUARY

WEEKLY EVENT CHECKLIST

Job meetings and preparation ___
Special meetings ___
Dinners and seminars ___
Assemble schedule information ___
Complete schedule updates ___
Requests out for all required information ___
Outstanding sub/supplier responses ___
Outstanding owner responses ___
Outstanding architect/engineer responses ___
Critical material deliveries confirmed ___
Shop drawings for ongoing work in/appr ___

Submittals for pending work in/appr ___
All other submittals in/approved ___
Shop drawing log up to date ___
All sub change proposals in ___
All change proposals to owner prep'd ___
Submitted change proposals appr ___
Change order logs up to date ___
Required bonds received for all subs ___
Certificates of insurance rec'd for all subs (proper amounts) ___
Equipment/scaffolding release forms in ___

All permits in place ___
Req testing/inspections arranged ___
Inspection certificates received ___
Safety inspections performed ___
Safety recommendations acted on ___
Field reports complete ___
Special photos taken ___
_____ ___
_____ ___
_____ ___

TO DO

Item	Job No.	Item	Job No.

WEEKLY MILESTONE UPDATE

	Planned Date	Actual Date	Variance

DAILY MINDER

√All required design info. received?

√January invoice(s) received?

√Schedule updates complete?

√Verify approval of outstanding change orders.

KEY EVENTS

Meetings

Schedule Updates

Cost Report Updates

Change Proposals

Material Deliveries

Special Information/Instructions

Arch./Owner Direction Received

DAILY DIARY

WEATHER/TEMP.   8A.M.   12NOON   4P.M.

EXPENSES

	WORK	CAL
MONTH TO DATE	2	4
MONTH REMAINING	18	27
YEAR TO DATE	24	35
YEAR REMAINING	230	330

FEBRUARY

4

MONDAY

JOB NO. APPOINTMENTS/EVENTS/CALLS

7A.M.

8A.M.

9A.M.

10A.M.

11A.M.

12NOON

1P.M.

2P.M.

3P.M.

4P.M.

5P.M.

6P.M.

JANUARY						
S	M	T	W	T	F	S
		1	2	3	4	5
6	7	8	9	10	11	12
13	14	15	16	17	18	19
20	21	22	23	24	25	26
27	28	29	30	31		

FEBRUARY						
S	M	T	W	T	F	S
					1	2
3	4	5	6	7	8	9
10	11	12	13	14	15	16
17	18	19	20	21	22	23
24	25	26	27	28		

MARCH						
S	M	T	W	T	F	S
					1	2
3	4	5	6	7	8	9
10	11	12	13	14	15	16
17	18	19	20	21	22	23
24	25	26	27	28	29	30
31						

5 FEBRUARY
TUESDAY

WORK	CAL
MONTH TO DATE	3	5
MONTH REMAINING	17	27
YEAR TO DATE	25	36
YEAR REMAINING	229	329

DAILY MINDER

√Key material deliveries confirmed?

√Field reports up-to-date?

√Last week's schedule commitments in-process?

√Cost reports complete?

JOB NO. APPOINTMENTS/EVENTS/CALLS

7 A.M.

8 A.M.

9 A.M.

10 A.M.

11 A.M.

12 NOON

1 P.M.

2 P.M.

3 P.M.

4 P.M.

5 P.M.

6 P.M.

KEY EVENTS

Meetings

Schedule Updates

Cost Report Updates

Change Proposals

Material Deliveries

Special Information/Instructions

Arch./Owner Direction Received

DAILY DIARY

WEATHER/TEMP.   8 A.M.   12 NOON   4 P.M.

EXPENSES

Laminar Flow: Fluid or air flow in which each particle moves in a smooth path substantially parallel to all other particles.

DAILY MINDER

√All requests for change proposals out?

√January invoices received?

√Cost reports complete?

	WORK	CAL
MONTH TO DATE	4	6
MONTH REMAINING	16	25
YEAR TO DATE	26	37
YEAR REMAINING	228	328

FEBRUARY

6

WEDNESDAY

KEY EVENTS

Meetings

Schedule Updates

Cost Report Updates

Change Proposals

Material Deliveries

Special Information/Instructions

Arch./Owner Direction Received

DAILY DIARY

WEATHER/TEMP.   8A.M.   12NOON   4P.M.

EXPENSES

JOB NO.   APPOINTMENTS/EVENTS/CALLS

7 A.M.

8 A.M.

9 A.M.

10 A.M.

11 A.M.

12 NOON

1 P.M.

2 P.M.

3 P.M.

4 P.M.

5 P.M.

6 P.M.

	JANUARY							FEBRUARY							MARCH					
S	M	T	W	T	F	S	S	M	T	W	T	F	S	S	M	T	W	T	F	S
		1	2	3	4	5						1	2						1	2
6	7	8	9	10	11	12	3	4	5	6	7	8	9	3	4	5	6	7	8	9
13	14	15	16	17	18	19	10	11	12	13	14	15	16	10	11	12	13	14	15	16
20	21	22	23	24	25	26	17	18	19	20	21	22	23	17	18	19	20	21	22	23
27	28	29	30	31			24	25	26	27	28			24	25	26	27	28	29	30
														31						

7 FEBRUARY
THURSDAY

	WORK	CAL
MONTH TO DATE	5	7
MONTH REMAINING	15	24
YEAR TO DATE	27	38
YEAR REMAINING	227	327

JOB NO. APPOINTMENTS/EVENTS/CALLS

7 A.M.

8 A.M.

9 A.M.

10 A.M.

11 A.M.

12 NOON

1 P.M.

2 P.M.

3 P.M.

4 P.M.

5 P.M.

6 P.M.

DAILY MINDER

✓ Job meeting minutes and reports complete?
✓ Key material deliveries confirmed?
✓ Meeting minutes prepared or received?
✓ Safety reviews performed?

KEY EVENTS

Meetings

Schedule Updates

Cost Report Updates

Change Proposals

Material Deliveries

Special Information/Instructions

Arch./Owner Direction Received

DAILY DIARY

WEATHER/TEMP.   8 A.M.   12 NOON   4 P.M.

EXPENSES

Parkerizing: Corrosion protector for internal parts that transforms the steel surface into a nonmetallic, nonconducting surface.

DAILY MINDER

√ Job meeting minutes and reports complete?

√ All change proposals submitted?

√ January invoice(s) received?

	WORK	CAL
MONTH TO DATE	6	8
MONTH REMAINING	14	23
YEAR TO DATE	28	39
YEAR REMAINING	226	326

FEBRUARY

8

FRIDAY

KEY EVENTS

Meetings

Schedule Updates

Cost Report Updates

Change Proposals

Material Deliveries

Special Information/Instructions

Arch./Owner Direction Received

DAILY DIARY

WEATHER/TEMP.   8A.M.   12NOON   4P.M.

EXPENSES

JOB NO. APPOINTMENTS/EVENTS/CALLS

7 A.M.

8 A.M.

9 A.M.

10 A.M.

11 A.M.

12 NOON

1 P.M.

2 P.M.

3 P.M.

4 P.M.

5 P.M.

6 P.M.

JANUARY						
S	M	T W T		F	S	
		1	2	3	4	5
6	7	8	9	10	11	12
13	14	15	16	17	18	19
20	21	22	23	24	25	26
27	28	29	30	31		

FEBRUARY						
S	M	T W T		F	S	
					1	2
3	4	5	6	7	8	9
10	11	12	13	14	15	16
17	18	19	20	21	22	23
24	25	26	27	28		

MARCH						
S	M	T W T		F	S	
					1	2
3	4	5	6	7	8	9
10	11	12	13	14	15	16
17	18	19	20	21	22	23
24	25	26	27	28	29	30
31						

9

FEBRUARY

SATURDAY

	WORK	CAL
MONTH TO DATE	6	9
MONTH REMAINING	14	22
YEAR TO DATE	28	40
YEAR REMAINING	226	325

JOB NO. APPOINTMENTS/EVENTS/CALLS

DAILY DIARY

FEBRUARY

SUNDAY

10

	WORK	CAL
MONTH TO DATE	6	10
MONTH REMAINING	14	21
YEAR TO DATE	28	41
YEAR REMAINING	226	324

JOB NO. APPOINTMENTS/EVENTS/CALLS

DAILY DIARY

WEEK Beginning 11 FEBRUARY
Ending 17 FEBRUARY

WEEKLY EVENT CHECKLIST

Job meetings and preparation —
Special meetings —
Dinners and seminars —
Assemble schedule information —
Complete schedule updates —
Requests out for all required information —
Outstanding sub/supplier responses —
Outstanding owner responses —
Outstanding architect/engineer responses —
Critical material deliveries confirmed —
Shop drawings for ongoing work in/appr —

Submittals for pending work in/appr —
All other submittals in/approved —
Shop drawing log up to date —
All sub change proposals in —
All change proposals to owner prep'd —
Submitted change proposals appr —
Change order logs up to date —
Required bonds received for all subs —
Certificates of insurance rec'd for all subs (proper amounts) —
Equipment/scaffolding release forms in —

All permits in place —
Req testing/inspections arranged —
Inspection certificates received —
Safety inspections performed —
Safety recommendations acted on —
Field reports complete —
Special photos taken —
_____ —
_____ —
_____ —
_____ —

TO DO

Item	Job No.	Item	Job No.

WEEKLY MILESTONE UPDATE

	Planned Date	Actual Date	Variance

11 FEBRUARY

MONDAY

WORK CAL		
MONTH TO DATE	7	11
MONTH REMAINING	13	20
YEAR TO DATE	29	42
YEAR REMAINING	225	323

DAILY MINDER

√ Verify approval of outstanding change orders.

√ Key material deliveries confirmed?

√ Jobsite safety reviews performed?

JOB NO. APPOINTMENTS/EVENTS/CALLS

7 A.M.

8 A.M.

9 A.M.

10 A.M.

11 A.M.

12 NOON

1 P.M.

2 P.M.

3 P.M.

4 P.M.

5 P.M.

6 P.M.

KEY EVENTS

Meetings

Schedule Updates

Cost Report Updates

Change Proposals

Material Deliveries

Special Information/Instructions

Arch./Owner Direction Received

DAILY DIARY

WEATHER/TEMP.   8 A.M.   12 NOON   4 P.M.

EXPENSES

Permeameter: Instrument to measure permeability, generally for soils.

DAILY MINDER

√ Assemble all schedule update information.

√ Winter precautions maintained at jobsite?

√ Preparing for spring-start work?

	WORK	CAL
MONTH TO DATE	8	12
MONTH REMAINING	12	19
YEAR TO DATE	30	43
YEAR REMAINING	224	322

FEBRUARY
Lincoln's
Birthday
TUESDAY

12

KEY EVENTS

Meetings

Schedule Updates

Cost Report Updates

Change Proposals

Material Deliveries

Special Information/Instructions

Arch./Owner Direction Received

DAILY DIARY

WEATHER/TEMP.   8A.M.   12NOON   4P.M.

EXPENSES

JOB NO.   APPOINTMENTS/EVENTS/CALLS

7A.M.

8A.M.

9A.M.

10A.M.

11A.M.

12NOON

1P.M.

2P.M.

3P.M.

4P.M.

5P.M.

6P.M.

JANUARY								FEBRUARY								MARCH						
S	M	T	W	T	F	S		S	M	T	W	T	F	S		S	M	T	W	T	F	S
		1	2	3	4	5							1	2							1	2
6	7	8	9	10	11	12		3	4	5	6	7	8	9		3	4	5	6	7	8	9
13	14	15	16	17	18	19		10	11	12	13	14	15	16		10	11	12	13	14	15	16
20	21	22	23	24	25	26		17	18	19	20	21	22	23		17	18	19	20	21	22	23
27	28	29	30	31				24	25	26	27	28				24	25	26	27	28	29	30
																31						

13 FEBRUARY
Ash
Wednesday
WEDNESDAY

WORK CAL

MONTH TO DATE	9	13
MONTH REMAINING	11	18
YEAR TO DATE	31	44
YEAR REMAINING	223	321

DAILY MINDER

√ Key material deliveries confirmed?

√ Last week's schedule commitments in-process?

√ Current change-orders prepared/submitted?

JOB NO. APPOINTMENTS/EVENTS/CALLS

7 A.M.

8 A.M.

9 A.M.

10 A.M.

11 A.M.

12 NOON

1 P.M.

2 P.M.

3 P.M.

4 P.M.

5 P.M.

6 P.M.

KEY EVENTS

Meetings

Schedule Updates

Cost Report Updates

Change Proposals

Material Deliveries

Special Information/Instructions

Arch./Owner Direction Received

DAILY DIARY

WEATHER/TEMP.   8 A.M.   12 NOON   4 P.M.

EXPENSES

Gumbe: A highly plastic clay, sticky when wet, which develops large shrinkage cracks upon drying.

DAILY MINDER

√ Assemble all schedule update information.

√ Job meeting minutes and reports complete?

√ All cost report information assembled?

	WORK	CAL
MONTH TO DATE	10	14
MONTH REMAINING	10	17
YEAR TO DATE	32	45
YEAR REMAINING	222	320

FEBRUARY
Valentine's
Day
THURSDAY

14

KEY EVENTS

Meetings

Schedule Updates

Cost Report Updates

Change Proposals

Material Deliveries

Special Information/Instructions

Arch./Owner Direction Received

DAILY DIARY

WEATHER/TEMP.   8 A.M.   12 NOON   4 P.M.

EXPENSES

JOB NO.   APPOINTMENTS/EVENTS/CALLS

7 A.M.

8 A.M.

9 A.M.

10 A.M.

11 A.M.

12 NOON

1 P.M.

2 P.M.

3 P.M.

4 P.M.

5 P.M.

6 P.M.

JANUARY							**FEBRUARY**							**MARCH**						
S	M	T	W	T	F	S	S	M	T	W	T	F	S	S	M	T	W	T	F	S
		1	2	3	4	5						1	2						1	2
6	7	8	9	10	11	12	3	4	5	6	7	8	9	3	4	5	6	7	8	9
13	14	15	16	17	18	19	10	11	12	13	14	15	16	10	11	12	13	14	15	16
20	21	22	23	24	25	26	17	18	19	20	21	22	23	17	18	19	20	21	22	23
27	28	29	30	31			24	25	26	27	28			24	25	26	27	28	29	30
														31						

15 FEBRUARY
FRIDAY

WORK CAL		
MONTH TO DATE	11	15
MONTH REMAINING	9	16
YEAR TO DATE	33	46
YEAR REMAINING	221	319

DAILY MINDER

√ Verify approval of outstanding change orders.
√ Schedule update complete?
√ Job meeting minutes and reports complete?
√ Make preparations to relieve winter protection?

JOB NO. APPOINTMENTS/EVENTS/CALLS

7 A.M.

8 A.M.

9 A.M.

10 A.M.

11 A.M.

12 NOON

1 P.M.

2 P.M.

3 P.M.

4 P.M.

5 P.M.

6 P.M.

KEY EVENTS

Meetings

Schedule Updates

Cost Report Updates

Change Proposals

Material Deliveries

Special Information/Instructions

Arch./Owner Direction Received

DAILY DIARY

WEATHER/TEMP.   8 A.M.   12 NOON   4 P.M.

EXPENSES

Direct Shear Test: Test for determining the strength (bearing value) of a soil.

16
FEBRUARY
SATURDAY

FEBRUARY
SUNDAY
17

JOB NO.   APPOINTMENTS/EVENTS/CALLS

JOB NO.   APPOINTMENTS/EVENTS/CALLS

DAILY DIARY

DAILY DIARY

WEEK Beginning 18 FEBRUARY
Ending 24 FEBRUARY

WEEKLY EVENT CHECKLIST

Job meetings and preparation   Submittals for pending work in/appr   All permits in place

Special meetings   All other submittals in/approved   Req testing/inspections arranged

Dinners and seminars   Shop drawing log up to date   Inspection certificates received

Assemble schedule information   All sub change proposals in   Safety inspections performed

Complete schedule updates   All change proposals to owner prep'd   Safety recommendations acted on

Requests out for all required information   Submitted change proposals appr   Field reports complete

Outstanding sub/supplier responses   Change order logs up to date   Special photos taken

Outstanding owner responses   Required bonds received for all subs

Outstanding architect/engineer responses   Certificates of insurance rec'd for all

Critical material deliveries confirmed   subs (proper amounts)

Shop drawings for ongoing work in/appr   Equipment/scaffolding release forms in

TO DO

Item	Job No.	Item	Job No.

WEEKLY MILESTONE UPDATE

	Planned Date	Actual Date	Variance

DAILY MINDER

√ Verify approval of outstanding change orders.

√ Verify receipt of all sub and supplier payment requisitions.

√ Authorize/approve sub and supplier payments.

√ All cost report information assembled?

WORK CAL

MONTH TO DATE	12	18
MONTH REMAINING	8	13
YEAR TO DATE	34	49
YEAR REMAINING	220	316

FEBRUARY
Washington's
Birthday Obsvd.
MONDAY

18

KEY EVENTS

Meetings

Schedule Updates

Cost Report Updates

Change Proposals

Material Deliveries

Special Information/Instructions

Arch./Owner Direction Received

DAILY DIARY

WEATHER/TEMP.   8A.M.   12NOON   4P.M.

EXPENSES

JOB NO. APPOINTMENTS/EVENTS/CALLS

7A.M.

8A.M.

9A.M.

10A.M.

11A.M.

12NOON

1P.M.

2P.M.

3P.M.

4P.M.

5P.M.

6P.M.

JANUARY						
S	M T W T	F	S
		1 2 3	4 5
6	7 8 9 10	11	12
13	14 15 16 17	18	19
20	21 22 23 24	25	26
27	28 29 30 31		

FEBRUARY						
S	M T W T	F	S
			1 2
3	4 5 6 7	8	9
10	11 12 13 14	15	16
17	18 19 20 21	22	23
24	25 26 27 28		

MARCH						
S	M T W T	F	S
			1 2
3	4 5 6 7	8	9
10	11 12 13 14	15	16
17	18 19 20 21	22	23
24	25 26 27 28	29	30
31			

19 FEBRUARY

TUESDAY

WORK	CAL
MONTH TO DATE	13	19
MONTH REMAINING	7	12
YEAR TO DATE	35	50
YEAR REMAINING	219	315

JOB NO. APPOINTMENTS/EVENTS/CALLS

7 A.M.

8 A.M.

9 A.M.

10 A.M.

11 A.M.

12 NOON

1 P.M.

2 P.M.

3 P.M.

4 P.M.

5 P.M.

6 P.M.

DAILY MINDER

√ Assemble all schedule update information.

√ All monthly reports and narratives complete?

√ Key material deliveries confirmed?

√ All cost information assembled?

KEY EVENTS

Meetings

Schedule Updates

Cost Report Updates

Change Proposals

Material Deliveries

Special Information/Instructions

Arch./Owner Direction Received

DAILY DIARY

WEATHER/TEMP.   8 A.M.   12 NOON   4 P.M.

EXPENSES

Hydronics: A coined word meaning the art and practice of heating and cooling with water.

DAILY MINDER

√ Verify approval of outstanding change orders.

√ Verify receipt of all sub and supplier payment requisitions.

√ Submit requisition(s) to owner(s).

√ Authorize/approve sub and supplier payments.

WORK CAL		
MONTH TO DATE	14	20
MONTH REMAINING	6	11
YEAR TO DATE	36	51
YEAR REMAINING	218	314

FEBRUARY

20

WEDNESDAY

KEY EVENTS

Meetings

Schedule Updates

Cost Report Updates

Change Proposals

Material Deliveries

Special Information/Instructions

Arch./Owner Direction Received

DAILY DIARY

WEATHER/TEMP.   8 A.M.   12 NOON   4 P.M.

EXPENSES

JOB NO.   APPOINTMENTS/EVENTS/CALLS

7 A.M.

8 A.M.

9 A.M.

10 A.M.

11 A.M.

12 NOON

1 P.M.

2 P.M.

3 P.M.

4 P.M.

5 P.M.

6 P.M.

	JANUARY							FEBRUARY							MARCH					
S	M	T	W	T	F	S	S	M	T	W	T	F	S	S	M	T	W	T	F	S
		1	2	3	4	5						1	2						1	2
6	7	8	9	10	11	12	3	4	5	6	7	8	9	3	4	5	6	7	8	9
13	14	15	16	17	18	19	10	11	12	13	14	15	16	10	11	12	13	14	15	16
20	21	22	23	24	25	26	17	18	19	20	21	22	23	17	18	19	20	21	22	23
27	28	29	30	31			24	25	26	27	28			24	25	26	27	28	29	30
														31						

21

FEBRUARY

THURSDAY

DAILY MINDER

√ Submit requisition(s) to owner(s).

√ Schedule update complete?

√ Job meeting minutes and reports complete?

√ Cost report complete?

JOB NO. APPOINTMENTS/EVENTS/CALLS

7 A.M.

8 A.M.

9 A.M.

10 A.M.

11 A.M.

12 NOON

1 P.M.

2 P.M.

3 P.M.

4 P.M.

5 P.M.

6 P.M.

KEY EVENTS

Meetings

Schedule Updates

Cost Report Updates

Change Proposals

Material Deliveries

Special Information/Instructions

Arch./Owner Direction Received

DAILY DIARY

WEATHER/TEMP.   8 A.M.   12 NOON   4 P.M.

EXPENSES

Coulomb: A quantity of electric charge, equivalent to that transported by a current of one ampere flowing for one second.

DAILY MINDER

√ Verify approval of outstanding change orders.

√ Submit requisition(s) to owner(s).

√ Authorize/approve sub and supplier payments.

√ Cost report complete?

WORK CAL

MONTH TO DATE	16	22
MONTH REMAINING	4	9
YEAR TO DATE	38	53
YEAR REMAINING	216	312

FEBRUARY 22
Washington's Birthday
FRIDAY

KEY EVENTS

Meetings

Schedule Updates

Cost Report Updates

Change Proposals

Material Deliveries

Special Information/Instructions

Arch./Owner Direction Received

DAILY DIARY

WEATHER/TEMP.   8A.M.   12NOON   4P.M.

EXPENSES

JOB NO. APPOINTMENTS/EVENTS/CALLS

7 A.M.

8 A.M.

9 A.M.

10 A.M.

11 A.M.

12 NOON

1 P.M.

2 P.M.

3 P.M.

4 P.M.

5 P.M.

6 P.M.

	JANUARY							FEBRUARY							MARCH					
S	M	T	W	T	F	S	S	M	T	W	T	F	S	S	M	T	W	T	F	S
		1	2	3	4	5						1	2						1	2
6	7	8	9	10	11	12	3	4	5	6	7	8	9	3	4	5	6	7	8	9
13	14	15	16	17	18	19	10	11	12	13	14	15	16	10	11	12	13	14	15	16
20	21	22	23	24	25	26	17	18	19	20	21	22	23	17	18	19	20	21	22	23
27	28	29	30	31			24	25	26	27	28			24	25	26	27	28	29	30
														31						

23

FEBRUARY

SATURDAY

JOB NO. APPOINTMENTS/EVENTS/CALLS

DAILY DIARY

24

FEBRUARY

SUNDAY

JOB NO. APPOINTMENTS/EVENTS/CALLS

DAILY DIARY

WEEK Beginning 25 FEBRUARY
Ending 3 MARCH

WEEKLY EVENT CHECKLIST

Job meetings and preparation	Submittals for pending work in/appr ___	All permits in place ___
Special meetings	All other submittals in/approved ___	Req testing/inspections arranged ___
Dinners and seminars	Shop drawing log up to date ___	Inspection certificates received ___
Assemble schedule information	All sub change proposals in ___	Safety inspections performed ___
Complete schedule updates	All change proposals to owner prep'd ___	Safety recommendations acted on ___
Requests out for all required information ___	Submitted change proposals appr ___	Field reports complete ___
Outstanding sub/supplier responses	Change order logs up to date ___	Special photos taken ___
Outstanding owner responses	Required bonds received for all subs ___	_____ ___
Outstanding architect/engineer responses ___	Certificates of insurance rec'd for all	_____ ___
Critical material deliveries confirmed ___	subs (proper amounts) ___	_____ ___
Shop drawings for ongoing work in/appr ___	Equipment/scaffolding release forms in ___	_____ ___

TO DO

Item	Job No.	Item	Job No.

WEEKLY MILESTONE UPDATE

	Planned Date	Actual Date	Variance

25 FEBRUARY
MONDAY

DAILY MINDER

√ This month's schedule update complete?
√ This month's reports and narratives complete?
√ Key material deliveries confirmed?
√ Invoices prepared/submitted?

JOB NO. APPOINTMENTS/EVENTS/CALLS

7 A.M.

8 A.M.

9 A.M.

10 A.M.

11 A.M.

12 NOON

1 P.M.

2 P.M.

3 P.M.

4 P.M.

5 P.M.

6 P.M.

KEY EVENTS

Meetings

Schedule Updates

Cost Report Updates

Change Proposals

Material Deliveries

Special Information/Instructions

Arch./Owner Direction Received

DAILY DIARY

WEATHER/TEMP.   8 A.M.   12 NOON   4 P.M.

EXPENSES

Magnaflux: Mechanical means of locating minute cracks in metal which are usually caused by heat treating or fatigue.

DAILY MINDER

√ Schedule update complete?
√ Reports and narratives complete?
√ Progress photos taken?
√ Cost-report info assembled?

WORK	CAL	
MONTH TO DATE	18	26
MONTH REMAINING	2	5
YEAR TO DATE	40	57
YEAR REMAINING	214	308

FEBRUARY
26
TUESDAY

KEY EVENTS

Meetings

Schedule Updates

Cost Report Updates

Change Proposals

Material Deliveries

Special Information/Instructions

Arch./Owner Direction Received

DAILY DIARY

WEATHER/TEMP.   8A.M.   12NOON   4P.M.

EXPENSES

JOB NO. APPOINTMENTS/EVENTS/CALLS

7A.M.

8A.M.

9A.M.

10A.M.

11A.M.

12NOON

1P.M.

2P.M.

3P.M.

4P.M.

5P.M.

6P.M.

	JANUARY							FEBRUARY							MARCH					
S	M	T	W	T	F	S	S	M	T	W	T	F	S	S	M	T	W	T	F	S
		1	2	3	4	5						1	2						1	2
6	7	8	9	10	11	12	3	4	5	6	7	8	9	3	4	5	6	7	8	9
13	14	15	16	17	18	19	10	11	12	13	14	15	16	10	11	12	13	14	15	16
20	21	22	23	24	25	26	17	18	19	20	21	22	23	17	18	19	20	21	22	23
27	28	29	30	31			24	25	26	27	28			24	25	26	27	28	29	30
														31						

27 FEBRUARY
WEDNESDAY

DAILY MINDER

√Schedule updates complete?
√Reports and narratives complete?
√Key material deliveries confirmed?
√Progress photos taken?

JOB NO. APPOINTMENTS/EVENTS/CALLS

7 A.M.

8 A.M.

9 A.M.

10 A.M.

11 A.M.

12 NOON

1 P.M.

2 P.M.

3 P.M.

4 P.M.

5 P.M.

6 P.M.

KEY EVENTS

Meetings

Schedule Updates

Cost Report Updates

Change Proposals

Material Deliveries

Special Information/Instructions

Arch./Owner Direction Received

DAILY DIARY

WEATHER/TEMP.   8 A.M.   12 NOON   4 P.M.

EXPENSES

Friction Loss: A loss of pressure between the inlet and outlet of a pipe or duct due to frictional resistance, or drag.

DAILY MINDER

✓ Job meeting minutes and reports complete?

✓ Progress photos taken?

✓ Attend any professional development seminars?

WORK	CAL
MONTH TO DATE	20	28
MONTH REMAINING	0	3
YEAR TO DATE	42	59
YEAR REMAINING	212	306

FEBRUARY

28

THURSDAY

KEY EVENTS

Meetings

Schedule Updates

Cost Report Updates

Change Proposals

Material Deliveries

Special Information/Instructions

Arch./Owner Direction Received

DAILY DIARY

WEATHER/TEMP.   8 A.M.   12 NOON   4 P.M.

EXPENSES

JOB NO. APPOINTMENTS/EVENTS/CALLS

7 A.M.

8 A.M.

9 A.M.

10 A.M.

11 A.M.

12 NOON

1 P.M.

2 P.M.

3 P.M.

4 P.M.

5 P.M.

6 P.M.

JANUARY							
S	M	T	W	T	F	S
		1	2	3	4	5
6	7	8	9	10	11	12
13	14	15	16	17	18	19
20	21	22	23	24	25	26
27	28	29	30	31		

FEBRUARY							
S	M	T	W	T	F	S
					1	2
3	4	5	6	7	8	9
10	11	12	13	14	15	16
17	18	19	20	21	22	23
24	25	26	27	28		

MARCH							
S	M	T	W	T	F	S
					1	2
3	4	5	6	7	8	9
10	11	12	13	14	15	16
17	18	19	20	21	22	23
24	25	26	27	28	29	30
31						

MARCH

20 Working Days

31 Calendar Days

FEBRUARY

S	M	T	W	T	F	S
					1	2
3	4	5	6	7	8	9
10	11	12	13	14	15	16
17	18	19	20	21	22	23
24	25	26	27	28		

MARCH

S	M	T	W	T	F	S
					1	2
3	4	5	6	7	8	9
10	11	12	13	14	15	16
17	18	19	20	21	22	23
24	25	26	27	28	29	30
31						

APRIL

S	M	T	W	T	F	S
	1	2	3	4	5	6
7	8	9	10	11	12	13
14	15	16	17	18	19	20
21	22	23	24	25	26	27
28	29	30				

MONTHLY KEY ACTIVITY UPDATE

Job/C.O. No.	Description	Planned Date	Actual Date	Variance	Remarks

MONTHLY SCHEDULE UPDATE SUMMARY

Job/C.O. No.	Activities	Original Duration	Days Spent	Days Remaining	Status/Remarks

MONTHLY RECAP

	S	M	T	W	T	F	S
						1	2
	3	4	5	6	7	8	9
	10	11	12	13	14	15	16
	17	18	19	20	21	22	23
	24	25	26	27	28	29	30
	31						

MARCH

MONTHLY EVENT CHECKLIST

Schedule updates complete	☐ All sub change proposals in	☐ Sub/supplier contract(s) rec'd
Requests out for all required info.	☐ All change proposals to owner prepared	☐ Requisition(s) submitted to owner(s)
Outstanding sub/supplier responses rec'd	☐ Submitted change proposals approved	☐ Sub/supplier adjustments complete
Outstanding owner responses rec'd	☐ Guarantees/warrantees rec'd	☐ Progress photos taken
Outstanding arch./eng. responses rec'd	☐ Inspection certificates rec'd	☐ Job cost report info. assembled
Critical material deliveries confirmed	☐ As-built drawings rec'd	☐ Job cost reports complete
Shop drawings for ongoing work in/appr	☐ Safety inspections performed	☐ Other:
Submittals for pending work in/appr	☐ Safety reports complete	☐ _____
All other submittals in/approved	☐ Narratives complete	☐ _____

CRITICAL ITEM COST REPORT SUMMARY

Job/CO No.	Description	(A) Budget $ Amount	(B) Cost To Date	(C) Cost Remaining	(D) Total Commitment (B + C)	(E) +/− (A − D)

CHANGE ORDER SUMMARY

Job No.	C.O. No.	Description	Submission Date Required	Submission Date Actual	Approval Date Required	Approval Date Actual	Remarks

1 MARCH

FRIDAY

WORK CAL		
MONTH TO DATE	1	1
MONTH REMAINING	19	30
YEAR TO DATE	43	60
YEAR REMAINING	211	305

JOB NO. APPOINTMENTS/EVENTS/CALLS

7 A.M.

8 A.M.

9 A.M.

10 A.M.

11 A.M.

12 NOON

1 P.M.

2 P.M.

3 P.M.

4 P.M.

5 P.M.

6 P.M.

KEY EVENTS

Meetings

Schedule Updates

Cost Report Updates

Change Proposals

Material Deliveries

Special Information/Instructions

Arch./Owner Direction Received

DAILY DIARY

WEATHER/TEMP.	8 A.M.	12 NOON	4 P.M.

EXPENSES

Caisson: Watertight steel or concrete shell that can be lowered into water or ground water to allow construction of a foundation within it.

2 MARCH
SATURDAY

	WORK	CAL
MONTH TO DATE	1	2
MONTH REMAINING	19	29
YEAR TO DATE	43	61
YEAR REMAINING	211	304

JOB NO. APPOINTMENTS/EVENTS/CALLS

DAILY DIARY

3 MARCH
SUNDAY

	WORK	CAL
MONTH TO DATE	1	3
MONTH REMAINING	19	28
YEAR TO DATE	43	62
YEAR REMAINING	211	303

JOB NO. APPOINTMENTS/EVENTS/CALLS

DAILY DIARY

WEEK Beginning 4 MARCH
Ending 10 MARCH

WEEKLY EVENT CHECKLIST

Job meetings and preparation ___   Submittals for pending work in/appr ___   All permits in place ___

Special meetings ___   All other submittals in/approved ___   Req testing/inspections arranged ___

Dinners and seminars ___   Shop drawing log up to date ___   Inspection certificates received ___

Assemble schedule information ___   All sub change proposals in ___   Safety inspections performed ___

Complete schedule updates ___   All change proposals to owner prep'd ___   Safety recommendations acted on ___

Requests out for all required information ___   Submitted change proposals appr ___   Field reports complete ___

Outstanding sub/supplier responses ___   Change order logs up to date ___   Special photos taken ___

Outstanding owner responses ___   Required bonds received for all subs ___   _____ ___

Outstanding architect/engineer responses ___   Certificates of insurance rec'd for all   _____ ___

Critical material deliveries confirmed ___   subs (proper amounts) ___   _____ ___

Shop drawings for ongoing work in/appr ___   Equipment/scaffolding release forms in ___   _____ ___

TO DO

Item	Job No.	Item	Job No.

WEEKLY MILESTONE UPDATE

	Planned Date	Actual Date	Variance

DAILY MINDER

√ Verify receipt of last month's payment.
√ All requests for change proposals out?
√ Last week's schedule commitments in-process?
√ Last month reports & narratives complete?

KEY EVENTS

Meetings

Schedule Updates

Cost Report Updates

Change Proposals

Material Deliveries

Special Information/Instructions

Arch./Owner Direction Received

DAILY DIARY

WEATHER/TEMP.   8A.M.   12NOON   4P.M.

EXPENSES

	WORK	CAL
MONTH TO DATE	2	4
MONTH REMAINING	18	27
YEAR TO DATE	44	63
YEAR REMAINING	210	302

MARCH

MONDAY

4

JOB NO.   APPOINTMENTS/EVENTS/CALLS

7A.M.

8A.M.

9A.M.

10A.M.

11A.M.

12NOON

1P.M.

2P.M.

3P.M.

4P.M.

5P.M.

6P.M.

	FEBRUARY					
S	M	T	W	T	F	S
					1	2
3	4	5	6	7	8	9
10	11	12	13	14	15	16
17	18	19	20	21	22	23
24	25	26	27	28		

	MARCH					
S	M	T	W	T	F	S
					1	2
3	4	5	6	7	8	9
10	11	12	13	14	15	16
17	18	19	20	21	22	23
24	25	26	27	28	29	30
31						

	APRIL					
S	M	T	W	T	F	S
	1	2	3	4	5	6
7	8	9	10	11	12	13
14	15	16	17	18	19	20
21	22	23	24	25	26	27
28	29	30				

5 MARCH
TUESDAY

DAILY MINDER

√ Key material deliveries confirmed?
√ All requests for change proposals out?
√ Current change orders prepared/submitted?

JOB NO.   APPOINTMENTS/EVENTS/CALLS

7 A.M.

8 A.M.

9 A.M.

10 A.M.

11 A.M.

12 NOON

1 P.M.

2 P.M.

3 P.M.

4 P.M.

5 P.M.

6 P.M.

KEY EVENTS

Meetings

Schedule Updates

Cost Report Updates

Change Proposals

Material Deliveries

Special Information/Instructions

Arch./Owner Direction Received

DAILY DIARY

WEATHER/TEMP.   8 A.M.   12 NOON   4 P.M.

EXPENSES

Heterogeneous: Consisting of several different materials.

DAILY MINDER

√ Scheduled a complete physical examination this year?

√ All change order proposals submitted?

√ February's invoice(s) received?

	WORK	CAL
MONTH TO DATE	4	6
MONTH REMAINING	16	25
YEAR TO DATE	46	65
YEAR REMAINING	208	300

MARCH

WEDNESDAY

6

KEY EVENTS

Meetings

Schedule Updates

Cost Report Updates

Change Proposals

Material Deliveries

Special Information/Instructions

Arch./Owner Direction Received

DAILY DIARY

WEATHER/TEMP.   8A.M.   12NOON   4P.M.

EXPENSES

JOB NO. APPOINTMENTS/EVENTS/CALLS

7A.M.

8A.M.

9A.M.

10A.M.

11A.M.

12NOON

1P.M.

2P.M.

3P.M.

4P.M.

5P.M.

6P.M.

FEBRUARY							MARCH							APRIL						
S	M	T	W	T	F	S	S	M	T	W	T	F	S	S	M	T	W	T	F	S
					1	2						1	2		1	2	3	4	5	6
3	4	5	6	7	8	9	3	4	5	6	7	8	9	7	8	9	10	11	12	13
10	11	12	13	14	15	16	10	11	12	13	14	15	16	14	15	16	17	18	19	20
17	18	19	20	21	22	23	17	18	19	20	21	22	23	21	22	23	24	25	26	27
24	25	26	27	28			24	25	26	27	28	29	30	28	29	30				
							31													

7 MARCH
THURSDAY

DAILY MINDER

√ Job meeting minutes and reports complete?
√ Key material deliveries confirmed?
√ Request/receive outstanding design info?

JOB NO.   APPOINTMENTS/EVENTS/CALLS

7 A.M.

8 A.M.

9 A.M.

10 A.M.

11 A.M.

12 NOON

1 P.M.

2 P.M.

3 P.M.

4 P.M.

5 P.M.

6 P.M.

KEY EVENTS

Meetings

Schedule Updates

Cost Report Updates

Change Proposals

Material Deliveries

Special Information/Instructions

Arch./Owner Direction Received

DAILY DIARY

WEATHER/TEMP.   8A.M.   12NOON   4P.M.

EXPENSES

Rheostat: Electrical device to vary the amount of resistance in a circuit, thereby changing the quantity of current flowing.

DAILY MINDER

√ Job meetintg minutes and reports complete?

√ Jobsite safety reviews performed?

√ Current schedule commitments in-process?

	WORK	CAL
MONTH TO DATE	6	8
MONTH REMAINING	14	23
YEAR TO DATE	48	67
YEAR REMAINING	206	298

MARCH

FRIDAY

8

KEY EVENTS

Meetings

Schedule Updates

Cost Report Updates

Change Proposals

Material Deliveries

Special Information/Instructions

Arch./Owner Direction Received

DAILY DIARY

WEATHER/TEMP.   8A.M.   12NOON   4P.M.

EXPENSES

JOB NO.   APPOINTMENTS/EVENTS/CALLS

7 A.M.

8 A.M.

9 A.M.

10 A.M.

11 A.M.

12 NOON

1 P.M.

2 P.M.

3 P.M.

4 P.M.

5 P.M.

6 P.M.

9 MARCH

SATURDAY

	WORK	CAL
MONTH TO DATE	6	9
MONTH REMAINING	14	22
YEAR TO DATE	48	68
YEAR REMAINING	206	297

JOB NO.   APPOINTMENTS/EVENTS/CALLS

DAILY DIARY

	WORK	CAL
MONTH TO DATE	6	10
MONTH REMAINING	14	21
YEAR TO DATE	48	69
YEAR REMAINING	206	296

MARCH 10

SUNDAY

JOB NO.   APPOINTMENTS/EVENTS/CALLS

DAILY DIARY

WEEK Beginning 11 MARCH
Ending 17 MARCH

WEEKLY EVENT CHECKLIST

Job meetings and preparation
Special meetings
Dinners and seminars
Assemble schedule information
Complete schedule updates
Requests out for all required information
Outstanding sub/supplier responses
Outstanding owner responses
Outstanding architect/engineer responses
Critical material deliveries confirmed
Shop drawings for ongoing work in/appr

___ Submittals for pending work in/appr
___ All other submittals in/approved
___ Shop drawing log up to date
___ All sub change proposals in
___ All change proposals to owner prep'd
___ Submitted change proposals appr
___ Change order logs up to date
___ Required bonds received for all subs
___ Certificates of insurance rec'd for all
     subs (proper amounts)
___ Equipment/scaffolding release forms in

___ All permits in place
___ Req testing/inspections arranged
___ Inspection certificates received
___ Safety inspections performed
___ Safety recommendations acted on
___ Field reports complete
___ Special photos taken
___ _____
___ _____
___ _____

TO DO

Item	Job No.	Item	Job No.

WEEKLY MILESTONE UPDATE

	Planned Date	Actual Date	Variance

11 MARCH

MONDAY

DAILY MINDER

√ Key material deliveries confirmed?

√ Quarterly report info. assembled?

√ Current schedule commitments in-process?

JOB NO. APPOINTMENTS/EVENTS/CALLS

7 A.M.

8 A.M.

9 A.M.

10 A.M.

11 A.M.

12 NOON

1 P.M.

2 P.M.

3 P.M.

4 P.M.

5 P.M.

6 P.M.

KEY EVENTS

Meetings

Schedule Updates

Cost Report Updates

Change Proposals

Material Deliveries

Special Information/Instructions

Arch./Owner Direction Received

DAILY DIARY

WEATHER/TEMP.   8A.M.   12NOON   4P.M.

EXPENSES

Optimum Moisture Content: Water content at which a given soil can be compacted to its maximum density.

DAILY MINDER

√ Assemble all schedule update information.
√ Meeting minutes prepared/received?
√ Current change orders prepared/submitted?

<table>
<tr><td></td><td>WORK</td><td>CAL</td></tr>
<tr><td>MONTH TO DATE</td><td>8</td><td>12</td></tr>
<tr><td>MONTH REMAINING</td><td>12</td><td>19</td></tr>
<tr><td>YEAR TO DATE</td><td>50</td><td>71</td></tr>
<tr><td>YEAR REMAINING</td><td>204</td><td>294</td></tr>
</table>

MARCH

12

TUESDAY

KEY EVENTS

Meetings

Schedule Updates

Cost Report Updates

Change Proposals

Material Deliveries

Special Information/Instructions

Arch./Owner Direction Received

DAILY DIARY

WEATHER/TEMP.   8A.M.   12NOON   4P.M.

EXPENSES

JOB NO. APPOINTMENTS/EVENTS/CALLS

7A.M.

8A.M.

9A.M.

10A.M.

11A.M.

12NOON

1P.M.

2P.M.

3P.M.

4P.M.

5P.M.

6P.M.

<table>
<tr><th colspan="7">FEBRUARY</th></tr>
<tr><td>S</td><td>M</td><td>T</td><td>W</td><td>T</td><td>F</td><td>S</td></tr>
<tr><td></td><td></td><td></td><td></td><td></td><td>1</td><td>2</td></tr>
<tr><td>3</td><td>4</td><td>5</td><td>6</td><td>7</td><td>8</td><td>9</td></tr>
<tr><td>10</td><td>11</td><td>12</td><td>13</td><td>14</td><td>15</td><td>16</td></tr>
<tr><td>17</td><td>18</td><td>19</td><td>20</td><td>21</td><td>22</td><td>23</td></tr>
<tr><td>24</td><td>25</td><td>26</td><td>27</td><td>28</td><td></td><td></td></tr>
</table>

<table>
<tr><th colspan="7">MARCH</th></tr>
<tr><td>S</td><td>M</td><td>T</td><td>W</td><td>T</td><td>F</td><td>S</td></tr>
<tr><td></td><td></td><td></td><td></td><td></td><td>1</td><td>2</td></tr>
<tr><td>3</td><td>4</td><td>5</td><td>6</td><td>7</td><td>8</td><td>9</td></tr>
<tr><td>10</td><td>11</td><td>12</td><td>13</td><td>14</td><td>15</td><td>16</td></tr>
<tr><td>17</td><td>18</td><td>19</td><td>20</td><td>21</td><td>22</td><td>23</td></tr>
<tr><td>24</td><td>25</td><td>26</td><td>27</td><td>28</td><td>29</td><td>30</td></tr>
<tr><td>31</td><td></td><td></td><td></td><td></td><td></td><td></td></tr>
</table>

<table>
<tr><th colspan="7">APRIL</th></tr>
<tr><td>S</td><td>M</td><td>T</td><td>W</td><td>T</td><td>F</td><td>S</td></tr>
<tr><td></td><td></td><td>1</td><td>2</td><td>3</td><td>4</td><td>5</td><td>6</td></tr>
<tr><td>7</td><td>8</td><td>9</td><td>10</td><td>11</td><td>12</td><td>13</td></tr>
<tr><td>14</td><td>15</td><td>16</td><td>17</td><td>18</td><td>19</td><td>20</td></tr>
<tr><td>21</td><td>22</td><td>23</td><td>24</td><td>25</td><td>26</td><td>27</td></tr>
<tr><td>28</td><td>29</td><td>30</td><td></td><td></td><td></td><td></td></tr>
</table>

13 MARCH
WEDNESDAY

DAILY MINDER

√ Key material deliveries confirmed?
√ Field reports up-to-date?
√ Outstanding design info requested/received?

JOB NO. APPOINTMENTS/EVENTS/CALLS

7 A.M.

8 A.M.

9 A.M.

10 A.M.

11 A.M.

12 NOON

1 P.M.

2 P.M.

3 P.M.

4 P.M.

5 P.M.

6 P.M.

KEY EVENTS

Meetings

Schedule Updates

Cost Report Updates

Change Proposals

Material Deliveries

Special Information/Instructions

Arch./Owner Direction Received

DAILY DIARY

WEATHER/TEMP.   8 A.M.   12 NOON   4 P.M.

EXPENSES

Hygrometer: Instrument for measuring relative humidity.

DAILY MINDER

√ Assemble all schedule update information.
√ Job meeting minutes and reports complete?
√ Current changes submitted/approved?

	WORK	CAL
MONTH TO DATE	10	14
MONTH REMAINING	10	17
YEAR TO DATE	52	73
YEAR REMAINING	202	292

MARCH

THURSDAY

14

KEY EVENTS

Meetings

Schedule Updates

Cost Report Updates

Change Proposals

Material Deliveries

Special Information/Instructions

Arch./Owner Direction Received

DAILY DIARY

WEATHER/TEMP.   8A.M.   12NOON   4P.M.

EXPENSES

JOB NO.   APPOINTMENTS/EVENTS/CALLS

7 A.M.

8 A.M.

9 A.M.

10 A.M.

11 A.M.

12 NOON

1 P.M.

2 P.M.

3 P.M.

4 P.M.

5 P.M.

6 P.M.

15 MARCH FRIDAY

WORK	CAL	
MONTH TO DATE	11	15
MONTH REMAINING	9	16
YEAR TO DATE	53	74
YEAR REMAINING	201	291

DAILY MINDER

√ Job meeting minutes and reports complete?
√ Current schedule commitments in-process?
√ Key material deliveries confirmed?

JOB NO. APPOINTMENTS/EVENTS/CALLS

7 A.M.

8 A.M.

9 A.M.

10 A.M.

11 A.M.

12 NOON

1 P.M.

2 P.M.

3 P.M.

4 P.M.

5 P.M.

6 P.M.

KEY EVENTS

Meetings

Schedule Updates

Cost Report Updates

Change Proposals

Material Deliveries

Special Information/Instructions

Arch./Owner Direction Received

DAILY DIARY

WEATHER/TEMP.   8 A.M.   12 NOON   4 P.M.

EXPENSES

Anemometer: Instrument for measuring air velocity.

16 MARCH
SATURDAY

	WORK	CAL
MONTH TO DATE	11	16
MONTH REMAINING	9	15
YEAR TO DATE	53	75
YEAR REMAINING	201	290

JOB NO. APPOINTMENTS/EVENTS/CALLS

DAILY DIARY

	WORK	CAL
MONTH TO DATE	11	17
MONTH REMAINING	9	14
YEAR TO DATE	53	76
YEAR REMAINING	201	289

17 MARCH
St. Patrick's Day
SUNDAY

JOB NO. APPOINTMENTS/EVENTS/CALLS

DAILY DIARY

WEEK Beginning 18 MARCH
Ending 24 MARCH

WEEKLY EVENT CHECKLIST

Job meetings and preparation ___
Special meetings ___
Dinners and seminars ___
Assemble schedule information ___
Complete schedule updates ___
Requests out for all required information ___
Outstanding sub/supplier responses ___
Outstanding owner responses ___
Outstanding architect/engineer responses ___
Critical material deliveries confirmed ___
Shop drawings for ongoing work in/appr ___

Submittals for pending work in/appr ___
All other submittals in/approved ___
Shop drawing log up to date ___
All sub change proposals in ___
All change proposals to owner prep'd ___
Submitted change proposals appr ___
Change order logs up to date ___
Required bonds received for all subs ___
Certificates of insurance rec'd for all subs (proper amounts) ___
Equipment/scaffolding release forms in ___

All permits in place ___
Req testing/inspections arranged ___
Inspection certificates received ___
Safety inspections performed ___
Safety recommendations acted on ___
Field reports complete ___
Special photos taken ___
_____ ___
_____ ___
_____ ___
_____ ___

TO DO

Item	Job No.	Item	Job No.

WEEKLY MILESTONE UPDATE

	Planned Date	Actual Date	Variance

DAILY MINDER

√ Verify approval of outstanding change orders.
√ Verify receipt of all sub and supplier payment requisitions.
√ Schedule commitments in-process?
√ Current change orders prepared/submitted?

	WORK CAL		MARCH
MONTH TO DATE	12	18	
MONTH REMAINING	8	13	
YEAR TO DATE	54	77	
YEAR REMAINING	200	288	MONDAY

18

KEY EVENTS

Meetings

Schedule Updates

Cost Report Updates

Change Proposals

Material Deliveries

Special Information/Instructions

Arch./Owner Direction Received

DAILY DIARY

WEATHER/TEMP.   8 A.M.   12 NOON   4 P.M.

EXPENSES

JOB NO. APPOINTMENTS/EVENTS/CALLS

7 A.M.

8 A.M.

9 A.M.

10 A.M.

11 A.M.

12 NOON

1 P.M.

2 P.M.

3 P.M.

4 P.M.

5 P.M.

6 P.M.

		FEBRUARY								MARCH								APRIL				
S	M	T	W	T	F	S	S	M	T	W	T	F	S	S	M	T	W	T	F	S
					1	2						1	2			1	2	3	4	5	6
3	4	5	6	7	8	9	3	4	5	6	7	8	9	7	8	9	10	11	12	13
10	11	12	13	14	15	16	10	11	12	13	14	15	16	14	15	16	17	18	19	20
17	18	19	20	21	22	23	17	18	19	20	21	22	23	21	22	23	24	25	26	27
24	25	26	27	28			24	25	26	27	28	29	30	28	29	30				
							31													

19

MARCH
TUESDAY

DAILY MINDER

√ Verify receipt of all sub and supplier payment requisitions.
√ Assemble all schedule update information.
√ Key material deliveries confirmed?
√ Quarterly report info. assembled?

JOB NO. APPOINTMENTS/EVENTS/CALLS

7 A.M.

8 A.M.

9 A.M.

10 A.M.

11 A.M.

12 NOON

1 P.M.

2 P.M.

3 P.M.

4 P.M.

5 P.M.

6 P.M.

KEY EVENTS

Meetings

Schedule Updates

Cost Report Updates

Change Proposals

Material Deliveries

Special Information/Instructions

Arch./Owner Direction Received

DAILY DIARY

WEATHER/TEMP.   8 A.M.   12 NOON   4 P.M.

EXPENSES

Drift Pin: Round spikelike tool used to align holes in structural steel members to be joined.

DAILY MINDER

√Verify approval of outstanding change orders.

√Schedule update complete?

√All cost report information assembled?

√Outstanding design info. requested/received?

	WORK	CAL
MONTH TO DATE	14	20
MONTH REMAINING	6	11
YEAR TO DATE	56	79
YEAR REMAINING	198	286

MARCH
WEDNESDAY 20

KEY EVENTS

Meetings

Schedule Updates

Cost Report Updates

Change Proposals

Material Deliveries

Special Information/Instructions

Arch./Owner Direction Received

DAILY DIARY

WEATHER/TEMP.   8 A.M.   12 NOON   4 P.M.

EXPENSES

JOB NO.   APPOINTMENTS/EVENTS/CALLS

7 A.M.

8 A.M.

9 A.M.

10 A.M.

11 A.M.

12 NOON

1 P.M.

2 P.M.

3 P.M.

4 P.M.

5 P.M.

6 P.M.

FEBRUARY							MARCH							APRIL						
S	M	T	W	T	F	S	S	M	T	W	T	F	S	S	M	T	W	T	F	S
					1	2						1	2			1	2	3	4	5	6
3	4	5	6	7	8	9	3	4	5	6	7	8	9	7	8	9	10	11	12	13
10	11	12	13	14	15	16	10	11	12	13	14	15	16	14	15	16	17	18	19	20
17	18	19	20	21	22	23	17	18	19	20	21	22	23	21	22	23	24	25	26	27
24	25	26	27	28			24	25	26	27	28	29	30	28	29	30				
							31													

21 MARCH
THURSDAY

WORK	CAL
MONTH TO DATE	15	21
MONTH REMAINING	5	10
YEAR TO DATE	57	80
YEAR REMAINING	197	285

DAILY MINDER

√ Authorize/approve sub and supplier payments.
√ Job meeting minutes and reports complete?
√ All monthly reports and narratives complete?
√ Key material deliveries confirmed?

JOB NO. APPOINTMENTS/EVENTS/CALLS

7 A.M.

8 A.M.

9 A.M.

10 A.M.

11 A.M.

12 NOON

1 P.M.

2 P.M.

3 P.M.

4 P.M.

5 P.M.

6 P.M.

KEY EVENTS

Meetings

Schedule Updates

Cost Report Updates

Change Proposals

Material Deliveries

Special Information/Instructions

Arch./Owner Direction Received

DAILY DIARY

WEATHER/TEMP.   8 A.M.   12 NOON   4 P.M.

EXPENSES

Broaching: A means of making holes in metal by removing bits of metal at a time with a reaming tool.

DAILY MINDER

√ Verify approval of outstanding change orders.
√ Authorize/approve sub and supplier payments.
√ Job meeting minutes and reports complete?
√ Assemble sub/supplier requisitions?

KEY EVENTS

Meetings

Schedule Updates

Cost Report Updates

Change Proposals

Material Deliveries

Special Information/Instructions

Arch./Owner Direction Received

DAILY DIARY

WEATHER/TEMP.   8 A.M.   12 NOON   4 P.M.

EXPENSES

WORK CAL

MONTH TO DATE	16	22
MONTH REMAINING	4	9
YEAR TO DATE	58	81
YEAR REMAINING	196	284

MARCH

22

FRIDAY

JOB NO.   APPOINTMENTS/EVENTS/CALLS

7 A.M.

8 A.M.

9 A.M.

10 A.M.

11 A.M.

12 NOON

1 P.M.

2 P.M.

3 P.M.

4 P.M.

5 P.M.

6 P.M.

FEBRUARY						
S	M	T	W	T	F	S
					1	2
3	4	5	6	7	8	9
10	11	12	13	14	15	16
17	18	19	20	21	22	23
24	25	26	27	28		

MARCH						
S	M	T	W	T	F	S
					1	2
3	4	5	6	7	8	9
10	11	12	13	14	15	16
17	18	19	20	21	22	23
24	25	26	27	28	29	30
31						

APRIL						
S	M	T	W	T	F	S
	1	2	3	4	5	6
7	8	9	10	11	12	13
14	15	16	17	18	19	20
21	22	23	24	25	26	27
28	29	30				

23

	WORK	CAL
MONTH TO DATE	16	23
MONTH REMAINING	4	8
YEAR TO DATE	58	82
YEAR REMAINING	196	283

	WORK	CAL
MONTH TO DATE	16	24
MONTH REMAINING	4	7
YEAR TO DATE	58	83
YEAR REMAINING	196	282

24

JOB NO. APPOINTMENTS/EVENTS/CALLS

JOB NO. APPOINTMENTS/EVENTS/CALLS

DAILY DIARY

DAILY DIARY

WEEK Beginning 25 MARCH
Ending 31 MARCH

WEEKLY EVENT CHECKLIST

Job meetings and preparation ___
Special meetings ___
Dinners and seminars ___
Assemble schedule information ___
Complete schedule updates ___
Requests out for all required information ___
Outstanding sub/supplier responses ___
Outstanding owner responses ___
Outstanding architect/engineer responses ___
Critical material deliveries confirmed ___
Shop drawings for ongoing work in/appr ___

___ Submittals for pending work in/appr
___ All other submittals in/approved
___ Shop drawing log up to date
___ All sub change proposals in
___ All change proposals to owner prep'd
___ Submitted change proposals appr
___ Change order logs up to date
___ Required bonds received for all subs
___ Certificates of insurance rec'd for all subs (proper amounts)
___ Equipment/scaffolding release forms in

___ All permits in place ___
___ Req testing/inspections arranged ___
___ Inspection certificates received ___
___ Safety inspections performed ___
___ Safety recommendations acted on ___
___ Field reports complete ___
___ Special photos taken ___
___ _____ ___
___ _____ ___
___ _____ ___

TO DO

Item	Job No.	Item	Job No.

WEEKLY MILESTONE UPDATE

	Planned Date	Actual Date	Variance

25

MARCH
MONDAY

WORK CAL		
MONTH TO DATE	17	25
MONTH REMAINING	3	6
YEAR TO DATE	59	84
YEAR REMAINING	195	281

JOB NO. APPOINTMENTS/EVENTS/CALLS

7 A.M.

8 A.M.

9 A.M.

10 A.M.

11 A.M.

12 NOON

1 P.M.

2 P.M.

3 P.M.

4 P.M.

5 P.M.

6 P.M.

DAILY MINDER

√ Verify approval of outstanding change orders.

√ Submit requisition(s) to owner(s).

√ Schedule update complete?

√ Cost report complete?

KEY EVENTS

Meetings

Schedule Updates

Cost Report Updates

Change Proposals

Material Deliveries

Special Information/Instructions

Arch./Owner Direction Received

DAILY DIARY

WEATHER/TEMP.   8A.M.   12NOON   4P.M.

EXPENSES

Mansard Roof: Roof having two pitches on all four sides, the lower of which is steeper than the upper.

DAILY MINDER

√ Submit requisition(s) to owner(s).

√ Authorize/approve sub and supplier payments.

√ All monthly reports and narratives complete?

√ Cost report complete?

KEY EVENTS

Meetings

Schedule Updates

Cost Report Updates

Change Proposals

Material Deliveries

Special Information/Instructions

Arch./Owner Direction Received

DAILY DIARY

WEATHER/TEMP.   8A.M.   12NOON   4P.M.

EXPENSES

	WORK	CAL
MONTH TO DATE	18	26
MONTH REMAINING	2	5
YEAR TO DATE	60	85
YEAR REMAINING	194	280

MARCH
26
TUESDAY

JOB NO.   APPOINTMENTS/EVENTS/CALLS

7A.M.

8A.M.

9A.M.

10A.M.

11A.M.

12NOON

1P.M.

2P.M.

3P.M.

4P.M.

5P.M.

6P.M.

	FEBRUARY						
S	M	T	W	T	F	S
					1	2
3	4	5	6	7	8	9
10	11	12	13	14	15	16
17	18	19	20	21	22	23
24	25	26	27	28		

	MARCH						
S	M	T	W	T	F	S
					1	2
3	4	5	6	7	8	9
10	11	12	13	14	15	16
17	18	19	20	21	22	23
24	25	26	27	28	29	30
31						

	APRIL						
S	M	T	W	T	F	S
	1	2	3	4	5	6
7	8	9	10	11	12	13
14	15	16	17	18	19	20
21	22	23	24	25	26	27
28	29	30				

27

MARCH
WEDNESDAY

WORK	CAL
MONTH TO DATE	19	27
MONTH REMAINING	1	4
YEAR TO DATE	61	86
YEAR REMAINING	193	279

JOB NO. APPOINTMENTS/EVENTS/CALLS

7 A.M.

8 A.M.

9 A.M.

10 A.M.

11 A.M.

12 NOON

1 P.M.

2 P.M.

3 P.M.

4 P.M.

5 P.M.

6 P.M.

KEY EVENTS

Meetings

Schedule Updates

Cost Report Updates

Change Proposals

Material Deliveries

Special Information/Instructions

Arch./Owner Direction Received

DAILY DIARY

WEATHER/TEMP.   8 A.M.   12 NOON   4 P.M.

EXPENSES

Yield Point: The point on a stress-strain curve where, for a given material, an increase in stress causes a permanent deformation.

DAILY MINDER

√ Schedule updates complete?

√ Job meeting minutes and reports complete?

√ Reports and narratives complete?

√ Quarterly reports prepared?

KEY EVENTS

Meetings

Schedule Updates

Cost Report Updates

Change Proposals

Material Deliveries

Special Information/Instructions

Arch./Owner Direction Received

DAILY DIARY

WEATHER/TEMP.   8A.M.   12NOON   4P.M.

EXPENSES

	WORK	CAL
MONTH TO DATE	20	28
MONTH REMAINING	0	3
YEAR TO DATE	62	87
YEAR REMAINING	192	278

MARCH
28
THURSDAY

JOB NO.   APPOINTMENTS/EVENTS/CALLS

7A.M.

8A.M.

9A.M.

10A.M.

11A.M.

12NOON

1P.M.

2P.M.

3P.M.

4P.M.

5P.M.

6P.M.

FEBRUARY							MARCH							APRIL						
S	M	T	W	T	F	S	S	M	T	W	T	F	S	S	M	T	W	T	F	S
					1	2						1	2			1	2	3	4	5	6
3	4	5	6	7	8	9	3	4	5	6	7	8	9	7	8	9	10	11	12	13
10	11	12	13	14	15	16	10	11	12	13	14	15	16	14	15	16	17	18	19	20
17	18	19	20	21	22	23	17	18	19	20	21	22	23	21	22	23	24	25	26	27
24	25	26	27	28			24	25	26	27	28	29	30	28	29	30				
							31													

29

MARCH
Good
Friday
FRIDAY

		WORK	CAL
MONTH TO DATE		20	29
MONTH REMAINING		0	2
YEAR TO DATE		62	88
YEAR REMAINING		192	277

JOB NO. APPOINTMENTS/EVENTS/CALLS

7 A.M.

8 A.M.

9 A.M.

10 A.M.

11 A.M.

12 NOON

1 P.M.

2 P.M.

3 P.M.

4 P.M.

5 P.M.

6 P.M.

DAILY MINDER

KEY EVENTS

Meetings

Schedule Updates

Cost Report Updates

Change Proposals

Material Deliveries

Special Information/Instructions

Arch./Owner Direction Received

DAILY DIARY

WEATHER/TEMP.	8 A.M.	12 NOON	4 P.M.

EXPENSES

Newel Post: An end post supporting a run of handrail.

30 MARCH
Passover

SATURDAY

	WORK	CAL
MONTH TO DATE	20	30
MONTH REMAINING	0	1
YEAR TO DATE	62	89
YEAR REMAINING	192	276

	WORK	CAL
MONTH TO DATE	20	31
MONTH REMAINING	0	0
YEAR TO DATE	62	90
YEAR REMAINING	192	275

MARCH
Easter

SUNDAY

31

JOB NO. APPOINTMENTS/EVENTS/CALLS

JOB NO. APPOINTMENTS/EVENTS/CALLS

DAILY DIARY

DAILY DIARY

APRIL

22 Working Days

30 Calendar Days

MARCH						
S	M	T	W	T	F	S
					1	2
3	4	5	6	7	8	9
10	11	12	13	14	15	16
17	18	19	20	21	22	23
24	25	26	27	28	29	30
31						

APRIL						
S	M	T	W	T	F	S
	1	2	3	4	5	6
7	8	9	10	11	12	13
14	15	16	17	18	19	20
21	22	23	24	25	26	27
28	29	30				

MAY						
S	M	T	W	T	F	S
			1	2	3	4
5	6	7	8	9	10	11
12	13	14	15	16	17	18
19	20	21	22	23	24	25
26	27	28	29	30	31	

MONTHLY KEY ACTIVITY UPDATE

Job/C.O. No.	Description	Planned Date	Actual Date	Variance	Remarks

MONTHLY SCHEDULE UPDATE SUMMARY

Job/C.O. No.	Activities	Original Duration	Days Spent	Days Remaining	Status/Remarks

MONTHLY RECAP

S	M	T	W	T	F	S
	1	2	3	4	5	6
7	8	9	10	11	12	13
14	15	16	17	18	19	20
21	22	23	24	25	26	27
28	29	30				

APRIL

MONTHLY EVENT CHECKLIST

Schedule updates complete

Requests out for all required info.

Outstanding sub/supplier responses rec'd

Outstanding owner responses rec'd

Outstanding arch./eng. responses rec'd

Critical material deliveries confirmed

Shop drawings for ongoing work in/appr

Submittals for pending work in/appr

All other submittals in/approved

All sub change proposals in

All change proposals to owner prepared

Submitted change proposals approved

Guarantees/warrantees rec'd

Inspection certificates rec'd

As-built drawings rec'd

Safety inspections performed

Safety reports complete

Narratives complete

Sub/supplier contract(s) rec'd

Requisition(s) submitted to owner(s)

Sub/supplier adjustments complete

Progress photos taken

Job cost report info. assembled

Job cost reports complete

Other:

_____

_____

CRITICAL ITEM COST REPORT SUMMARY

Job/CO No.	Description	(A) Budget $ Amount	(B) Cost To Date	(C) Cost Remaining	(D) Total Commitment (B + C)	(E) +/− (A − D)

CHANGE ORDER SUMMARY

Job No.	C.O. No.	Description	Submission Date Required	Submission Date Actual	Approval Date Required	Approval Date Actual	Remarks

WEEK Beginning 1 APRIL
Ending 7 APRIL

WEEKLY EVENT CHECKLIST

Job meetings and preparation ___
Special meetings ___
Dinners and seminars ___
Assemble schedule information ___
Complete schedule updates ___
Requests out for all required information ___
Outstanding sub/supplier responses ___
Outstanding owner responses ___
Outstanding architect/engineer responses ___
Critical material deliveries confirmed ___
Shop drawings for ongoing work in/appr ___

Submittals for pending work in/appr ___
All other submittals in/approved ___
Shop drawing log up to date ___
All sub change proposals in ___
All change proposals to owner prep'd ___
Submitted change proposals appr ___
Change order logs up to date ___
Required bonds received for all subs ___
Certificates of insurance rec'd for all subs (proper amounts) ___
Equipment/scaffolding release forms in ___

All permits in place ___
Req testing/inspections arranged ___
Inspection certificates received ___
Safety inspections performed ___
Safety recommendations acted on ___
Field reports complete ___
Special photos taken ___
_____ ___
_____ ___
_____ ___
_____ ___

TO DO

Item	Job No.	Item	Job No.

WEEKLY MILESTONE UPDATE

	Planned Date	Actual Date	Variance

DAILY MINDER

√ Verify receipt of last month's payment.
√ Progress photos taken?
√ Required submittals in and approved?
√ Cost report prepared?

KEY EVENTS

Meetings

Schedule Updates

Cost Report Updates

Change Proposals

Material Deliveries

Special Information/Instructions

Arch./Owner Direction Received

DAILY DIARY

WEATHER/TEMP.   8 A.M.   12 NOON   4 P.M.

EXPENSES

	MARCH						
S	M	T	W	T	F	S	
					1	2	
3	4	5	6	7	8	9	
10	11	12	13	14	15	16	
17	18	19	20	21	22	23	
24	25	26	27	28	29	30	
31							

	APRIL						
S	M	T	W	T	F	S	
		1	2	3	4	5	6
7	8	9	10	11	12	13	
14	15	16	17	18	19	20	
21	22	23	24	25	26	27	
28	29	30					

	MAY						
S	M	T	W	T	F	S	
				1	2	3	4
5	6	7	8	9	10	11	
12	13	14	15	16	17	18	
19	20	21	22	23	24	25	
26	27	28	29	30	31		

WORK	CAL		
MONTH TO DATE	1	1	
MONTH REMAINING	21	30	
YEAR TO DATE	63	91	
YEAR REMAINING	191	274	

APRIL

MONDAY

1

JOB NO.   APPOINTMENTS/EVENTS/CALLS

7 A.M.

8 A.M.

9 A.M.

10 A.M.

11 A.M.

12 NOON

1 P.M.

2 P.M.

3 P.M.

4 P.M.

5 P.M.

6 P.M.

2 APRIL
TUESDAY

	WORK	CAL
MONTH TO DATE	2	2
MONTH REMAINING	20	29
YEAR TO DATE	64	92
YEAR REMAINING	190	273

JOB NO. APPOINTMENTS/EVENTS/CALLS

7 A.M.

8 A.M.

9 A.M.

10 A.M.

11 A.M.

12 NOON

1 P.M.

2 P.M.

3 P.M.

4 P.M.

5 P.M.

6 P.M.

KEY EVENTS

Meetings

Schedule Updates

Cost Report Updates

Change Proposals

Material Deliveries

Special Information/Instructions

Arch./Owner Direction Received

DAILY DIARY

WEATHER/TEMP.   8 A.M.   12 NOON   4 P.M.

EXPENSES

Hydrometer: Calibrated float designed to determine the specific gravity of liquids.

DAILY MINDER

√ Requests for change proposals out?
√ All change proposals submitted?
√ Last month's reports/narratives complete?
√ Last month's schedule updates complete?

KEY EVENTS

Meetings

Schedule Updates

Cost Report Updates

Change Proposals

Material Deliveries

Special Information/Instructions

Arch./Owner Direction Received

DAILY DIARY

WEATHER/TEMP.   8A.M.   12NOON   4P.M.

EXPENSES

WORK CAL		
MONTH TO DATE	3	3
MONTH REMAINING	19	28
YEAR TO DATE	65	93
YEAR REMAINING	189	272

APRIL

WEDNESDAY

3

JOB NO. APPOINTMENTS/EVENTS/CALLS

7A.M.

8A.M.

9A.M.

10A.M.

11A.M.

12NOON

1P.M.

2P.M.

3P.M.

4P.M.

5P.M.

6P.M.

	MARCH					
S	M	T	W	T	F	S
					1	2
3	4	5	6	7	8	9
10	11	12	13	14	15	16
17	18	19	20	21	22	23
24	25	26	27	28	29	30
31						

	APRIL					
S	M	T	W	T	F	S
	1	2	3	4	5	6
7	8	9	10	11	12	13
14	15	16	17	18	19	20
21	22	23	24	25	26	27
28	29	30				

	MAY					
S	M	T	W	T	F	S
			1	2	3	4
5	6	7	8	9	10	11
12	13	14	15	16	17	18
19	20	21	22	23	24	25
26	27	28	29	30	31	

4 APRIL THURSDAY

	WORK	CAL
MONTH TO DATE	4	4
MONTH REMAINING	18	27
YEAR TO DATE	66	94
YEAR REMAINING	188	271

DAILY MINDER

√ Job meeting minutes and reports complete?
√ Key material deliveries confirmed?
√ Current change orders prepared/submitted?
√ Current schedule commitments in-process?

JOB NO. APPOINTMENTS/EVENTS/CALLS

7 A.M.

8 A.M.

9 A.M.

10 A.M.

11 A.M.

12 NOON

1 P.M.

2 P.M.

3 P.M.

4 P.M.

5 P.M.

6 P.M.

KEY EVENTS

Meetings

Schedule Updates

Cost Report Updates

Change Proposals

Material Deliveries

Special Information/Instructions

Arch./Owner Direction Received

DAILY DIARY

WEATHER/TEMP.   8 A.M.   12 NOON   4 P.M.

EXPENSES

Eave Strut: Structural member spanning between columns at the edge of a roof. Usually applies to preengineered steel buildings.

DAILY MINDER

√ Job meeting minutes and reports complete?

√ Key material deliveries confirmed?

√ Field reports up-to-date?

√ Request/receive outstanding design job?

KEY EVENTS

Meetings

Schedule Updates

Cost Report Updates

Change Proposals

Material Deliveries

Special Information/Instructions

Arch./Owner Direction Received

DAILY DIARY

WEATHER/TEMP.   8A.M.   12NOON   4P.M.

EXPENSES

	WORK	CAL	**APRIL**
MONTH TO DATE	5	5	
MONTH REMAINING	17	27	
YEAR TO DATE	67	95	
YEAR REMAINING	187	270	**FRIDAY**

5

JOB NO.   APPOINTMENTS/EVENTS/CALLS

7A.M.

8A.M.

9A.M.

10A.M.

11A.M.

12NOON

1P.M.

2P.M.

3P.M.

4P.M.

5P.M.

6P.M.

	MARCH							APRIL							MAY					
S	M	T	W	T	F	S	S	M	T	W	T	F	S	S	M	T	W	T	F	S
					1	2			1	2	3	4	5	6				1	2	3	4
3	4	5	6	7	8	9	7	8	9	10	11	12	13	5	6	7	8	9	10	11
10	11	12	13	14	15	16	14	15	16	17	18	19	20	12	13	14	15	16	17	18
17	18	19	20	21	22	23	21	22	23	24	25	26	27	19	20	21	22	23	24	25
24	25	26	27	28	29	30	28	29	30					26	27	28	29	30	31	
31																				

6 APRIL

SATURDAY

	WORK	CAL
MONTH TO DATE	5	6
MONTH REMAINING	17	25
YEAR TO DATE	67	96
YEAR REMAINING	187	269

JOB NO. APPOINTMENTS/EVENTS/CALLS

DAILY DIARY

7 APRIL

SUNDAY

	WORK	CAL
MONTH TO DATE	5	7
MONTH REMAINING	17	24
YEAR TO DATE	67	97
YEAR REMAINING	187	268

JOB NO. APPOINTMENTS/EVENTS/CALLS

DAILY DIARY

WEEK Beginning 8 APRIL
Ending 14 APRIL

WEEKLY EVENT CHECKLIST

- Job meetings and preparation
- Special meetings
- Dinners and seminars
- Assemble schedule information
- Complete schedule updates
- Requests out for all required information
- Outstanding sub/supplier responses
- Outstanding owner responses
- Outstanding architect/engineer responses
- Critical material deliveries confirmed
- Shop drawings for ongoing work in/appr

- [ ] Submittals for pending work in/appr
- [ ] All other submittals in/approved
- [ ] Shop drawing log up to date
- [ ] All sub change proposals in
- [ ] All change proposals to owner prep'd
- [ ] Submitted change proposals appr
- [ ] Change order logs up to date
- [ ] Required bonds received for all subs
- [ ] Certificates of insurance rec'd for all subs (proper amounts)
- [ ] Equipment/scaffolding release forms in

- [ ] All permits in place
- [ ] Req testing/inspections arranged
- [ ] Inspection certificates received
- [ ] Safety inspections performed
- [ ] Safety recommendations acted on
- [ ] Field reports complete
- [ ] Special photos taken
- [ ] _____
- [ ] _____
- [ ] _____
- [ ] _____

TO DO

Item	Job No.	Item	Job No.

WEEKLY MILESTONE UPDATE

	Planned Date	Actual Date	Variance

8 APRIL
MONDAY

WORK	CAL
MONTH TO DATE	6	8
MONTH REMAINING	16	23
YEAR TO DATE	68	98
YEAR REMAINING	186	267

JOB NO. APPOINTMENTS/EVENTS/CALLS

7 A.M.

8 A.M.

9 A.M.

10 A.M.

11 A.M.

12 NOON

1 P.M.

2 P.M.

3 P.M.

4 P.M.

5 P.M.

6 P.M.

DAILY MINDER

√ Verify receipt of last month's payment.

√ Key material deliveries confirmed?

√ Requests for change proposals out?

√ Current schedule commitments in-process?

KEY EVENTS

Meetings

Schedule Updates

Cost Report Updates

Change Proposals

Material Deliveries

Special Information/Instructions

Arch./Owner Direction Received

DAILY DIARY

WEATHER/TEMP.   8 A.M.   12 NOON   4 P.M.

EXPENSES

Plasticizer: An admixture for mortar or plaster mixes to give a more plastic (workable) quality.

DAILY MINDER

√Scheduled a physical examination?
√Personal income tax prepared?
√Current change orders submitted?
√Outstanding design info. requested/received?

KEY EVENTS

Meetings

Schedule Updates

Cost Report Updates

Change Proposals

Material Deliveries

Special Information/Instructions

Arch./Owner Direction Received

DAILY DIARY

WEATHER/TEMP.   8A.M.   12NOON   4P.M.

EXPENSES

	WORK	CAL
MONTH TO DATE	7	9
MONTH REMAINING	15	22
YEAR TO DATE	69	99
YEAR REMAINING	185	266

APRIL

TUESDAY

9

JOB NO.   APPOINTMENTS/EVENTS/CALLS

7A.M.

8A.M.

9A.M.

10A.M.

11A.M.

12NOON

1P.M.

2P.M.

3P.M.

4P.M.

5P.M.

6P.M.

	MARCH							APRIL							MAY					
S	M	T	W	T	F	S	S	M	T	W	T	F	S	S	M	T	W	T	F	S
					1	2		1	2	3	4	5	6				1	2	3	4
3	4	5	6	7	8	9	7	8	9	10	11	12	13	5	6	7	8	9	10	11
10	11	12	13	14	15	16	14	15	16	17	18	19	20	12	13	14	15	16	17	18
17	18	19	20	21	22	23	21	22	23	24	25	26	27	19	20	21	22	23	24	25
24	25	26	27	28	29	30	28	29	30					26	27	28	29	30	31	
31																				

10 APRIL
WEDNESDAY

WORK	CAL	
MONTH TO DATE	8	10
MONTH REMAINING	14	21
YEAR TO DATE	70	100
YEAR REMAINING	184	265

JOB NO. APPOINTMENTS/EVENTS/CALLS

7 A.M.

8 A.M.

9 A.M.

10 A.M.

11 A.M.

12 NOON

1 P.M.

2 P.M.

3 P.M.

4 P.M.

5 P.M.

6 P.M.

DAILY MINDER

√ Key material deliveries confirmed?
√ Personal income tax prepared?
√ Requests for change proposals out?
√ Schedule commitments in-process?

KEY EVENTS

Meetings

Schedule Updates

Cost Report Updates

Change Proposals

Material Deliveries

Special Information/Instructions

Arch./Owner Direction Received

DAILY DIARY

WEATHER/TEMP.   8 A.M.   12 NOON   4 P.M.

EXPENSES

Jack Rafter: Short rafters framing into a hip or valley.

DAILY MINDER

√ Assemble all schedule update information?
√ Job meeting minutes and reports complete?
√ Personal income tax prepared?
√ Current schedule commitments in-process?

	WORK	CAL	**APRIL**
MONTH TO DATE	9	11	
MONTH REMAINING	11	20	
YEAR TO DATE	71	101	
YEAR REMAINING	183	264	**THURSDAY**

11

KEY EVENTS

Meetings

Schedule Updates

Cost Report Updates

Change Proposals

Material Deliveries

Special Information/Instructions

Arch./Owner Direction Received

DAILY DIARY

WEATHER/TEMP.   8 A.M.   12 NOON   4 P.M.

EXPENSES

JOB NO.   APPOINTMENTS/EVENTS/CALLS

7 A.M.

8 A.M.

9 A.M.

10 A.M.

11 A.M.

12 NOON

1 P.M.

2 P.M.

3 P.M.

4 P.M.

5 P.M.

6 P.M.

	MARCH							APRIL							MAY					
S	M	T	W	T	F	S	S	M	T	W	T	F	S	S	M	T	W	T	F	S
					1	2			1	2	3	4	5	6				1	2	3	4
3	4	5	6	7	8	9	7	8	9	10	11	12	13	5	6	7	8	9	10	11
10	11	12	13	14	15	16	14	15	16	17	18	19	20	12	13	14	15	16	17	18
17	18	19	20	21	22	23	21	22	23	24	25	26	27	19	20	21	22	23	24	25
24	25	26	27	28	29	30	28	29	30					26	27	28	29	30	31	
31																				

12 APRIL

FRIDAY

	WORK	CAL
MONTH TO DATE	10	12
MONTH REMAINING	10	19
YEAR TO DATE	72	102
YEAR REMAINING	182	263

DAILY MINDER

√ Job meeting minutes and reports complete?

√ Change proposals prepared/submitted?

√ Required submittals in/approved?

JOB NO. APPOINTMENTS/EVENTS/CALLS

7 A.M.

8 A.M.

9 A.M.

10 A.M.

11 A.M.

12 NOON

1 P.M.

2 P.M.

3 P.M.

4 P.M.

5 P.M.

6 P.M.

KEY EVENTS

Meetings

Schedule Updates

Cost Report Updates

Change Proposals

Material Deliveries

Special Information/Instructions

Arch./Owner Direction Received

DAILY DIARY

WEATHER/TEMP.   8 A.M.   12 NOON   4 P.M.

EXPENSES

Dado Joint: A joint having a rectangular groove cut into the surface of one board, and into which the end of a joining board is fitted.

13 APRIL
SATURDAY

	WORK	CAL
MONTH TO DATE	10	13
MONTH REMAINING	12	18
YEAR TO DATE	72	103
YEAR REMAINING	182	262

JOB NO. APPOINTMENTS/EVENTS/CALLS

DAILY DIARY

APRIL 14
SUNDAY

	WORK	CAL
MONTH TO DATE	10	14
MONTH REMAINING	12	17
YEAR TO DATE	72	104
YEAR REMAINING	182	261

JOB NO. APPOINTMENTS/EVENTS/CALLS

DAILY DIARY

WEEK Beginning 15 APRIL
Ending 21 APRIL

WEEKLY EVENT CHECKLIST

Job meetings and preparation ⬚
Special meetings ⬚
Dinners and seminars ⬚
Assemble schedule information ⬚
Complete schedule updates ⬚
Requests out for all required information ⬚
Outstanding sub/supplier responses ⬚
Outstanding owner responses ⬚
Outstanding architect/engineer responses ⬚
Critical material deliveries confirmed ⬚
Shop drawings for ongoing work in/appr ⬚

Submittals for pending work in/appr ⬚
All other submittals in/approved ⬚
Shop drawing log up to date ⬚
All sub change proposals in ⬚
All change proposals to owner prep'd ⬚
Submitted change proposals appr ⬚
Change order logs up to date ⬚
Required bonds received for all subs ⬚
Certificates of insurance rec'd for all subs (proper amounts) ⬚
Equipment/scaffolding release forms in ⬚

All permits in place ⬚
Req testing/inspections arranged ⬚
Inspection certificates received ⬚
Safety inspections performed ⬚
Safety recommendations acted on ⬚
Field reports complete ⬚
Special photos taken ⬚
⬚ _____ ⬚
⬚ _____ ⬚
⬚ _____ ⬚
⬚ _____ ⬚

TO DO

Item	Job No.	Item	Job No.

WEEKLY MILESTONE UPDATE

	Planned Date	Actual Date	Variance

DAILY MINDER

√Verify approval of outstanding change orders.

√All required design info. received?

√Current schedule commitments in-process?

√Midnight deadline to file income tax.

WORK	CAL	APRIL
MONTH TO DATE	11 15	
MONTH REMAINING	11 16	
YEAR TO DATE	73 105	
YEAR REMAINING	181 260	**MONDAY**

15

KEY EVENTS

Meetings

Schedule Updates

Cost Report Updates

Change Proposals

Material Deliveries

Special Information/Instructions

Arch./Owner Direction Received

DAILY DIARY

WEATHER/TEMP.   8A.M.   12NOON   4P.M.

EXPENSES

JOB NO. APPOINTMENTS/EVENTS/CALLS

7A.M.

8A.M.

9A.M.

10A.M.

11A.M.

12NOON

1P.M.

2P.M.

3P.M.

4P.M.

5P.M.

6P.M.

MARCH							APRIL							MAY						
S	M	T	W	T	F	S	S	M	T	W	T	F	S	S	M	T	W	T	F	S
					1	2			1	2	3	4	5					1	2	3
3	4	5	6	7	8	9	6	7	8	9	10	11	12	4	5	6	7	8	9	10
10	11	12	13	14	15	16	13	14	15	16	17	18	19	11	12	13	14	15	16	17
17	18	19	20	21	22	23	20	21	22	23	24	25	26	18	19	20	21	22	23	24
24	25	26	27	28	29	30	27	28	29	30				25	26	27	28	29	30	31
31																				

16 APRIL
TUESDAY

DAILY MINDER

√Assemble all schedule update information.
√Key material deliveries confirmed?
√Requests for changes out?
√Your income tax is late.

JOB NO. APPOINTMENTS/EVENTS/CALLS

7 A.M.
8 A.M.
9 A.M.
10 A.M.
11 A.M.
12 NOON
1 P.M.
2 P.M.
3 P.M.
4 P.M.
5 P.M.
6 P.M.

KEY EVENTS

Meetings

Schedule Updates

Cost Report Updates

Change Proposals

Material Deliveries

Special Information/Instructions

Arch./Owner Direction Received

DAILY DIARY

WEATHER/TEMP.   8 A.M.   12 NOON   4 P.M.

EXPENSES

Trimmer: A stud supporting a lintel or a header; a short wood member into which joists or rafters are framed.

DAILY MINDER

√Verify approval of outstanding change orders.

√Schedule update info. assembled?

√Requests for change proposals out?

√Outstanding design info. requested/received?

KEY EVENTS

Meetings

Schedule Updates

Cost Report Updates

Change Proposals

Material Deliveries

Special Information/Instructions

Arch./Owner Direction Received

DAILY DIARY

WEATHER/TEMP.   8A.M.   12NOON   4P.M.

EXPENSES

	WORK CAL		APRIL
MONTH TO DATE	13	17	
MONTH REMAINING	9	14	
YEAR TO DATE		75 107	
YEAR REMAINING		179 258	WEDNESDAY

17

JOB NO.   APPOINTMENTS/EVENTS/CALLS

7A.M.

8A.M.

9A.M.

10A.M.

11A.M.

12NOON

1P.M.

2P.M.

3P.M.

4P.M.

5P.M.

6P.M.

MARCH							APRIL							MAY						
S	M	T	W	T	F	S	S	M	T	W	T	F	S	S	M	T	W	T	F	S
					1	2		1	2	3	4	5	6				1	2	3	4
3	4	5	6	7	8	9	7	8	9	10	11	12	13	5	6	7	8	9	10	11
10	11	12	13	14	15	16	14	15	16	17	18	19	20	12	13	14	15	16	17	18
17	18	19	20	21	22	23	21	22	23	24	25	26	27	19	20	21	22	23	24	25
24	25	26	27	28	29	30	28	29	30					26	27	28	29	30	31	
31																				

18 APRIL THURSDAY

WORK		CAL
MONTH TO DATE	14	18
MONTH REMAINING	8	13
YEAR TO DATE	76	108
YEAR REMAINING	178	257

DAILY MINDER

✓ Request/receive outstanding design info?
✓ Assemble all schedule update information.
✓ Job meeting minutes and reports complete?
✓ Key material deliveries confirmed?

JOB NO. APPOINTMENTS/EVENTS/CALLS

7 A.M.

8 A.M.

9 A.M.

10 A.M.

11 A.M.

12 NOON

1 P.M.

2 P.M.

3 P.M.

4 P.M.

5 P.M.

6 P.M.

KEY EVENTS

Meetings

Schedule Updates

Cost Report Updates

Change Proposals

Material Deliveries

Special Information/Instructions

Arch./Owner Direction Received

DAILY DIARY

WEATHER/TEMP.   8A.M.   12NOON   4P.M.

EXPENSES

Hydration: The chemical action resulting from combining a material with water; usually refers to hardening process of cement.

DAILY MINDER

√Authorize sub/supplier payments?

√Schedule update prepared?

√Job meeting minutes and reports prepared?

√All monthly reports and narratives prepared?

KEY EVENTS

Meetings

Schedule Updates

Cost Report Updates

Change Proposals

Material Deliveries

Special Information/Instructions

Arch./Owner Direction Received

DAILY DIARY

WEATHER/TEMP.   8A.M.   12NOON   4P.M.

EXPENSES

	WORK CAL		**APRIL**
MONTH TO DATE	15	19	
MONTH REMAINING	7	12	
YEAR TO DATE	77	109	
YEAR REMAINING	177	256	**FRIDAY**

19

JOB NO. APPOINTMENTS/EVENTS/CALLS

7A.M.

8A.M.

9A.M.

10A.M.

11A.M.

12NOON

1P.M.

2P.M.

3P.M.

4P.M.

5P.M.

6P.M.

	MARCH							APRIL							MAY					
S	M	T	W	T	F	S	S	M	T	W	T	F	S	S	M	T	W	T	F	S
					1	2		1	2	3	4	5	6				1	2	3	4
3	4	5	6	7	8	9	7	8	9	10	11	12	13	5	6	7	8	9	10	11
10	11	12	13	14	15	16	14	15	16	17	18	19	20	12	13	14	15	16	17	18
17	18	19	20	21	22	23	21	22	23	24	25	26	27	19	20	21	22	23	24	25
24	25	26	27	28	29	30	28	29	30					26	27	28	29	30	31	
31																				

20 APRIL

SATURDAY

JOB NO. APPOINTMENTS/EVENTS/CALLS

DAILY DIARY

21 APRIL

SUNDAY

JOB NO. APPOINTMENTS/EVENTS/CALLS

DAILY DIARY

WEEK Beginning 22 APRIL
Ending 28 APRIL

WEEKLY EVENT CHECKLIST

Job meetings and preparation
Special meetings
Dinners and seminars
Assemble schedule information
Complete schedule updates
Requests out for all required information
Outstanding sub/supplier responses
Outstanding owner responses
Outstanding architect/engineer responses
Critical material deliveries confirmed
Shop drawings for ongoing work in/appr

Submittals for pending work in/appr
All other submittals in/approved
Shop drawing log up to date
All sub change proposals in
All change proposals to owner prep'd
Submitted change proposals appr
Change order logs up to date
Required bonds received for all subs
Certificates of insurance rec'd for all subs (proper amounts)
Equipment/scaffolding release forms in

All permits in place
Req testing/inspections arranged
Inspection certificates received
Safety inspections performed
Safety recommendations acted on
Field reports complete
Special photos taken

TO DO

Item	Job No.	Item	Job No.

WEEKLY MILESTONE UPDATE

	Planned Date	Actual Date	Variance

22 APRIL
MONDAY

DAILY MINDER

√ Verify approval of outstanding change orders.
√ Authorize/approve sub and supplier payments.
√ Key material deliveries confirmed?
√ All cost report information assembled?

JOB NO. APPOINTMENTS/EVENTS/CALLS

7 A.M.

8 A.M.

9 A.M.

10 A.M.

11 A.M.

12 NOON

1 P.M.

2 P.M.

3 P.M.

4 P.M.

5 P.M.

6 P.M.

KEY EVENTS

Meetings

Schedule Updates

Cost Report Updates

Change Proposals

Material Deliveries

Special Information/Instructions

Arch./Owner Direction Received

DAILY DIARY

WEATHER/TEMP.   8 A.M.   12 NOON   4 P.M.

EXPENSES

Chaining: Measuring horizontal distances by means of a steel tape.

DAILY MINDER

√ Submit requisition(s) to owner(s).
√ Assemble all schedule update information.
√ Schedule update complete?
√ All monthly reports and narratives complete?

WORK CAL			APRIL
MONTH TO DATE	17	23	
MONTH REMAINING	5	8	
YEAR TO DATE	79	113	
YEAR REMAINING	175	252	TUESDAY

23

KEY EVENTS

Meetings

Schedule Updates

Cost Report Updates

Change Proposals

Material Deliveries

Special Information/Instructions

Arch./Owner Direction Received

DAILY DIARY

WEATHER/TEMP.   8A.M.   12NOON   4P.M.

EXPENSES

JOB NO.   APPOINTMENTS/EVENTS/CALLS

7 A.M.

8 A.M.

9 A.M.

10 A.M.

11 A.M.

12 NOON

1 P.M.

2 P.M.

3 P.M.

4 P.M.

5 P.M.

6 P.M.

MARCH						
S	M	T	W	T	F	S
					1	2
3	4	5	6	7	8	9
10	11	12	13	14	15	16
17	18	19	20	21	22	23
24	25	26	27	28	29	30
31						

APRIL						
S	M	T	W	T	F	S
		1	2	3	4	5	6
7	8	9	10	11	12	13
14	15	16	17	18	19	20
21	22	23	24	25	26	27
28	29	30				

MAY						
S	M	T	W	T	F	S
			1	2	3	4
5	6	7	8	9	10	11
12	13	14	15	16	17	18
19	20	21	22	23	24	25
26	27	28	29	30	31	

24 APRIL
WEDNESDAY

WORK CAL		
MONTH TO DATE	18	24
MONTH REMAINING	4	7
YEAR TO DATE	80	114
YEAR REMAINING	174	251

DAILY MINDER

√ Verify approval of outstanding change orders.

√ Submit requisition(s) to owner(s).

√ Key material deliveries confirmed?

√ Cost report complete?

JOB NO. APPOINTMENTS/EVENTS/CALLS

7 A.M.

8 A.M.

9 A.M.

10 A.M.

11 A.M.

12 NOON

1 P.M.

2 P.M.

3 P.M.

4 P.M.

5 P.M.

6 P.M.

KEY EVENTS

Meetings

Schedule Updates

Cost Report Updates

Change Proposals

Material Deliveries

Special Information/Instructions

Arch./Owner Direction Received

DAILY DIARY

WEATHER/TEMP.	8 A.M.	12 NOON	4 P.M.

EXPENSES

Fish Tape: Electrician's device to aid in pulling wires through a conduit.

DAILY MINDER

√ Submit requisition(s) to owner(s).
√ Authorize sub and supplier payments?
√ Job meeting minutes and reports complete?
√ Cost report complete?

	WORK	CAL
MONTH TO DATE	19	25
MONTH REMAINING	3	6
YEAR TO DATE	81	115
YEAR REMAINING	173	250

APRIL

25

THURSDAY

KEY EVENTS

Meetings

Schedule Updates

Cost Report Updates

Change Proposals

Material Deliveries

Special Information/Instructions

Arch./Owner Direction Received

DAILY DIARY

WEATHER/TEMP.   8A.M.   12NOON   4P.M.

EXPENSES

JOB NO.   APPOINTMENTS/EVENTS/CALLS

7 A.M.

8 A.M.

9 A.M.

10 A.M.

11 A.M.

12 NOON

1 P.M.

2 P.M.

3 P.M.

4 P.M.

5 P.M.

6 P.M.

MARCH						
S	M	T	W	T	F	S
					1	2
3	4	5	6	7	8	9
10	11	12	13	14	15	16
17	18	19	20	21	22	23
24	25	26	27	28	29	30
31						

APRIL						
S	M	T	W	T	F	S
	1	2	3	4	5	6
7	8	9	10	11	12	13
14	15	16	17	18	19	20
21	22	23	24	25	26	27
28	29	30				

MAY						
S	M	T	W	T	F	S
			1	2	3	4
5	6	7	8	9	10	11
12	13	14	15	16	17	18
19	20	21	22	23	24	25
26	27	28	29	30	31	

26
APRIL
FRIDAY

DAILY MINDER

√This month's schedule update complete?
√Job meeting minutes and reports complete?
√This month's reports and narratives complete?
√Authorize sub/supplier payment requisitions?

JOB NO. APPOINTMENTS/EVENTS/CALLS

7 A.M.

8 A.M.

9 A.M.

10 A.M.

11 A.M.

12 NOON

1 P.M.

2 P.M.

3 P.M.

4 P.M.

5 P.M.

6 P.M.

KEY EVENTS

Meetings

Schedule Updates

Cost Report Updates

Change Proposals

Material Deliveries

Special Information/Instructions

Arch./Owner Direction Received

DAILY DIARY

WEATHER/TEMP.   8A.M.   12NOON   4P.M.

EXPENSES

Parapet: The top of an exterior wall which is aove the roof line.

27 APRIL
SATURDAY

28 APRIL
SUNDAY

JOB NO. APPOINTMENTS/EVENTS/CALLS

JOB NO. APPOINTMENTS/EVENTS/CALLS

DAILY DIARY

DAILY DIARY

WEEK Beginning 29 APRIL
Ending 5 MAY

WEEKLY EVENT CHECKLIST

Job meetings and preparation ___
Special meetings ___
Dinners and seminars ___
Assemble schedule information ___
Complete schedule updates ___
Requests out for all required information ___
Outstanding sub/supplier responses ___
Outstanding owner responses ___
Outstanding architect/engineer responses ___
Critical material deliveries confirmed ___
Shop drawings for ongoing work in/appr ___

Submittals for pending work in/appr ___
All other submittals in/approved ___
Shop drawing log up to date ___
All sub change proposals in ___
All change proposals to owner prep'd ___
Submitted change proposals appr ___
Change order logs up to date ___
Required bonds received for all subs ___
Certificates of insurance rec'd for all subs (proper amounts) ___
Equipment/scaffolding release forms in ___

All permits in place ___
Req testing/inspections arranged ___
Inspection certificates received ___
Safety inspections performed ___
Safety recommendations acted on ___
Field reports complete ___
Special photos taken ___
_____ ___
_____ ___
_____ ___
_____ ___

TO DO

Item	Job No.	Item	Job No.

WEEKLY MILESTONE UPDATE

	Planned Date	Actual Date	Variance

DAILY MINDER

√ Schedule update complete?

√ Reports and narratives complete?

√ Progress photos taken?

√ Current schedule commitments in-process?

KEY EVENTS

Meetings

Schedule Updates

Cost Report Updates

Change Proposals

Material Deliveries

Special Information/Instructions

Arch./Owner Direction Received

DAILY DIARY

WEATHER/TEMP.   8A.M.   12NOON   4P.M.

EXPENSES

29

JOB NO.   APPOINTMENTS/EVENTS/CALLS

7 A.M.

8 A.M.

9 A.M.

10 A.M.

11 A.M.

12 NOON

1 P.M.

2 P.M.

3 P.M.

4 P.M.

5 P.M.

6 P.M.

MARCH							APRIL							MAY						
S	M	T	W	T	F	S	S	M	T	W	T	F	S	S	M	T	W	T	F	S
					1	2			1	2	3	4	5	6				1	2	3	4
3	4	5	6	7	8	9	7	8	9	10	11	12	13	5	6	7	8	9	10	11
10	11	12	13	14	15	16	14	15	16	17	18	19	20	12	13	14	15	16	17	18
17	18	19	20	21	22	23	21	22	23	24	25	26	27	19	20	21	22	23	24	25
24	25	26	27	28	29	30	28	29	30					26	27	28	29	30	31	
31																				

30 APRIL
TUESDAY

DAILY MINDER
√ Key material deliveries confirmed?
√ Progress photos taken?
√ Jobsite safety reviews performed?
√ April reports & narratives complete?

JOB NO. APPOINTMENTS/EVENTS/CALLS

7 A.M.

8 A.M.

9 A.M.

10 A.M.

11 A.M.

12 NOON

1 P.M.

2 P.M.

3 P.M.

4 P.M.

5 P.M.

6 P.M.

KEY EVENTS
Meetings

Schedule Updates

Cost Report Updates

Change Proposals

Material Deliveries

Special Information/Instructions

Arch./Owner Direction Received

DAILY DIARY

WEATHER/TEMP.   8 A.M.   12 NOON   4 P.M.

EXPENSES

Web: That portion of a beam or girder between the flanges.

MAY

22 Working Days

31 Calendar Days

APRIL						
S	M	T	W	T	F	S
		1	2	3	4	5	6
7	8	9	10	11	12	13
14	15	16	17	18	19	20
21	22	23	24	25	26	27
28	29	30				

MAY						
S	M	T	W	T	F	S
			1	2	3	4
5	6	7	8	9	10	11
12	13	14	15	16	17	18
19	20	21	22	23	24	25
26	27	28	29	30	31	

JUNE						
S	M	T	W	T	F	S
						1
2	3	4	5	6	7	8
9	10	11	12	13	14	15
16	17	18	19	20	21	22
23	24	25	26	27	28	29
30						

MONTHLY KEY ACTIVITY UPDATE

Job/C.O. No.	Description	Planned Date	Actual Date	Variance	Remarks

MONTHLY SCHEDULE UPDATE SUMMARY

Job/C.O. No.	Activities	Original Duration	Days Spent	Days Remaining	Status/Remarks

MONTHLY RECAP

S	M	T	W	T	F	S
				1	2	3	4
5	6	7	8	9	10	11
12	13	14	15	16	17	18
19	20	21	22	23	24	25
26	27	28	29	30	31	

MAY

MONTHLY EVENT CHECKLIST

Schedule updates complete ___

Requests out for all required info. ___

Outstanding sub/supplier responses rec'd ___

Outstanding owner responses rec'd ___

Outstanding arch./eng. responses rec'd ___

Critical material deliveries confirmed ___

Shop drawings for ongoing work in/appr ___

Submittals for pending work in/appr ___

All other submittals in/approved ___

All sub change proposals in ___

All change proposals to owner prepared ___

Submitted change proposals approved ___

Guarantees/warrantees rec'd ___

Inspection certificates rec'd ___

As-built drawings rec'd ___

Safety inspections performed ___

Safety reports complete ___

Narratives complete ___

Sub/supplier contract(s) rec'd ___

Requisition(s) submitted to owner(s) ___

Sub/supplier adjustments complete ___

Progress photos taken ___

Job cost report info. assembled ___

Job cost reports complete ___

Other: ___

_____ ___

_____ ___

CRITICAL ITEM COST REPORT SUMMARY

Job/CO No.	Description	(A) Budget $ Amount	(B) Cost To Date	(C) Cost Remaining	(D) Total Commitment (B + C)	(E) +/− (A − D)

CHANGE ORDER SUMMARY

Job No.	C.O. No.	Description	Submission Date Required	Submission Date Actual	Approval Date Required	Approval Date Actual	Remarks

DAILY MINDER

√ Last month's schedule update complete?
√ Last month's reports and narratives complete?
√ Progress photos taken?
√ Request/receive outstanding design info?

KEY EVENTS

Meetings

Schedule Updates

Cost Report Updates

Change Proposals

Material Deliveries

Special Information/Instructions

Arch./Owner Direction Received

DAILY DIARY

WEATHER/TEMP.   8 A.M.   12 NOON   4 P.M.

EXPENSES

	WORK	CAL
MONTH TO DATE	1	1
MONTH REMAINING	21	30
YEAR TO DATE	85	121
YEAR REMAINING	169	244

MAY

WEDNESDAY

1

JOB NO. APPOINTMENTS/EVENTS/CALLS

7 A.M.

8 A.M.

9 A.M.

10 A.M.

11 A.M.

12 NOON

1 P.M.

2 P.M.

3 P.M.

4 P.M.

5 P.M.

6 P.M.

APRIL								MAY								JUNE						
S	M	T	W	T	F	S		S	M	T	W	T	F	S		S	M	T	W	T	F	S
	1	2	3	4	5	6					1	2	3	4								1
7	8	9	10	11	12	13		5	6	7	8	9	10	11		2	3	4	5	6	7	8
14	15	16	17	18	19	20		12	13	14	15	16	17	18		9	10	11	12	13	14	15
21	22	23	24	25	26	27		19	20	21	22	23	24	25		16	17	18	19	20	21	22
28	29	30						26	27	28	29	30	31			23	24	25	26	27	28	29
																30						

2 MAY
THURSDAY

WORK CAL		
MONTH TO DATE	2	2
MONTH REMAINING	20	29
YEAR TO DATE	86	122
YEAR REMAINING	168	243

DAILY MINDER

√ All requests for change proposals out?
√ Key material deliveries confirmed?
√ April payments received?
√ Current change orders prepared/submitted?

JOB NO. APPOINTMENTS/EVENTS/CALLS

7 A.M.

8 A.M.

9 A.M.

10 A.M.

11 A.M.

12 NOON

1 P.M.

2 P.M.

3 P.M.

4 P.M.

5 P.M.

6 P.M.

KEY EVENTS

Meetings

Schedule Updates

Cost Report Updates

Change Proposals

Material Deliveries

Special Information/Instructions

Arch./Owner Direction Received

DAILY DIARY

WEATHER/TEMP.   8 A.M.   12 NOON   4 P.M.

EXPENSES

Zenith: A point directly overhead; the upward extension of a plumb line.

DAILY MINDER

√ Last month's schedule update complete?
√ Last month's reports and narratives complete?
√ Progress photos taken?
√ Request/receive outstanding design info?

	WORK	CAL
MONTH TO DATE	3	3
MONTH REMAINING	19	28
YEAR TO DATE	87	123
YEAR REMAINING	167	242

MAY

3

FRIDAY

KEY EVENTS

Meetings

Schedule Updates

Cost Report Updates

Change Proposals

Material Deliveries

Special Information/Instructions

Arch./Owner Direction Received

DAILY DIARY

WEATHER/TEMP.   8A.M.   12NOON   4P.M.

EXPENSES

JOB NO.   APPOINTMENTS/EVENTS/CALLS

7 A.M.

8 A.M.

9 A.M.

10 A.M.

11 A.M.

12 NOON

1 P.M.

2 P.M.

3 P.M.

4 P.M.

5 P.M.

6 P.M.

APRIL								MAY								JUNE						
S	M	T	W	T	F	S		S	M	T	W	T	F	S		S	M	T	W	T	F	S
	1	2	3	4	5	6				1	2	3	4									1
7	8	9	10	11	12	13		5	6	7	8	9	10	11		2	3	4	5	6	7	8
14	15	16	17	18	19	20		12	13	14	15	16	17	18		9	10	11	12	13	14	15
21	22	23	24	25	26	27		19	20	21	22	23	24	25		16	17	18	19	20	21	22
28	29	30						26	27	28	29	30	31			23	24	25	26	27	28	29
																30						

4

MAY

SATURDAY

MAY

SUNDAY

5

JOB NO. APPOINTMENTS/EVENTS/CALLS

JOB NO. APPOINTMENTS/EVENTS/CALLS

DAILY DIARY

DAILY DIARY

WEEK Beginning   6 MAY
Ending   12 MAY

WEEKLY EVENT CHECKLIST

Job meetings and preparation

Special meetings

Dinners and seminars

Assemble schedule information

Complete schedule updates

Requests out for all required information

Outstanding sub/supplier responses

Outstanding owner responses

Outstanding architect/engineer responses

Critical material deliveries confirmed

Shop drawings for ongoing work in/appr

Submittals for pending work in/appr

All other submittals in/approved

Shop drawing log up to date

All sub change proposals in

All change proposals to owner prep'd

Submitted change proposals appr

Change order logs up to date

Required bonds received for all subs

Certificates of insurance rec'd for all subs (proper amounts)

Equipment/scaffolding release forms in

All permits in place

Req testing/inspections arranged

Inspection certificates received

Safety inspections performed

Safety recommendations acted on

Field reports complete

Special photos taken

_____

_____

_____

_____

TO DO

Item	Job No.	Item	Job No.

WEEKLY MILESTONE UPDATE

	Planned Date	Actual Date	Variance

6 MAY
MONDAY

DAILY MINDER

√ Key material deliveries confirmed?
√ Field reports up-to-date?
√ Current schedule commitments in-process?
√ Receive all April payments?

JOB NO. APPOINTMENTS/EVENTS/CALLS

7 A.M.

8 A.M.

9 A.M.

10 A.M.

11 A.M.

12 NOON

1 P.M.

2 P.M.

3 P.M.

4 P.M.

5 P.M.

6 P.M.

KEY EVENTS

Meetings

Schedule Updates

Cost Report Updates

Change Proposals

Material Deliveries

Special Information/Instructions

Arch./Owner Direction Received

DAILY DIARY

WEATHER/TEMP. 8 A.M.   12 NOON   4 P.M.

EXPENSES

Obelisk: A pyramid-topped four-sided pillar, usually of stone or concrete.

DAILY MINDER

√ All required submittals in and approved?
√ All change proposals submitted?
√ Received outstanding design info?
√ Current schedule commitments in-process?

KEY EVENTS

Meetings

Schedule Updates

Cost Report Updates

Change Proposals

Material Deliveries

Special Information/Instructions

Arch./Owner Direction Received

DAILY DIARY

WEATHER/TEMP.   8A.M.   12NOON   4P.M.

EXPENSES

	WORK CAL	**MAY**
MONTH TO DATE	5 7	
MONTH REMAINING	17 24	
YEAR TO DATE	89 127	
YEAR REMAINING	165 238	**TUESDAY**

7

JOB NO.   APPOINTMENTS/EVENTS/CALLS

7A.M.

8A.M.

9A.M.

10A.M.

11A.M.

12NOON

1P.M.

2P.M.

3P.M.

4P.M.

5P.M.

6P.M.

	APRIL							MAY							JUNE					
S	M	T	W	T	F	S	S	M	T	W	T	F	S	S	M	T	W	T	F	S
	1	2	3	4	5	6				1	2	3	4							1
7	8	9	10	11	12	13	5	6	7	8	9	10	11	2	3	4	5	6	7	8
14	15	16	17	18	19	20	12	13	14	15	16	17	18	9	10	11	12	13	14	15
21	22	23	24	25	26	27	19	20	21	22	23	24	25	16	17	18	19	20	21	22
28	29	30					26	27	28	29	30	31		23	24	25	26	27	28	29
														30						

8 MAY WEDNESDAY

WORK	CAL
MONTH TO DATE	6	8
MONTH REMAINING	16	23
YEAR TO DATE	90	128
YEAR REMAINING	164	237

DAILY MINDER

√Key material deliveries confirmed?
√All requests for change proposals out?
√April payments received?
√Schedule commitments in-process?

JOB NO. APPOINTMENTS/EVENTS/CALLS

7 A.M.

8 A.M.

9 A.M.

10 A.M.

11 A.M.

12 NOON

1 P.M.

2 P.M.

3 P.M.

4 P.M.

5 P.M.

6 P.M.

KEY EVENTS

Meetings

Schedule Updates

Cost Report Updates

Change Proposals

Material Deliveries

Special Information/Instructions

Arch./Owner Direction Received

DAILY DIARY

WEATHER/TEMP.   8A.M.   12NOON   4P.M.

EXPENSES

Nitrocellulose: Cotton or wood fibers treated with nitric acid, major ingredient of most lacquers.

DAILY MINDER

√Scheduled a complete physical examination this year?
√Required submittals in/approved?
√Jobsite safety reviews performed?
√Current changes submitted/approved?

WORK	CAL	**MAY**
MONTH TO DATE	7	9
MONTH REMAINING	15	22
YEAR TO DATE	91	129
YEAR REMAINING	163	236

MAY

9

THURSDAY

KEY EVENTS

Meetings

Schedule Updates

Cost Report Updates

Change Proposals

Material Deliveries

Special Information/Instructions

Arch./Owner Direction Received

DAILY DIARY

WEATHER/TEMP.   8A.M.   12NOON   4P.M.

EXPENSES

JOB NO.   APPOINTMENTS/EVENTS/CALLS

7A.M.

8A.M.

9A.M.

10A.M.

11A.M.

12NOON

1P.M.

2P.M.

3P.M.

4P.M.

5P.M.

6P.M.

	APRIL							MAY								JUNE					
S	M	T	W	T	F	S	S	M	T	W	T	F	S	S	M	T	W	T	F	S
	1	2	3	4	5	6				1	2	3	4							1
7	8	9	10	11	12	13	5	6	7	8	9	10	11	2	3	4	5	6	7	8
14	15	16	17	18	19	20	12	13	14	15	16	17	18	9	10	11	12	13	14	15
21	22	23	24	25	26	27	19	20	21	22	23	24	25	16	17	18	19	20	21	22
28	29	30					26	27	28	29	30	31		23	24	25	26	27	28	29
														30						

10 MAY
FRIDAY

WORK	CAL		
MONTH TO DATE	8	10	
MONTH REMAINING	14	21	
YEAR TO DATE	92	130	
YEAR REMAINING	162	235	

DAILY MINDER

√ Job meeting minutes and reports complete?
√ Key material deliveries confirmed?
√ Schedules in-process for next week?
√ Outstanding design info. requested/received?

JOB NO. APPOINTMENTS/EVENTS/CALLS

7 A.M.

8 A.M.

9 A.M.

10 A.M.

11 A.M.

12 NOON

1 P.M.

2 P.M.

3 P.M.

4 P.M.

5 P.M.

6 P.M.

KEY EVENTS

Meetings

Schedule Updates

Cost Report Updates

Change Proposals

Material Deliveries

Special Information/Instructions

Arch./Owner Direction Received

DAILY DIARY

WEATHER/TEMP.   8 A.M.   12 NOON   4 P.M.

EXPENSES

Hydrostatic Pressure: Pressure exerted by water.

11

MAY

SATURDAY

	WORK	CAL
MONTH TO DATE	8	11
MONTH REMAINING	14	20
YEAR TO DATE	92	131
YEAR REMAINING	162	234

	WORK	CAL
MONTH TO DATE	8	12
MONTH REMAINING	14	19
YEAR TO DATE	92	132
YEAR REMAINING	162	233

MAY

Mother's
Day

SUNDAY

12

JOB NO. APPOINTMENTS/EVENTS/CALLS

JOB NO. APPOINTMENTS/EVENTS/CALLS

DAILY DIARY

DAILY DIARY

WEEK Beginning 13 MAY
Ending 19 MAY

WEEKLY EVENT CHECKLIST

Job meetings and preparation	Submittals for pending work in/appr ___	All permits in place ___
Special meetings	All other submittals in/approved ___	Req testing/inspections arranged ___
Dinners and seminars	Shop drawing log up to date ___	Inspection certificates received ___
Assemble schedule information	All sub change proposals in ___	Safety inspections performed ___
Complete schedule updates	All change proposals to owner prep'd ___	Safety recommendations acted on ___
Requests out for all required information ___	Submitted change proposals appr ___	Field reports complete ___
Outstanding sub/supplier responses	Change order logs up to date ___	Special photos taken ___
Outstanding owner responses	Required bonds received for all subs ___	___
Outstanding architect/engineer responses ___	Certificates of insurance rec'd for all	___
Critical material deliveries confirmed ___	subs (proper amounts) ___	___
Shop drawings for ongoing work in/appr ___	Equipment/scaffolding release forms in ___	___

TO DO

Item	Job No.	Item	Job No.

WEEKLY MILESTONE UPDATE

	Planned Date	Actual Date	Variance

DAILY MINDER

√ Job meeting minutes and reports complete?
√ Current schedule commitments in-process?
√ Change proposals requested.

	WORK	CAL	**MAY**
MONTH TO DATE	9	13	
MONTH REMAINING	13	18	
YEAR TO DATE		93	133
YEAR REMAINING	161	232	**MONDAY**

13

KEY EVENTS

Meetings

Schedule Updates

Cost Report Updates

Change Proposals

Material Deliveries

Special Information/Instructions

Arch./Owner Direction Received

DAILY DIARY

WEATHER/TEMP.   8A.M.   12NOON   4P.M.

EXPENSES

7A.M.

8A.M.

9A.M.

10A.M.

11A.M.

12NOON

1P.M.

2P.M.

3P.M.

4P.M.

5P.M.

6P.M.

APRIL						
S	M	T	W	T	F	S
	1	2	3	4	5	6
7	8	9	10	11	12	13
14	15	16	17	18	19	20
21	22	23	24	25	26	27
28	29	30				

MAY						
S	M	T	W	T	F	S
			1	2	3	4
5	6	7	8	9	10	11
12	13	14	15	16	17	18
19	20	21	22	23	24	25
26	27	28	29	30	31	

JUNE						
S	M	T	W	T	F	S
						1
2	3	4	5	6	7	8
9	10	11	12	13	14	15
16	17	18	19	20	21	22
23	24	25	26	27	28	29
30						

14 MAY
TUESDAY

WORK	CAL
MONTH TO DATE	10	14
MONTH REMAINING	12	17
YEAR TO DATE	94	134
YEAR REMAINING	160	231

DAILY MINDER

√ Verify approval of outstanding change orders.
√ Key material deliveries confirmed?
√ Required submittals in/approved?

JOB NO. APPOINTMENTS/EVENTS/CALLS

7 A.M.

8 A.M.

9 A.M.

10 A.M.

11 A.M.

12 NOON

1 P.M.

2 P.M.

3 P.M.

4 P.M.

5 P.M.

6 P.M.

KEY EVENTS

Meetings

Schedule Updates

Cost Report Updates

Change Proposals

Material Deliveries

Special Information/Instructions

Arch./Owner Direction Received

DAILY DIARY

WEATHER/TEMP.   8 A.M.   12 NOON   4 P.M.

EXPENSES

Grade Beam: A continuous footing reinforced to act as a beam.

DAILY MINDER

√ Assemble all schedule update information.
√ All requests for change proposals out?
√ Current schedule commitments in-process?
√ Meeting minutes received/prepared?

WORK	CAL		MAY
MONTH TO DATE	11	15	
MONTH REMAINING	11	16	
YEAR TO DATE	95	135	
YEAR REMAINING	159	230	WEDNESDAY

15

KEY EVENTS

Meetings

Schedule Updates

Cost Report Updates

Change Proposals

Material Deliveries

Special Information/Instructions

Arch./Owner Direction Received

DAILY DIARY

WEATHER/TEMP.   8A.M.   12NOON   4P.M.

EXPENSES

	APRIL							MAY							JUNE					
S	M	T	W	T	F	S	S	M	T	W	T	F	S	S	M	T	W	T	F	S
	1	2	3	4	5	6				1	2	3	4							1
7	8	9	10	11	12	13	5	6	7	8	9	10	11	2	3	4	5	6	7	8
14	15	16	17	18	19	20	12	13	14	15	16	17	18	9	10	11	12	13	14	15
21	22	23	24	25	26	27	19	20	21	22	23	24	25	16	17	18	19	20	21	22
28	29	30					26	27	28	29	30	31		23	24	25	26	27	28	29
														30						

JOB NO.   APPOINTMENTS/EVENTS/CALLS

7 A.M.

8 A.M.

9 A.M.

10 A.M.

11 A.M.

12 NOON

1 P.M.

2 P.M.

3 P.M.

4 P.M.

5 P.M.

6 P.M.

16 MAY
THURSDAY

	WORK	CAL
MONTH TO DATE	12	16
MONTH REMAINING	10	15
YEAR TO DATE	96	136
YEAR REMAINING	158	229

DAILY MINDER

√ Key material deliveries confirmed?
√ All change proposals submitted?
√ Schedules in-process for next week?

JOB NO. APPOINTMENTS/EVENTS/CALLS

7A.M.

8A.M.

9A.M.

10A.M.

11A.M.

12NOON

1P.M.

2P.M.

3P.M.

4P.M.

5P.M.

6P.M.

KEY EVENTS

Meetings

Schedule Updates

Cost Report Updates

Change Proposals

Material Deliveries

Special Information/Instructions

Arch./Owner Direction Received

DAILY DIARY

WEATHER/TEMP.	8A.M.	12NOON	4P.M.

EXPENSES

Tall Joist: A joist framing perpendicularly into a header joist.

DAILY MINDER

√ Assemble all schedule update information.
√ Schedule update info assembled?
√ Job meeting minutes and reports complete?
√ Next week's schedules confirmed?

KEY EVENTS

Meetings

Schedule Updates

Cost Report Updates

Change Proposals

Material Deliveries

Special Information/Instructions

Arch./Owner Direction Received

DAILY DIARY

WEATHER/TEMP.   8A.M.   12NOON   4P.M.

EXPENSES

WORK	CAL

	WORK	CAL
MONTH TO DATE	13	17
MONTH REMAINING	9	14
YEAR TO DATE	97	137
YEAR REMAINING	157	228

MAY

FRIDAY

17

JOB NO. APPOINTMENTS/EVENTS/CALLS

7 A.M.

8 A.M.

9 A.M.

10 A.M.

11 A.M.

12 NOON

1 P.M.

2 P.M.

3 P.M.

4 P.M.

5 P.M.

6 P.M.

APRIL								MAY								JUNE						
S	M	T	W	T	F	S		S	M	T	W	T	F	S		S	M	T	W	T	F	S
	1	2	3	4	5	6					1	2	3	4								1
7	8	9	10	11	12	13		5	6	7	8	9	10	11		2	3	4	5	6	7	8
14	15	16	17	18	19	20		12	13	14	15	16	17	18		9	10	11	12	13	14	15
21	22	23	24	25	26	27		19	20	21	22	23	24	25		16	17	18	19	20	21	22
28	29	30						26	27	28	29	30	31			23	24	25	26	27	28	29
																30						

18 MAY
SATURDAY

	WORK	CAL
MONTH TO DATE	13	18
MONTH REMAINING	9	13
YEAR TO DATE	97	138
YEAR REMAINING	157	227

JOB NO. APPOINTMENTS/EVENTS/CALLS

DAILY DIARY

MAY 19
SUNDAY

	WORK	CAL
MONTH TO DATE	13	19
MONTH REMAINING	9	12
YEAR TO DATE	97	139
YEAR REMAINING	157	226

JOB NO. APPOINTMENTS/EVENTS/CALLS

DAILY DIARY

WEEK Beginning 20 MAY
Ending 26 MAY

WEEKLY EVENT CHECKLIST

Job meetings and preparation
Special meetings
Dinners and seminars
Assemble schedule information
Complete schedule updates
Requests out for all required information
Outstanding sub/supplier responses
Outstanding owner responses
Outstanding architect/engineer responses
Critical material deliveries confirmed
Shop drawings for ongoing work in/appr

Submittals for pending work in/appr
All other submittals in/approved
Shop drawing log up to date
All sub change proposals in
All change proposals to owner prep'd
Submitted change proposals appr
Change order logs up to date
Required bonds received for all subs
Certificates of insurance rec'd for all subs (proper amounts)
Equipment/scaffolding release forms in

All permits in place
Req testing/inspections arranged
Inspection certificates received
Safety inspections performed
Safety recommendations acted on
Field reports complete
Special photos taken

TO DO

Item	Job No.	Item	Job No.

WEEKLY MILESTONE UPDATE

	Planned Date	Actual Date	Variance

20
MAY

MONDAY

JOB NO. APPOINTMENTS/EVENTS/CALLS

7 A.M.

8 A.M.

9 A.M.

10 A.M.

11 A.M.

12 NOON

1 P.M.

2 P.M.

3 P.M.

4 P.M.

5 P.M.

6 P.M.

DAILY MINDER

√ Verify approval of outstanding orders.
√ Authorize/approve sub and supplier payments.
√ Job meeting minutes and reports complete?
√ Requests for change proposals out?

KEY EVENTS

Meetings

Schedule Updates

Cost Report Updates

Change Proposals

Material Deliveries

Special Information/Instructions

Arch./Owner Direction Received

DAILY DIARY

WEATHER/TEMP.   8 A.M.   12 NOON   4 P.M.

EXPENSES

Latent Heat: Heat necessary to produce a change of state of material at a constant temperature.

DAILY MINDER

√ Verify receipt of sub and supplier payment requisitions.

√ Schedule update info assembled?

√ Cost report info assembled?

WORK CAL			**MAY**
MONTH TO DATE	15	21	
MONTH REMAINING	7	10	
YEAR TO DATE	99	141	
YEAR REMAINING	155	224	**TUESDAY**

21

KEY EVENTS

Meetings

Schedule Updates

Cost Report Updates

Change Proposals

Material Deliveries

Special Information/Instructions

Arch./Owner Direction Received

DAILY DIARY

WEATHER/TEMP.   8 A.M.   12 NOON   4 P.M.

EXPENSES

JOB NO.   APPOINTMENTS/EVENTS/CALLS

7 A.M.

8 A.M.

9 A.M.

10 A.M.

11 A.M.

12 NOON

1 P.M.

2 P.M.

3 P.M.

4 P.M.

5 P.M.

6 P.M.

	APRIL							MAY							JUNE					
S	M	T	W	T	F	S	S	M	T	W	T	F	S	S	M	T	W	T	F	S
	1	2	3	4	5	6				1	2	3	4							1
7	8	9	10	11	12	13	5	6	7	8	9	10	11	2	3	4	5	6	7	8
14	15	16	17	18	19	20	12	13	14	15	16	17	18	9	10	11	12	13	14	15
21	22	23	24	25	26	27	19	20	21	22	23	24	25	16	17	18	19	20	21	22
28	29	30					26	27	28	29	30	31		23	24	25	26	27	28	29
														30						

22 MAY
WEDNESDAY

DAILY MINDER

√Key material deliveries confirmed?
√All required design info. received?
√Current change orders prepared/submitted?
√May schedule updates complete?

JOB NO. APPOINTMENTS/EVENTS/CALLS

7 A.M.

8 A.M.

9 A.M.

10 A.M.

11 A.M.

12 NOON

1 P.M.

2 P.M.

3 P.M.

4 P.M.

5 P.M.

6 P.M.

KEY EVENTS

Meetings

Schedule Updates

Cost Report Updates

Change Proposals

Material Deliveries

Special Information/Instructions

Arch./Owner Direction Received

DAILY DIARY

WEATHER/TEMP.   8 A.M.   12 NOON   4 P.M.

EXPENSES

Shrinkage Limit: Water content at which a soil has minimum volume.

DAILY MINDER

√ Submit requisition(s) to owner(s).

√ Authorize/approve sub and supplier payments.

√ Schedule update info assembled?

√ Cost report info assembled?

KEY EVENTS

Meetings

Schedule Updates

Cost Report Updates

Change Proposals

Material Deliveries

Special Information/Instructions

Arch./Owner Direction Received

DAILY DIARY

WEATHER/TEMP.   8A.M.   12NOON   4P.M.

EXPENSES

	WORK CAL	
MONTH TO DATE	17	23
MONTH REMAINING	5	8
YEAR TO DATE	101	143
YEAR REMAINING	153	222

MAY

23

THURSDAY

JOB NO.   APPOINTMENTS/EVENTS/CALLS

7 A.M.

8 A.M.

9 A.M.

10 A.M.

11 A.M.

12 NOON

1 P.M.

2 P.M.

3 P.M.

4 P.M.

5 P.M.

6 P.M.

APRIL						
S	M	T	W	T	F	S
	1	2	3	4	5	6
7	8	9	10	11	12	13
14	15	16	17	18	19	20
21	22	23	24	25	26	27
28	29	30				

MAY						
S	M	T	W	T	F	S
			1	2	3	4
5	6	7	8	9	10	11
12	13	14	15	16	17	18
19	20	21	22	23	24	25
26	27	28	29	30	31	

JUNE						
S	M	T	W	T	F	S
						1
2	3	4	5	6	7	8
9	10	11	12	13	14	15
16	17	18	19	20	21	22
23	24	25	26	27	28	29
30						

24 MAY FRIDAY

DAILY MINDER

√ Schedule update complete?
√ All monthly reports and narratives complete?
√ Key material deliveries confirmed?
√ Cost report complete?

JOB NO. APPOINTMENTS/EVENTS/CALLS

7 A.M.

8 A.M.

9 A.M.

10 A.M.

11 A.M.

12 NOON

1 P.M.

2 P.M.

3 P.M.

4 P.M.

5 P.M.

6 P.M.

KEY EVENTS

Meetings

Schedule Updates

Cost Report Updates

Change Proposals

Material Deliveries

Special Information/Instructions

Arch./Owner Direction Received

DAILY DIARY

WEATHER/TEMP.   8 A.M.   12 NOON   4 P.M.

EXPENSES

Blade: Slang for a grader. Also the implement in a tractor or grader used to push earth.

25 MAY SATURDAY

	WORK	CAL
MONTH TO DATE	18	25
MONTH REMAINING	4	6
YEAR TO DATE	102	145
YEAR REMAINING	152	220

JOB NO. APPOINTMENTS/EVENTS/CALLS

DAILY DIARY

MAY 26 SUNDAY

	WORK	CAL
MONTH TO DATE	18	26
MONTH REMAINING	4	5
YEAR TO DATE	102	146
YEAR REMAINING	152	219

JOB NO. APPOINTMENTS/EVENTS/CALLS

DAILY DIARY

WEEK Beginning 27 MAY
Ending 2 JUNE

WEEKLY EVENT CHECKLIST

Job meetings and preparation
Special meetings
Dinners and seminars
Assemble schedule information
Complete schedule updates
Requests out for all required information
Outstanding sub/supplier responses
Outstanding owner responses
Outstanding architect/engineer responses
Critical material deliveries confirmed
Shop drawings for ongoing work in/appr

Submittals for pending work in/appr
All other submittals in/approved
Shop drawing log up to date
All sub change proposals in
All change proposals to owner prep'd
Submitted change proposals appr
Change order logs up to date
Required bonds received for all subs
Certificates of insurance rec'd for all subs (proper amounts)
Equipment/scaffolding release forms in

All permits in place
Req testing/inspections arranged
Inspection certificates received
Safety inspections performed
Safety recommendations acted on
Field reports complete
Special photos taken

TO DO

Item	Job No.	Item	Job No.

WEEKLY MILESTONE UPDATE

	Planned Date	Actual Date	Variance

DAILY MINDER

√ Verify approval of outstanding change orders.

√ Submit requisition(s) to owner(s).

√ Authorize/approve sub and supplier payments.

√ Cost report complete?

	WORK	CAL
MONTH TO DATE	18	27
MONTH REMAINING	4	4
YEAR TO DATE	102	147
YEAR REMAINING	152	218

MAY
Memorial
Day Obsvd.
MONDAY

27

KEY EVENTS

Meetings

Schedule Updates

Cost Report Updates

Change Proposals

Material Deliveries

Special Information/Instructions

Arch./Owner Direction Received

DAILY DIARY

WEATHER/TEMP.   8A.M.   12NOON   4P.M.

EXPENSES

JOB NO.   APPOINTMENTS/EVENTS/CALLS

7A.M.

8A.M.

9A.M.

10A.M.

11A.M.

12NOON

1P.M.

2P.M.

3P.M.

4P.M.

5P.M.

6P.M.

		APRIL							MAY							JUNE				
S	M	T	W	T	F	S	S	M	T	W	T	F	S	S	M	T	W	T	F	S
	1	2	3	4	5	6				1	2	3	4							1
7	8	9	10	11	12	13	5	6	7	8	9	10	11	2	3	4	5	6	7	8
14	15	16	17	18	19	20	12	13	14	15	16	17	18	9	10	11	12	13	14	15
21	22	23	24	25	26	27	19	20	21	22	23	24	25	16	17	18	19	20	21	22
28	29	30					26	27	28	29	30	31		23	24	25	26	27	28	29
														30						

28 MAY TUESDAY

WORK	CAL
MONTH TO DATE	19	28
MONTH REMAINING	3	3
YEAR TO DATE	103	148
YEAR REMAINING	151	217

DAILY MINDER

√ This month's schedule update complete?
√ This month's reports and narratives complete?
√ Key material deliveries confirmed?
√ All requisitions submitted to owner(s)?

JOB NO. APPOINTMENTS/EVENTS/CALLS

7 A.M.

8 A.M.

9 A.M.

10 A.M.

11 A.M.

12 NOON

1 P.M.

2 P.M.

3 P.M.

4 P.M.

5 P.M.

6 P.M.

KEY EVENTS

Meetings

Schedule Updates

Cost Report Updates

Change Proposals

Material Deliveries

Special Information/Instructions

Arch./Owner Direction Received

DAILY DIARY

WEATHER/TEMP.   8 A.M.   12 NOON   4 P.M.

EXPENSES

Tine: A tooth in the excavating mouth of a dragline, excavating bucket, or scraper loader.

DAILY MINDER

√ This month's schedule update complete?

√ This month's reports and narratives complete?

√ Progress photos taken?

√ Requests for change proposals out?

	WORK	CAL
MONTH TO DATE	20	29
MONTH REMAINING	2	2
YEAR TO DATE	104	149
YEAR REMAINING	150	216

MAY

WEDNESDAY **29**

KEY EVENTS

Meetings

Schedule Updates

Cost Report Updates

Change Proposals

Material Deliveries

Special Information/Instructions

Arch./Owner Direction Received

DAILY DIARY

WEATHER/TEMP.   8A.M.   12NOON   4P.M.

EXPENSES

JOB NO. APPOINTMENTS/EVENTS/CALLS

7 A.M.

8 A.M.

9 A.M.

10 A.M.

11 A.M.

12 NOON

1 P.M.

2 P.M.

3 P.M.

4 P.M.

5 P.M.

6 P.M.

	APRIL							MAY							JUNE					
S	M	T	W	T	F	S	S	M	T	W	T	F	S	S	M	T	W	T	F	S
	1	2	3	4	5	6				1	2	3	4							1
7	8	9	10	11	12	13	5	6	7	8	9	10	11	2	3	4	5	6	7	8
14	15	16	17	18	19	20	12	13	14	15	16	17	18	9	10	11	12	13	14	15
21	22	23	24	25	26	27	19	20	21	22	23	24	25	16	17	18	19	20	21	22
28	29	30					26	27	28	29	30	31		23	24	25	26	27	28	29
														30						

30 MAY THURSDAY

	WORK	CAL
MONTH TO DATE	21	30
MONTH REMAINING	1	1
YEAR TO DATE	105	150
YEAR REMAINING	149	215

DAILY MINDER

√ Schedule update coomplete?
√ Key material deliveries confirmed?
√ Progress photos taken?
√ Next week's schedules confirmed?

JOB NO. APPOINTMENTS/EVENTS/CALLS

7 A.M.

8 A.M.

9 A.M.

10 A.M.

11 A.M.

12 NOON

1 P.M.

2 P.M.

3 P.M.

4 P.M.

5 P.M.

6 P.M.

KEY EVENTS

Meetings

Schedule Updates

Cost Report Updates

Change Proposals

Material Deliveries

Special Information/Instructions

Arch./Owner Direction Received

DAILY DIARY

WEATHER/TEMP.   8 A.M.   12 NOON   4 P.M.

EXPENSES

Welsh Arch: A lintel design with a loose wedge in the middle.

DAILY MINDER

√ Job meeting minutes and reports complete?

√ Progress photos taken?

√ May schedule update(s) complete?

√ Sub change proposals received?

WORK	CAL
MONTH TO DATE	22	31
MONTH REMAINING	0	0
YEAR TO DATE	106	151
YEAR REMAINING	148	214

MAY

31

FRIDAY

KEY EVENTS

Meetings

Schedule Updates

Cost Report Updates

Change Proposals

Material Deliveries

Special Information/Instructions

Arch./Owner Direction Received

DAILY DIARY

WEATHER/TEMP.   8 A.M.   12 NOON   4 P.M.

EXPENSES

JOB NO.   APPOINTMENTS/EVENTS/CALLS

7 A.M.

8 A.M.

9 A.M.

10 A.M.

11 A.M.

12 NOON

1 P.M.

2 P.M.

3 P.M.

4 P.M.

5 P.M.

6 P.M.

APRIL						
S	M	T	W	T	F	S
	1	2	3	4	5	6
7	8	9	10	11	12	13
14	15	16	17	18	19	20
21	22	23	24	25	26	27
28	29	30				

MAY						
S	M	T	W	T	F	S
			1	2	3	4
5	6	7	8	9	10	11
12	13	14	15	16	17	18
19	20	21	22	23	24	25
26	27	28	29	30	31	

JUNE						
S	M	T	W	T	F	S
						1
2	3	4	5	6	7	8
9	10	11	12	13	14	15
16	17	18	19	20	21	22
23	24	25	26	27	28	29
30						

JUNE

20 Working Days

31 Calendar Days

MAY

S	M	T	W	T	F	S
				1	2	3	4
5	6	7	8	9	10	11
12	13	14	15	16	17	18
19	20	21	22	23	24	25
26	27	28	29	30	31	

JUNE

S	M	T	W	T	F	S
						1
2	3	4	5	6	7	8
9	10	11	12	13	14	15
16	17	18	19	20	21	22
23	24	25	26	27	28	29
30						

JULY

S	M	T	W	T	F	S
	1	2	3	4	5	6
7	8	9	10	11	12	13
14	15	16	17	18	19	20
21	22	23	24	25	26	27
28	29	30	31			

MONTHLY KEY ACTIVITY UPDATE

Job/C.O. No.	Description	Planned Date	Actual Date	Variance	Remarks

MONTHLY SCHEDULE UPDATE SUMMARY

Job/C.O. No.	Activities	Original Duration	Days Spent	Days Remaining	Status/Remarks

MONTHLY RECAP

JUNE

MONTHLY EVENT CHECKLIST

- ☐ Schedule updates complete
- ☐ Requests out for all required info.
- ☐ Outstanding sub/supplier responses rec'd
- ☐ Outstanding owner responses rec'd
- ☐ Outstanding arch./eng. responses rec'd
- ☐ Critical material deliveries confirmed
- ☐ Shop drawings for ongoing work in/appr
- ☐ Submittals for pending work in/appr
- ☐ All other submittals in/approved

- ☐ All sub change proposals in
- ☐ All change proposals to owner prepared
- ☐ Submitted change proposals approved
- ☐ Guarantees/warrantees rec'd
- ☐ Inspection certificates rec'd
- ☐ As-built drawings rec'd
- ☐ Safety inspections performed
- ☐ Safety reports complete
- ☐ Narratives complete

- ☐ Sub/supplier contract(s) rec'd ☐
- ☐ Requisition(s) submitted to owner(s) ☐
- ☐ Sub/supplier adjustments complete ☐
- ☐ Progress photos taken ☐
- ☐ Job cost report info. assembled ☐
- ☐ Job cost reports complete ☐
- ☐ Other: ☐
- ☐ _____ ☐
- ☐ _____ ☐

CRITICAL ITEM COST REPORT SUMMARY

Job/CO No.	Description	(A) Budget $ Amount	(B) Cost To Date	(C) Cost Remaining	(D) Total Commitment (B + C)	(E) +/− (A − D)

CHANGE ORDER SUMMARY

Job No.	C.O. No.	Description	Submission Date Required	Submission Date Actual	Approval Date Required	Approval Date Actual	Remarks

1

JUNE

SATURDAY

JUNE

SUNDAY

2

JOB NO. APPOINTMENTS/EVENTS/CALLS

JOB NO. APPOINTMENTS/EVENTS/CALLS

DAILY DIARY

DAILY DIARY

WEEK Beginning   3 JUNE
Ending   9 JUNE

WEEKLY EVENT CHECKLIST

Job meetings and preparation ___
Special meetings ___
Dinners and seminars ___
Assemble schedule information ___
Complete schedule updates ___
Requests out for all required information ___
Outstanding sub/supplier responses ___
Outstanding owner responses ___
Outstanding architect/engineer responses ___
Critical material deliveries confirmed ___
Shop drawings for ongoing work in/appr ___

Submittals for pending work in/appr ___
All other submittals in/approved ___
Shop drawing log up to date ___
All sub change proposals in ___
All change proposals to owner prep'd ___
Submitted change proposals appr ___
Change order logs up to date ___
Required bonds received for all subs ___
Certificates of insurance rec'd for all subs (proper amounts) ___
Equipment/scaffolding release forms in ___

All permits in place ___
Req testing/inspections arranged ___
Inspection certificates received ___
Safety inspections performed ___
Safety recommendations acted on ___
Field reports complete ___
Special photos taken ___
_____ ___
_____ ___
_____ ___

TO DO

Item	Job No.	Item	Job No.

WEEKLY MILESTONE UPDATE

	Planned Date	Actual Date	Variance

3
JUNE
MONDAY

	WORK	CAL
MONTH TO DATE	1	3
MONTH REMAINING	19	28
YEAR TO DATE	107	154
YEAR REMAINING	147	211

DAILY MINDER

√ Job meeting minutes and reports complete?

√ Jobsite safety reviews performed?

√ May schedule update(s) complete?

√ May cost reports complete?

KEY EVENTS

Meetings

Schedule Updates

Cost Report Updates

Change Proposals

Material Deliveries

Special Information/Instructions

Arch./Owner Direction Received

DAILY DIARY

JOB NO.   APPOINTMENTS/EVENTS/CALLS

7 A.M.

8 A.M.

9 A.M.

10 A.M.

11 A.M.

12 NOON

1 P.M.

2 P.M.

3 P.M.

4 P.M.

5 P.M.

6 P.M.

WEATHER/TEMP.   8 A.M.   12 NOON   4 P.M.

EXPENSES

Rod Buster: (Slang) Ironworker who installs concrete reinforcement.

DAILY MINDER

√ All requests for change proposals out?

√ Field reports up-to-date?

√ May narratives & reports complete?

√ Current schedules in-process?

KEY EVENTS

Meetings

Schedule Updates

Cost Report Updates

Change Proposals

Material Deliveries

Special Information/Instructions

Arch./Owner Direction Received

DAILY DIARY

WEATHER/TEMP.   8A.M.   12NOON   4P.M.

EXPENSES

	WORK	CAL
MONTH TO DATE	2	4
MONTH REMAINING	18	27
YEAR TO DATE	108	155
YEAR REMAINING	146	210

JUNE

TUESDAY

4

JOB NO. APPOINTMENTS/EVENTS/CALLS

7A.M.

8A.M.

9A.M.

10A.M.

11A.M.

12NOON

1P.M.

2P.M.

3P.M.

4P.M.

5P.M.

6P.M.

	MAY								JUNE								JULY					
S	M	T	W	T	F	S	S	M	T	W	T	F	S	S	M	T	W	T	F	S
			1	2	3	4							1			1	2	3	4	5	6
5	6	7	8	9	10	11	2	3	4	5	6	7	8	7	8	9	10	11	12	13
12	13	14	15	16	17	18	9	10	11	12	13	14	15	14	15	16	17	18	19	20
19	20	21	22	23	24	25	16	17	18	19	20	21	22	21	22	23	24	25	26	27
26	27	28	29	30	31		23	24	25	26	27	28	29	28	29	30	31			
							30													

5 JUNE
WEDNESDAY

DAILY MINDER

√ Key material deliveries confirmed?

√ All required design info received?

√ Current change orders prepared/submitted?

JOB NO. APPOINTMENTS/EVENTS/CALLS

7 A.M.

8 A.M.

9 A.M.

10 A.M.

11 A.M.

12 NOON

1 P.M.

2 P.M.

3 P.M.

4 P.M.

5 P.M.

6 P.M.

KEY EVENTS

Meetings

Schedule Updates

Cost Report Updates

Change Proposals

Material Deliveries

Special Information/Instructions

Arch./Owner Direction Received

DAILY DIARY

WEATHER/TEMP.   8 A.M.   12 NOON   4 P.M.

EXPENSES

Slewing: Rotation of a crane jib that moves the load horizontally through an arc.

DAILY MINDER

√ All change order proposals submitted?

√ Required submittals in/approved?

√ Next week's schedules confirmed?

√ May payments received?

KEY EVENTS

Meetings

Schedule Updates

Cost Report Updates

Change Proposals

Material Deliveries

Special Information/Instructions

Arch./Owner Direction Received

DAILY DIARY

WEATHER/TEMP.   8A.M.   12NOON   4P.M.

EXPENSES

	WORK	CAL
MONTH TO DATE	4	6
MONTH REMAINING	16	25
YEAR TO DATE	110	157
YEAR REMAINING	144	208

JUNE

THURSDAY

6

JOB NO.   APPOINTMENTS/EVENTS/CALLS

7A.M.

8A.M.

9A.M.

10A.M.

11A.M.

12NOON

1P.M.

2P.M.

3P.M.

4P.M.

5P.M.

6P.M.

	MAY							JUNE							JULY					
S	M	T	W	T	F	S	S	M	T	W	T	F	S	S	M	T	W	T	F	S
			1	2	3	4							1		1	2	3	4	5	6
5	6	7	8	9	10	11	2	3	4	5	6	7	8	7	8	9	10	11	12	13
12	13	14	15	16	17	18	9	10	11	12	13	14	15	14	15	16	17	18	19	20
19	20	21	22	23	24	25	16	17	18	19	20	21	22	21	22	23	24	25	26	27
26	27	28	29	30	31		23	24	25	26	27	28	29	28	29	30	31			
							30													

7 JUNE
FRIDAY

JOB NO. APPOINTMENTS/EVENTS/CALLS

7 A.M.

8 A.M.

9 A.M.

10 A.M.

11 A.M.

12 NOON

1 P.M.

2 P.M.

3 P.M.

4 P.M.

5 P.M.

6 P.M.

DAILY MINDER

√ Job meeting minutes and reports complete?

√ Key material deliveries confirmed?

√ Next week's schedules confirmed?

√ May payments prepared to subs?

KEY EVENTS

Meetings

Schedule Updates

Cost Report Updates

Change Proposals

Material Deliveries

Special Information/Instructions

Arch./Owner Direction Received

DAILY DIARY

WEATHER/TEMP.   8 A.M.   12 NOON   4 P.M.

EXPENSES

Brisance: Shattering or crushing effect of an explosive.

8 JUNE
SATURDAY

	WORK	CAL
MONTH TO DATE	5	8
MONTH REMAINING	15	23
YEAR TO DATE	111	159
YEAR REMAINING	143	206

JOB NO. APPOINTMENTS/EVENTS/CALLS

DAILY DIARY

JUNE 9
SUNDAY

	WORK	CAL
MONTH TO DATE	5	9
MONTH REMAINING	15	22
YEAR TO DATE	111	160
YEAR REMAINING	143	205

JOB NO. APPOINTMENTS/EVENTS/CALLS

DAILY DIARY

WEEK Beginning 10 JUNE
Ending 16 JUNE

WEEKLY EVENT CHECKLIST

Job meetings and preparation
Special meetings
Dinners and seminars
Assemble schedule information
Complete schedule updates
Requests out for all required information
Outstanding sub/supplier responses
Outstanding owner responses
Outstanding architect/engineer responses
Critical material deliveries confirmed
Shop drawings for ongoing work in/appr

Submittals for pending work in/appr
All other submittals in/approved
Shop drawing log up to date
All sub change proposals in
All change proposals to owner prep'd
Submitted change proposals appr
Change order logs up to date
Required bonds received for all subs
Certificates of insurance rec'd for all subs (proper amounts)
Equipment/scaffolding release forms in

All permits in place
Req testing/inspections arranged
Inspection certificates received
Safety inspections performed
Safety recommendations acted on
Field reports complete
Special photos taken

TO DO

Item	Job No.	Item	Job No.

WEEKLY MILESTONE UPDATE

	Planned Date	Actual Date	Variance

DAILY MINDER

√ Job meeting minutes and reports complete?

√ May payments prepared to subs?

√ May payments received?

√ Request/received outstanding design info?

KEY EVENTS

Meetings

Schedule Updates

Cost Report Updates

Change Proposals

Material Deliveries

Special Information/Instructions

Arch./Owner Direction Received

DAILY DIARY

WEATHER/TEMP.   8A.M.   12NOON   4P.M.

EXPENSES

WORK CAL		
MONTH TO DATE	6	10
MONTH REMAINING	14	21
YEAR TO DATE	112	161
YEAR REMAINING	142	204

JUNE

10

MONDAY

JOB NO. APPOINTMENTS/EVENTS/CALLS

7A.M.

8A.M.

9A.M.

10A.M.

11A.M.

12NOON

1P.M.

2P.M.

3P.M.

4P.M.

5P.M.

6P.M.

	MAY								JUNE								JULY					
S	M	T	W	T	F	S	S	M	T	W	T	F	S	S	M	T	W	T	F	S
			1	2	3	4							1			1	2	3	4	5	6
5	6	7	8	9	10	11	2	3	4	5	6	7	8	7	8	9	10	11	12	13
12	13	14	15	16	17	18	9	10	11	12	13	14	15	14	15	16	17	18	19	20
19	20	21	22	23	24	25	16	17	18	19	20	21	22	21	22	23	24	25	26	27
26	27	28	29	30	31		23	24	25	26	27	28	29	28	29	30	31			
							30													

11 JUNE
TUESDAY

DAILY MINDER

√ Key material deliveries confirmed?

√ All required submittals in and approved?

√ Current schedule commitments in-process?

JOB NO.   APPOINTMENTS/EVENTS/CALLS

7 A.M.

8 A.M.

9 A.M.

10 A.M.

11 A.M.

12 NOON

1 P.M.

2 P.M.

3 P.M.

4 P.M.

5 P.M.

6 P.M.

KEY EVENTS

Meetings

Schedule Updates

Cost Report Updates

Change Proposals

Material Deliveries

Special Information/Instructions

Arch./Owner Direction Received

DAILY DIARY

WEATHER/TEMP.   8 A.M.   12 NOON   4 P.M.

EXPENSES

Ammonal: A powdered explosive used for heavy blasts in boreholes and tunnels. It absorbs moisture and does not store easily.

DAILY MINDER

√ Assemble all schedule update information.

√ Meeting minutes received/prepared?

√ Change proposals requested?

WORK	CAL	
MONTH TO DATE	8	12
MONTH REMAINING	12	19
YEAR TO DATE	114	163
YEAR REMAINING	140	202

JUNE

12

WEDNESDAY

KEY EVENTS

Meetings

Schedule Updates

Cost Report Updates

Change Proposals

Material Deliveries

Special Information/Instructions

Arch./Owner Direction Received

DAILY DIARY

WEATHER/TEMP.   8A.M.   12NOON   4P.M.

EXPENSES

JOB NO. APPOINTMENTS/EVENTS/CALLS

7 A.M.

8 A.M.

9 A.M.

10 A.M.

11 A.M.

12 NOON

1 P.M.

2 P.M.

3 P.M.

4 P.M.

5 P.M.

6 P.M.

MAY						
S	M	T	W	T	F	S
				1	2	3	4
5	6	7	8	9	10	11
12	13	14	15	16	17	18
19	20	21	22	23	24	25
26	27	28	29	30	31	

JUNE						
S	M	T	W	T	F	S
						1
2	3	4	5	6	7	8
9	10	11	12	13	14	15
16	17	18	19	20	21	22
23	24	25	26	27	28	29
30						

JULY						
S	M	T	W	T	F	S
	1	2	3	4	5	6
7	8	9	10	11	12	13
14	15	16	17	18	19	20
21	22	23	24	25	26	27
28	29	30	31			

13 JUNE THURSDAY

DAILY MINDER

√ Key material deliveries confirmed?

√ Next week's schedules confirmed?

√ Request/received outstanding design info?

JOB NO. APPOINTMENTS/EVENTS/CALLS

7 A.M.

8 A.M.

9 A.M.

10 A.M.

11 A.M.

12 NOON

1 P.M.

2 P.M.

3 P.M.

4 P.M.

5 P.M.

6 P.M.

KEY EVENTS

Meetings

Schedule Updates

Cost Report Updates

Change Proposals

Material Deliveries

Special Information/Instructions

Arch./Owner Direction Received

DAILY DIARY

WEATHER/TEMP.   8 A.M.   12 NOON   4 P.M.

EXPENSES

Orio: A fillet at the top or bottom of a column or shaft.

DAILY MINDER

√ Assemble all schedule update information.

√ Job meeting minutes and reports complete?

√ Next week's schedules confirmed?

√ Submitted change orders approved?

	WORK	CAL
MONTH TO DATE	10	14
MONTH REMAINING	10	17
YEAR TO DATE	116	165
YEAR REMAINING	138	200

JUNE
Flag
Day
FRIDAY

14

KEY EVENTS

Meetings

Schedule Updates

Cost Report Updates

Change Proposals

Material Deliveries

Special Information/Instructions

Arch./Owner Direction Received

DAILY DIARY

WEATHER/TEMP. 8A.M.   12NOON   4P.M.

EXPENSES

JOB NO. APPOINTMENTS/EVENTS/CALLS

7 A.M.

8 A.M.

9 A.M.

10 A.M.

11 A.M.

12 NOON

1 P.M.

2 P.M.

3 P.M.

4 P.M.

5 P.M.

6 P.M.

	MAY							JUNE							JULY					
S	M	T	W	T	F	S	S	M	T	W	T	F	S	S	M	T	W	T	F	S
			1	2	3	4							1			1	2	3	4	5	6
5	6	7	8	9	10	11	2	3	4	5	6	7	8	7	8	9	10	11	12	13
12	13	14	15	16	17	18	9	10	11	12	13	14	15	14	15	16	17	18	19	20
19	20	21	22	23	24	25	16	17	18	19	20	21	22	21	22	23	24	25	26	27
26	27	28	29	30	31		23	24	25	26	27	28	29	28	29	30	31			
							30													

15 JUNE

SATURDAY

	WORK	CAL
MONTH TO DATE	10	15
MONTH REMAINING	10	16
YEAR TO DATE	116	166
YEAR REMAINING	138	199

JOB NO. APPOINTMENTS/EVENTS/CALLS

DAILY DIARY

	WORK	CAL
MONTH TO DATE	10	16
MONTH REMAINING	10	15
YEAR TO DATE	116	167
YEAR REMAINING	138	198

JUNE
Father's
Day

SUNDAY

16

JOB NO. APPOINTMENTS/EVENTS/CALLS

DAILY DIARY

WEEK Beginning 17 JUNE
Ending 23 JUNE

WEEKLY EVENT CHECKLIST

- [ ] Job meetings and preparation
- [ ] Special meetings
- [ ] Dinners and seminars
- [ ] Assemble schedule information
- [ ] Complete schedule updates
- [ ] Requests out for all required information
- [ ] Outstanding sub/supplier responses
- [ ] Outstanding owner responses
- [ ] Outstanding architect/engineer responses
- [ ] Critical material deliveries confirmed
- [ ] Shop drawings for ongoing work in/appr

- [ ] Submittals for pending work in/appr
- [ ] All other submittals in/approved
- [ ] Shop drawing log up to date
- [ ] All sub change proposals in
- [ ] All change proposals to owner prep'd
- [ ] Submitted change proposals appr
- [ ] Change order logs up to date
- [ ] Required bonds received for all subs
- [ ] Certificates of insurance rec'd for all subs (proper amounts)
- [ ] Equipment/scaffolding release forms in

- [ ] All permits in place
- [ ] Req testing/inspections arranged
- [ ] Inspection certificates received
- [ ] Safety inspections performed
- [ ] Safety recommendations acted on
- [ ] Field reports complete
- [ ] Special photos taken
- [ ] _____
- [ ] _____
- [ ] _____
- [ ] _____

TO DO

Item	Job No.	Item	Job No.

WEEKLY MILESTONE UPDATE

	Planned Date	Actual Date	Variance

17

JUNE

MONDAY

	WORK	CAL
MONTH TO DATE	11	17
MONTH REMAINING	9	14
YEAR TO DATE	117	168
YEAR REMAINING	137	197

DAILY MINDER

√ Job meeting minutes and reports complete?

√ All required design info. received?

√ Current schedule commitments in-process?

√ Change orders proposals submitted?

JOB NO. APPOINTMENTS/EVENTS/CALLS

7 A.M.

8 A.M.

9 A.M.

10 A.M.

11 A.M.

12 NOON

1 P.M.

2 P.M.

3 P.M.

4 P.M.

5 P.M.

6 P.M.

KEY EVENTS

Meetings

Schedule Updates

Cost Report Updates

Change Proposals

Material Deliveries

Special Information/Instructions

Arch./Owner Direction Received

DAILY DIARY

WEATHER/TEMP.   8 A.M.   12 NOON   4 P.M.

EXPENSES

Dogtro Wreath Piece: Curved section of the handrail string of a winding stair.

DAILY MINDER

√ Verify approval of outstanding change orders.
√ All cost report information assembled?
√ Quarterly report information assembled?
√ Sub change proposals received?

KEY EVENTS

Meetings

Schedule Updates

Cost Report Updates

Change Proposals

Material Deliveries

Special Information/Instructions

Arch./Owner Direction Received

DAILY DIARY

WEATHER/TEMP.   8A.M.   12NOON   4P.M.

EXPENSES

WORK	CAL
MONTH TO DATE	12	18
MONTH REMAINING	8	13
YEAR TO DATE	118	169
YEAR REMAINING	136	196

JUNE

18

TUESDAY

JOB NO. APPOINTMENTS/EVENTS/CALLS

7A.M.

8A.M.

9A.M.

10A.M.

11A.M.

12NOON

1P.M.

2P.M.

3P.M.

4P.M.

5P.M.

6P.M.

MAY						
S	M	T	W	T	F	S
			1	2	3	4
5	6	7	8	9	10	11
12	13	14	15	16	17	18
19	20	21	22	23	24	25
26	27	28	29	30	31	

JUNE						
S	M	T	W	T	F	S
						1
2	3	4	5	6	7	8
9	10	11	12	13	14	15
16	17	18	19	20	21	22
23	24	25	26	27	28	29
30						

JULY						
S	M	T	W	T	F	S
	1	2	3	4	5	6
7	8	9	10	11	12	13
14	15	16	17	18	19	20
21	22	23	24	25	26	27
28	29	30	31			

19 JUNE
WEDNESDAY

DAILY MINDER

√ Required submittals in/approved?
√ Schedule update info assembled?
√ Key material deliveries confirmed?
√ Meeting minutes received/prepared?

JOB NO. APPOINTMENTS/EVENTS/CALLS

7 A.M.

8 A.M.

9 A.M.

10 A.M.

11 A.M.

12 NOON

1 P.M.

2 P.M.

3 P.M.

4 P.M.

5 P.M.

6 P.M.

KEY EVENTS

Meetings

Schedule Updates

Cost Report Updates

Change Proposals

Material Deliveries

Special Information/Instructions

Arch./Owner Direction Received

DAILY DIARY

WEATHER/TEMP.   8 A.M.   12 NOON   4 P.M.

EXPENSES

Adiabatic Curing: Maintenance of conditions during the curing of concrete so that heat is neither gained nor lost from the surroundings.

DAILY MINDER

√ Verify approval of outstanding change orders.

√ Verify receipt of all sub and supplier payment requisitions.

√ Schedule update complete?

√ All cost report information assembled?

	WORK	CAL
MONTH TO DATE	14	20
MONTH REMAINING	6	11
YEAR TO DATE	120	171
YEAR REMAINING	134	194

JUNE
20
THURSDAY

KEY EVENTS

Meetings

Schedule Updates

Cost Report Updates

Change Proposals

Material Deliveries

Special Information/Instructions

Arch./Owner Direction Received

DAILY DIARY

WEATHER/TEMP.   8A.M.   12NOON   4P.M.

EXPENSES

JOB NO.   APPOINTMENTS/EVENTS/CALLS

7A.M.

8A.M.

9A.M.

10A.M.

11A.M.

12NOON

1P.M.

2P.M.

3P.M.

4P.M.

5P.M.

6P.M.

		MAY								JUNE								JULY				
S	M	T	W	T	F	S	S	M	T	W	T	F	S	S	M	T	W	T	F	S
			1	2	3	4							1			1	2	3	4	5	6
5	6	7	8	9	10	11	2	3	4	5	6	7	8	7	8	9	10	11	12	13
12	13	14	15	16	17	18	9	10	11	12	13	14	15	14	15	16	17	18	19	20
19	20	21	22	23	24	25	16	17	18	19	20	21	22	21	22	23	24	25	26	27
26	27	28	29	30	31		23	24	25	26	27	28	29	28	29	30	31			
							30													

21

JUNE
FRIDAY

	WORK	CAL
MONTH TO DATE	15	21
MONTH REMAINING	5	10
YEAR TO DATE	121	172
YEAR REMAINING	133	193

JOB NO. APPOINTMENTS/EVENTS/CALLS

Time	
7 A.M.	
8 A.M.	
9 A.M.	
10 A.M.	
11 A.M.	
12 NOON	
1 P.M.	
2 P.M.	
3 P.M.	
4 P.M.	
5 P.M.	
6 P.M.	

DAILY MINDER

√ Assemble all schedule update information.
√ Job meeting minutes and reports complete?
√ All monthly reports and narratives complete?
√ Key material deliveries confirmed?

KEY EVENTS

Meetings
Schedule Updates
Cost Report Updates
Change Proposals
Material Deliveries
Special Information/Instructions
Arch./Owner Direction Received

DAILY DIARY

WEATHER/TEMP.   8 A.M.   12 NOON   4 P.M.

EXPENSES

Pyranom Overgrainer: A brush used for graining and marble finishes.

22 JUNE
SATURDAY

JOB NO. APPOINTMENTS/EVENTS/CALLS

DAILY DIARY

JUNE 23
SUNDAY

JOB NO. APPOINTMENTS/EVENTS/CALLS

DAILY DIARY

WEEK Beginning 24 JUNE
Ending 30 JUNE

WEEKLY EVENT CHECKLIST

Job meetings and preparation ___	Submittals for pending work in/appr ___	All permits in place ___
Special meetings ___	All other submittals in/approved ___	Req testing/inspections arranged ___
Dinners and seminars ___	Shop drawing log up to date ___	Inspection certificates received ___
Assemble schedule information ___	All sub change proposals in ___	Safety inspections performed ___
Complete schedule updates ___	All change proposals to owner prep'd ___	Safety recommendations acted on ___
Requests out for all required information ___	Submitted change proposals appr ___	Field reports complete ___
Outstanding sub/supplier responses ___	Change order logs up to date ___	Special photos taken ___
Outstanding owner responses ___	Required bonds received for all subs ___	_____ ___
Outstanding architect/engineer responses ___	Certificates of insurance rec'd for all	_____ ___
Critical material deliveries confirmed ___	subs (proper amounts) ___	_____ ___
Shop drawings for ongoing work in/appr ___	Equipment/scaffolding release forms in ___	_____ ___

TO DO

Item	Job No.	Item	Job No.

WEEKLY MILESTONE UPDATE

	Planned Date	Actual Date	Variance

DAILY MINDER

√ Verify approval of outstanding change orders.

√ Submit requisition(s) to owner(s).

√ Authorize/approve sub and supplier payments.

√ Schedule update complete?

WORK CAL
JUNE

MONTH TO DATE	16	24
MONTH REMAINING	4	7
YEAR TO DATE	122	175
YEAR REMAINING	132	190

MONDAY

24

KEY EVENTS

Meetings

Schedule Updates

Cost Report Updates

Change Proposals

Material Deliveries

Special Information/Instructions

Arch./Owner Direction Received

DAILY DIARY

WEATHER/TEMP.   8A.M.   12NOON   4P.M.

EXPENSES

JOB NO. APPOINTMENTS/EVENTS/CALLS

7 A.M.

8 A.M.

9 A.M.

10 A.M.

11 A.M.

12 NOON

1 P.M.

2 P.M.

3 P.M.

4 P.M.

5 P.M.

6 P.M.

MAY								JUNE								JULY						
S	M	T	W	T	F	S		S	M	T	W	T	F	S		S	M	T	W	T	F	S
			1	2	3	4								1			1	2	3	4	5	6
5	6	7	8	9	10	11		2	3	4	5	6	7	8		7	8	9	10	11	12	13
12	13	14	15	16	17	18		9	10	11	12	13	14	15		14	15	16	17	18	19	20
19	20	21	22	23	24	25		16	17	18	19	20	21	22		21	22	23	24	25	26	27
26	27	28	29	30	31			23	24	25	26	27	28	29		28	29	30	31			
								30														

25 JUNE
TUESDAY

	WORK	CAL
MONTH TO DATE	17	25
MONTH REMAINING	3	6
YEAR TO DATE	123	176
YEAR REMAINING	131	189

DAILY MINDER

√ Submit requisition(s) to owner(s).
√ All monthly reports and narratives complete?
√ Quarterly reports prepared?
√ Cost report complete?

JOB NO. APPOINTMENTS/EVENTS/CALLS

7 A.M.

8 A.M.

9 A.M.

10 A.M.

11 A.M.

12 NOON

1 P.M.

2 P.M.

3 P.M.

4 P.M.

5 P.M.

6 P.M.

KEY EVENTS

Meetings

Schedule Updates

Cost Report Updates

Change Proposals

Material Deliveries

Special Information/Instructions

Arch./Owner Direction Received

DAILY DIARY

WEATHER/TEMP.   8 A.M.   12 NOON   4 P.M.

EXPENSES

Corbel: A piece of brick, stone, or wood that protrudes from the face of a wall to form a support for weight, such as a timber.

DAILY MINDER

√ Submit requisition(s) to owner(s).

√ Authorize/approve sub and supplier payments.

√ Schedule update complete?

√ Cost report complete?

KEY EVENTS

Meetings

Schedule Updates

Cost Report Updates

Change Proposals

Material Deliveries

Special Information/Instructions

Arch./Owner Direction Received

DAILY DIARY

WEATHER/TEMP.   8A.M.   12NOON   4P.M.

EXPENSES

WORK	CAL
MONTH TO DATE	18	26
MONTH REMAINING	2	5
YEAR TO DATE	124	177
YEAR REMAINING	130	188

JUNE
26
WEDNESDAY

JOB NO. APPOINTMENTS/EVENTS/CALLS

7 A.M.

8 A.M.

9 A.M.

10 A.M.

11 A.M.

12 NOON

1 P.M.

2 P.M.

3 P.M.

4 P.M.

5 P.M.

6 P.M.

	MAY							JUNE							JULY					
S	M	T	W	T	F	S	S	M	T	W	T	F	S	S	M	T	W	T	F	S
			1	2	3	4							1			1	2	3	4	5	6
5	6	7	8	9	10	11	2	3	4	5	6	7	8	7	8	9	10	11	12	13
12	13	14	15	16	17	18	9	10	11	12	13	14	15	14	15	16	17	18	19	20
19	20	21	22	23	24	25	16	17	18	19	20	21	22	21	22	23	24	25	26	27
26	27	28	29	30	31		23	24	25	26	27	28	29	28	29	30	31			
							30													

27 JUNE
THURSDAY

	WORK	CAL
MONTH TO DATE	19	27
MONTH REMAINING	1	4
YEAR TO DATE	125	178
YEAR REMAINING	129	187

JOB NO. APPOINTMENTS/EVENTS/CALLS

7 A.M.

8 A.M.

9 A.M.

10 A.M.

11 A.M.

12 NOON

1 P.M.

2 P.M.

3 P.M.

4 P.M.

5 P.M.

6 P.M.

DAILY MINDER

√ This month's schedule update complete?

√ This month's reports and narratives complete?

√ Quarterly reports prepared?

√ Current schedules in-process?

KEY EVENTS

Meetings

Schedule Updates

Cost Report Updates

Change Proposals

Material Deliveries

Special Information/Instructions

Arch./Owner Direction Received

DAILY DIARY

WEATHER/TEMP.   8 A.M.   12 NOON   4 P.M.

EXPENSES

Orchostyle: The placing of a series of columns in a straight row.

DAILY MINDER

√ This month's schedule update complete?
√ This month's reports and narratives complete?
√ Key material deliveries confirmed?
√ Progress photos taken?

KEY EVENTS

Meetings

Schedule Updates

Cost Report Updates

Change Proposals

Material Deliveries

Special Information/Instructions

Arch./Owner Direction Received

DAILY DIARY

WEATHER/TEMP.   8 A.M.   12 NOON   4 P.M.

EXPENSES

	WORK	CAL	**JUNE**
MONTH TO DATE	20	28	
MONTH REMAINING	0	3	
YEAR TO DATE	126	179	
YEAR REMAINING	128	186	**FRIDAY**

28

JOB NO. APPOINTMENTS/EVENTS/CALLS

7 A.M.

8 A.M.

9 A.M.

10 A.M.

11 A.M.

12 NOON

1 P.M.

2 P.M.

3 P.M.

4 P.M.

5 P.M.

6 P.M.

		MAY								JUNE								JULY				
S	M	T	W	T	F	S	S	M	T	W	T	F	S	S	M	T	W	T	F	S
			1	2	3	4							1		1	2	3	4	5	6
5	6	7	8	9	10	11	2	3	4	5	6	7	8	7	8	9	10	11	12	13
12	13	14	15	16	17	18	9	10	11	12	13	14	15	14	15	16	17	18	19	20
19	20	21	22	23	24	25	16	17	18	19	20	21	22	21	22	23	24	25	26	27
26	27	28	29	30	31		23	24	25	26	27	28	29	28	29	30	31			
							30													

29 JUNE SATURDAY

	WORK	CAL
MONTH TO DATE	20	29
MONTH REMAINING	0	2
YEAR TO DATE	126	180
YEAR REMAINING	128	185

JOB NO. APPOINTMENTS/EVENTS/CALLS

DAILY DIARY

JUNE 30 SUNDAY

	WORK	CAL
MONTH TO DATE	20	30
MONTH REMAINING	0	1
YEAR TO DATE	126	181
YEAR REMAINING	128	184

JOB NO. APPOINTMENTS/EVENTS/CALLS

DAILY DIARY

JULY

22 Working Days

31 Calendar Days

JUNE

S	M	T	W	T	F	S
						1
2	3	4	5	6	7	8
9	10	11	12	13	14	15
16	17	18	19	20	21	22
23	24	25	26	27	28	29
30						

JULY

S	M	T	W	T	F	S
		1	2	3	4	5	6
7	8	9	10	11	12	13
14	15	16	17	18	19	20
21	22	23	24	25	26	27
28	29	30	31			

AUGUST

S	M	T	W	T	F	S
					1	2	3
4	5	6	7	8	9	10
11	12	13	14	15	16	17
18	19	20	21	22	23	24
25	26	27	28	29	30	31

MONTHLY KEY ACTIVITY UPDATE

Job/C.O. No.	Description	Planned Date	Actual Date	Variance	Remarks

MONTHLY SCHEDULE UPDATE SUMMARY

Job/C.O. No.	Activities	Original Duration	Days Spent	Days Remaining	Status/Remarks

MONTHLY RECAP

S	M	T	W	T	F	S
		1	2	3	4	5	6
7	8	9	10	11	12	13
14	15	16	17	18	19	20
21	22	23	24	25	26	27
28	29	30	31			

JULY

MONTHLY EVENT CHECKLIST

Schedule updates complete
Requests out for all required info.
Outstanding sub/supplier responses rec'd
Outstanding owner responses rec'd
Outstanding arch./eng. responses rec'd
Critical material deliveries confirmed
Shop drawings for ongoing work in/appr
Submittals for pending work in/appr
All other submittals in/approved

All sub change proposals in
All change proposals to owner prepared
Submitted change proposals approved
Guarantees/warrantees rec'd
Inspection certificates rec'd
As-built drawings rec'd
Safety inspections performed
Safety reports complete
Narratives complete

Sub/supplier contract(s) rec'd
Requisition(s) submitted to owner(s)
Sub/supplier adjustments complete
Progress photos taken
Job cost report info. assembled
Job cost reports complete
Other:
_____
_____

CRITICAL ITEM COST REPORT SUMMARY

Job/CO No.	Description	(A) Budget $ Amount	(B) Cost To Date	(C) Cost Remaining	(D) Total Commitment (B + C)	(E) +/− (A − D)

CHANGE ORDER SUMMARY

Job No.	C.O. No.	Description	Submission Date Required	Submission Date Actual	Approval Date Required	Approval Date Actual	Remarks

WEEK Beginning 1 JULY
Ending 7 JULY

WEEKLY EVENT CHECKLIST

☐ Job meetings and preparation	☐ Submittals for pending work in/appr	☐ All permits in place
☐ Special meetings	☐ All other submittals in/approved	☐ Req testing/inspections arranged
☐ Dinners and seminars	☐ Shop drawing log up to date	☐ Inspection certificates received
☐ Assemble schedule information	☐ All sub change proposals in	☐ Safety inspections performed
☐ Complete schedule updates	☐ All change proposals to owner prep'd	☐ Safety recommendations acted on
☐ Requests out for all required information	☐ Submitted change proposals appr	☐ Field reports complete
☐ Outstanding sub/supplier responses	☐ Change order logs up to date	☐ Special photos taken
☐ Outstanding owner responses	☐ Required bonds received for all subs	☐ _____
☐ Outstanding architect/engineer responses	☐ Certificates of insurance rec'd for all subs (proper amounts)	☐ _____
☐ Critical material deliveries confirmed	☐ Equipment/scaffolding release forms in	☐ _____
☐ Shop drawings for ongoing work in/appr		

TO DO

Item	Job No.	Item	Job No.

WEEKLY MILESTONE UPDATE

	Planned Date	Actual Date	Variance

1 JULY
MONDAY

WORK CAL		
MONTH TO DATE	1	1
MONTH REMAINING	21	30
YEAR TO DATE	127	182
YEAR REMAINING	127	183

DAILY MINDER

√ Last month's schedule update complete?

√ Job meeting minutes and reports complete?

√ Key material deliveries confirmed?

√ Progress photos taken?

JOB NO. APPOINTMENTS/EVENTS/CALLS

7 A.M.

8 A.M.

9 A.M.

10 A.M.

11 A.M.

12 NOON

1 P.M.

2 P.M.

3 P.M.

4 P.M.

5 P.M.

6 P.M.

KEY EVENTS

Meetings

Schedule Updates

Cost Report Updates

Change Proposals

Material Deliveries

Special Information/Instructions

Arch./Owner Direction Received

DAILY DIARY

WEATHER/TEMP.   8 A.M.   12 NOON   4 P.M.

EXPENSES

Chalking: The breakdown of the surface of a paint film to a loose powder.

DAILY MINDER

√ Last month's schedule update complete?
√ Job meeting minutes and reports complete?
√ Key material deliveries confirmed?
√ Progress photos taken?

KEY EVENTS

Meetings

Schedule Updates

Cost Report Updates

Change Proposals

Material Deliveries

Special Information/Instructions

Arch./Owner Direction Received

DAILY DIARY

WEATHER/TEMP.   8A.M.   12NOON   4P.M.

EXPENSES

	WORK	CAL	**JULY**
MONTH TO DATE	3	2	
MONTH REMAINING	20	29	
YEAR TO DATE	128	183	
YEAR REMAINING	126	182	**TUESDAY**

2

JOB NO.   APPOINTMENTS/EVENTS/CALLS

7 A.M.

8 A.M.

9 A.M.

10 A.M.

11 A.M.

12 NOON

1 P.M.

2 P.M.

3 P.M.

4 P.M.

5 P.M.

6 P.M.

		JUNE				
S	M	T W	T	F	S	
						1
2	3	4 5	6	7	8	
9	10	11 12	13	14	15	
16	17	18 19	20	21	22	
23	24	25 26	27	28	29	
30						

		JULY				
S	M	T W	T	F	S	
	1	2 3	4	5	6	
7	8	9 10	11	12	13	
14	15	16 17	18	19	20	
21	22	23 24	25	26	27	
28	29	30 31				

		AUGUST				
S	M	T W	T	F	S	
				1	2	3
4	5	6 7	8	9	10	
11	12	13 14	15	16	17	
18	19	20 21	22	23	24	
25	26	27 28	29	30	31	

3 JULY
WEDNESDAY

WORK	CAL	
MONTH TO DATE	3	3
MONTH REMAINING	19	28
YEAR TO DATE	129	184
YEAR REMAINING	125	181

JOB NO. APPOINTMENTS/EVENTS/CALLS

7 A.M.

8 A.M.

9 A.M.

10 A.M.

11 A.M.

12 NOON

1 P.M.

2 P.M.

3 P.M.

4 P.M.

5 P.M.

6 P.M.

DAILY MINDER

√ Requested/received required design info?
√ Current schedules in-process?
√ Received June payment(s)?
√ Current change orders prepared/submitted?

KEY EVENTS

Meetings

Schedule Updates

Cost Report Updates

Change Proposals

Material Deliveries

Special Information/Instructions

Arch./Owner Direction Received

DAILY DIARY

WEATHER/TEMP.   8A.M.   12NOON   4P.M.

EXPENSES

Damper: Adjustable blades within an air duct to regulate the flow of air.

DAILY MINDER

√ Key material deliveries confirmed?
√ All requests for change proposals out?
√ Received June payment(s)?
√ Submitted change proposals approved?

KEY EVENTS

Meetings

Schedule Updates

Cost Report Updates

Change Proposals

Material Deliveries

Special Information/Instructions

Arch./Owner Direction Received

DAILY DIARY

WEATHER/TEMP.   8A.M.   12NOON   4P.M.

EXPENSES

	WORK CAL	
MONTH TO DATE	3	4
MONTH REMAINING	19	27
YEAR TO DATE	129	185
YEAR REMAINING	125	180

JULY
Independence
Day
THURSDAY

4

JOB NO. APPOINTMENTS/EVENTS/CALLS

7A.M.

8A.M.

9A.M.

10A.M.

11A.M.

12NOON

1P.M.

2P.M.

3P.M.

4P.M.

5P.M.

6P.M.

JUNE							JULY							AUGUST						
S	M	T	W	T	F	S	S	M	T	W	T	F	S	S	M	T	W	T	F	S
						1		1	2	3	4	5	6					1	2	3
2	3	4	5	6	7	8	7	8	9	10	11	12	13	4	5	6	7	8	9	10
9	10	11	12	13	14	15	14	15	16	17	18	19	20	11	12	13	14	15	16	17
16	17	18	19	20	21	22	21	22	23	24	25	26	27	18	19	20	21	22	23	24
23	24	25	26	27	28	29	28	29	30	31				25	26	27	28	29	30	31
30																				

5 JULY
FRIDAY

WORK	CAL
MONTH TO DATE	4	5
MONTH REMAINING	18	27
YEAR TO DATE	130	186
YEAR REMAINING	124	179

DAILY MINDER

√ Job meeting minutes and reports complete?

√ All required submittals in and approved?

√ Cost reports complete?

√ Next week's schedules confirmed?

JOB NO. APPOINTMENTS/EVENTS/CALLS

7 A.M.

8 A.M.

9 A.M.

10 A.M.

11 A.M.

12 NOON

1 P.M.

2 P.M.

3 P.M.

4 P.M.

5 P.M.

6 P.M.

KEY EVENTS

Meetings

Schedule Updates

Cost Report Updates

Change Proposals

Material Deliveries

Special Information/Instructions

Arch./Owner Direction Received

DAILY DIARY

WEATHER/TEMP.   8 A.M.   12 NOON   4 P.M.

EXPENSES

Mullion: A framing or separating member between adjacent door or window sections.

6 JULY
SATURDAY

	WORK	CAL
MONTH TO DATE	4	6
MONTH REMAINING	18	25
YEAR TO DATE	130	187
YEAR REMAINING	124	178

JOB NO. APPOINTMENTS/EVENTS/CALLS

DAILY DIARY

JULY 7
SUNDAY

	WORK	CAL
MONTH TO DATE	4	7
MONTH REMAINING	18	24
YEAR TO DATE	130	188
YEAR REMAINING	124	177

JOB NO. APPOINTMENTS/EVENTS/CALLS

DAILY DIARY

WEEK Beginning   8 JULY
Ending   14 JULY

WEEKLY EVENT CHECKLIST

Job meetings and preparation   ☐   Submittals for pending work in/appr   ☐   All permits in place   ☐

Special meetings   ☐   All other submittals in/approved   ☐   Req testing/inspections arranged   ☐

Dinners and seminars   ☐   Shop drawing log up to date   ☐   Inspection certificates received   ☐

Assemble schedule information   ☐   All sub change proposals in   ☐   Safety inspections performed   ☐

Complete schedule updates   ☐   All change proposals to owner prep'd   ☐   Safety recommendations acted on   ☐

Requests out for all required information   ☐   Submitted change proposals appr   ☐   Field reports complete   ☐

Outstanding sub/supplier responses   ☐   Change order logs up to date   ☐   Special photos taken   ☐

Outstanding owner responses   ☐   Required bonds received for all subs   ☐   _____ ☐

Outstanding architect/engineer responses   ☐   Certificates of insurance rec'd for all   _____ ☐

Critical material deliveries confirmed   ☐   subs (proper amounts)   _____ ☐

Shop drawings for ongoing work in/appr   ☐   Equipment/scaffolding release forms in   ☐   _____ ☐

TO DO

Item	Job No.	Item	Job No.

WEEKLY MILESTONE UPDATE

	Planned Date	Actual Date	Variance

DAILY MINDER

√ Job meeting minutes and reports complete?

√ June payment(s) received?

√ Submitted change proposals approved?

√ Current schedule commitments in-process?

KEY EVENTS

Meetings

Schedule Updates

Cost Report Updates

Change Proposals

Material Deliveries

Special Information/Instructions

Arch./Owner Direction Received

DAILY DIARY

WEATHER/TEMP.   8A.M.   12NOON   4P.M.

EXPENSES

	WORK	CAL
MONTH TO DATE	5	8
MONTH REMAINING	17	23
YEAR TO DATE	131	189
YEAR REMAINING	123	176

JULY

8

MONDAY

JOB NO.   APPOINTMENTS/EVENTS/CALLS

7 A.M.

8 A.M.

9 A.M.

10 A.M.

11 A.M.

12 NOON

1 P.M.

2 P.M.

3 P.M.

4 P.M.

5 P.M.

6 P.M.

	JUNE								JULY								AUGUST					
S	M	T	W	T	F	S		S	M	T	W	T	F	S		S	M	T	W	T	F	S
						1			1	2	3	4	5	6						1	2	3
2	3	4	5	6	7	8		7	8	9	10	11	12	13		4	5	6	7	8	9	10
9	10	11	12	13	14	15		14	15	16	17	18	19	20		11	12	13	14	15	16	17
16	17	18	19	20	21	22		21	22	23	24	25	26	27		18	19	20	21	22	23	24
23	24	25	26	27	28	29		28	29	30	31					25	26	27	28	29	30	31
30																						

9 JULY
TUESDAY

WORK CAL		
MONTH TO DATE	6	9
MONTH REMAINING	16	22
YEAR TO DATE	132	190
YEAR REMAINING	122	175

JOB NO. APPOINTMENTS/EVENTS/CALLS

7 A.M.

8 A.M.

9 A.M.

10 A.M.

11 A.M.

12 NOON

1 P.M.

2 P.M.

3 P.M.

4 P.M.

5 P.M.

6 P.M.

DAILY MINDER

√ Verify receipt of last month's payment.

√ All required change proposals out?

√ Required submittals in/approved?

KEY EVENTS

Meetings

Schedule Updates

Cost Report Updates

Change Proposals

Material Deliveries

Special Information/Instructions

Arch./Owner Direction Received

DAILY DIARY

WEATHER/TEMP.   8 A.M.   12 NOON   4 P.M.

EXPENSES

Heel: The part of timber, rafter, or beam resting on a wall plate.

DAILY MINDER

√ Key material deliveries confirmed?

√ All change proposals submitted?

√ Meeting minutes received/prepared?

WORK CAL		
MONTH TO DATE	7	10
MONTH REMAINING	15	21
YEAR TO DATE	133	191
YEAR REMAINING	121	174

JULY

WEDNESDAY

10

KEY EVENTS

Meetings

Schedule Updates

Cost Report Updates

Change Proposals

Material Deliveries

Special Information/Instructions

Arch./Owner Direction Received

DAILY DIARY

WEATHER/TEMP.   8A.M.   12NOON   4P.M.

EXPENSES

JOB NO. APPOINTMENTS/EVENTS/CALLS

7A.M.

8A.M.

9A.M.

10A.M.

11A.M.

12NOON

1P.M.

2P.M.

3P.M.

4P.M.

5P.M.

6P.M.

	JUNE							JULY							AUGUST					
S	M	T	W	T	F	S	S	M	T	W	T	F	S	S	M	T	W	T	F	S
						1			1	2	3	4	5	6					1	2	3
2	3	4	5	6	7	8	7	8	9	10	11	12	13	4	5	6	7	8	9	10
9	10	11	12	13	14	15	14	15	16	17	18	19	20	11	12	13	14	15	16	17
16	17	18	19	20	21	22	21	22	23	24	25	26	27	18	19	20	21	22	23	24
23	24	25	26	27	28	29	28	29	30	31				25	26	27	28	29	30	31
30																				

11 JULY
THURSDAY

WORK	CAL
MONTH TO DATE	8	11
MONTH REMAINING	14	20
YEAR TO DATE	134	192
YEAR REMAINING	120	173

DAILY MINDER

√ Scheduled a complete physical examination this year?

√ Next week's schedules confirmed?

√ Prepare payments to subs?

JOB NO. APPOINTMENTS/EVENTS/CALLS

7 A.M.

8 A.M.

9 A.M.

10 A.M.

11 A.M.

12 NOON

1 P.M.

2 P.M.

3 P.M.

4 P.M.

5 P.M.

6 P.M.

KEY EVENTS

Meetings

Schedule Updates

Cost Report Updates

Change Proposals

Material Deliveries

Special Information/Instructions

Arch./Owner Direction Received

DAILY DIARY

WEATHER/TEMP.   8 A.M.   12 NOON   4 P.M.

EXPENSES

Perron: An architectural term describing an out-of-doorway stair leading to the first floor of a building.

DAILY MINDER

√ Assemble all schedule update information.

√ Job meeting minutes and reports complete?

√ Key material deliveries confirmed?

	WORK	CAL
MONTH TO DATE	9	12
MONTH REMAINING	13	19
YEAR TO DATE	135	193
YEAR REMAINING	119	172

JULY

FRIDAY

12

KEY EVENTS

Meetings

Schedule Updates

Cost Report Updates

Change Proposals

Material Deliveries

Special Information/Instructions

Arch./Owner Direction Received

DAILY DIARY

WEATHER/TEMP. 8A.M.   12NOON   4P.M.

EXPENSES

JOB NO. APPOINTMENTS/EVENTS/CALLS

7A.M.

8A.M.

9A.M.

10A.M.

11A.M.

12NOON

1P.M.

2P.M.

3P.M.

4P.M.

5P.M.

6P.M.

JUNE						
S	M	T	W	T	F	S
						1
2	3	4	5	6	7	8
9	10	11	12	13	14	15
16	17	18	19	20	21	22
23	24	25	26	27	28	29
30						

JULY						
S	M	T	W	T	F	S
	1	2	3	4	5	6
7	8	9	10	11	12	13
14	15	16	17	18	19	20
21	22	23	24	25	26	27
28	29	30	31			

AUGUST						
S	M	T	W	T	F	S
				1	2	3
4	5	6	7	8	9	10
11	12	13	14	15	16	17
18	19	20	21	22	23	24
25	26	27	28	29	30	31

13

JULY

SATURDAY

	WORK	CAL
MONTH TO DATE	9	13
MONTH REMAINING	13	18
YEAR TO DATE	135	194
YEAR REMAINING	119	171

	WORK	CAL
MONTH TO DATE	9	14
MONTH REMAINING	13	17
YEAR TO DATE	135	195
YEAR REMAINING	119	170

JULY

SUNDAY

14

JOB NO. APPOINTMENTS/EVENTS/CALLS

JOB NO. APPOINTMENTS/EVENTS/CALLS

DAILY DIARY

DAILY DIARY

WEEK Beginning   15 JULY
Ending   21 JULY

WEEKLY EVENT CHECKLIST

Job meetings and preparation   ☐ Submittals for pending work in/appr   ☐ All permits in place

Special meetings   ☐ All other submittals in/approved   ☐ Req testing/inspections arranged

Dinners and seminars   ☐ Shop drawing log up to date   ☐ Inspection certificates received

Assemble schedule information   ☐ All sub change proposals in   ☐ Safety inspections performed

Complete schedule updates   ☐ All change proposals to owner prep'd   ☐ Safety recommendations acted on

Requests out for all required information   ☐ Submitted change proposals appr   ☐ Field reports complete

Outstanding sub/supplier responses   ☐ Change order logs up to date   ☐ Special photos taken

Outstanding owner responses   ☐ Required bonds received for all subs   ☐ _____

Outstanding architect/engineer responses   ☐ Certificates of insurance rec'd for all   ☐ _____

Critical material deliveries confirmed   ☐ subs (proper amounts)   ☐ _____

Shop drawings for ongoing work in/appr   ☐ Equipment/scaffolding release forms in   ☐ _____

TO DO	Item	Job No.	Item	Job No.

WEEKLY MILESTONE UPDATE

	Planned Date	Actual Date	Variance

15 JULY
MONDAY

DAILY MINDER

√ Job meeting minutes and reports complete?

√ All required design info. received?

√ Sub's change proposals received?

√ Current schedule commitments in-process?

JOB NO. APPOINTMENTS/EVENTS/CALLS

7 A.M.

8 A.M.

9 A.M.

10 A.M.

11 A.M.

12 NOON

1 P.M.

2 P.M.

3 P.M.

4 P.M.

5 P.M.

6 P.M.

KEY EVENTS

Meetings

Schedule Updates

Cost Report Updates

Change Proposals

Material Deliveries

Special Information/Instructions

Arch./Owner Direction Received

DAILY DIARY

WEATHER/TEMP.   8 A.M.   12 NOON   4 P.M.

EXPENSES

Joggle: A key, or pin, set in between two joining surfaces that reinforces the joint.

DAILY MINDER

√ Verify approval of outstanding change orders.

√ All required submittals in and approved?

√ Attend any professional development seminars?

<table>
<tr><td></td><td>WORK</td><td>CAL</td></tr>
<tr><td>MONTH TO DATE</td><td>11</td><td>16</td></tr>
<tr><td>MONTH REMAINING</td><td>11</td><td>15</td></tr>
<tr><td>YEAR TO DATE</td><td>137</td><td>197</td></tr>
<tr><td>YEAR REMAINING</td><td>117</td><td>168</td></tr>
</table>

JULY

TUESDAY

16

KEY EVENTS

Meetings

Schedule Updates

Cost Report Updates

Change Proposals

Material Deliveries

Special Information/Instructions

Arch./Owner Direction Received

DAILY DIARY

WEATHER/TEMP.   8A.M.   12NOON   4P.M.

EXPENSES

JOB NO.   APPOINTMENTS/EVENTS/CALLS

7A.M.

8A.M.

9A.M.

10A.M.

11A.M.

12NOON

1P.M.

2P.M.

3P.M.

4P.M.

5P.M.

6P.M.

	JUNE							JULY							AUGUST					
S	M	T	W	T	F	S	S	M	T	W	T	F	S	S	M	T	W	T	F	S
						1		1	2	3	4	5	6					1	2	3
2	3	4	5	6	7	8	7	8	9	10	11	12	13	4	5	6	7	8	9	10
9	10	11	12	13	14	15	14	15	16	17	18	19	20	11	12	13	14	15	16	17
16	17	18	19	20	21	22	21	22	23	24	25	26	27	18	19	20	21	22	23	24
23	24	25	26	27	28	29	28	29	30	31				25	26	27	28	29	30	31
30																				

17 JULY
WEDNESDAY

DAILY MINDER

√ Assemble all schedule update material.

√ Key material deliveries confirmed?

√ Meeting minutes received/prepared?

JOB NO. APPOINTMENTS/EVENTS/CALLS

7 A.M.

8 A.M.

9 A.M.

10 A.M.

11 A.M.

12 NOON

1 P.M.

2 P.M.

3 P.M.

4 P.M.

5 P.M.

6 P.M.

KEY EVENTS

Meetings

Schedule Updates

Cost Report Updates

Change Proposals

Material Deliveries

Special Information/Instructions

Arch./Owner Direction Received

DAILY DIARY

WEATHER/TEMP.   8 A.M.   12 NOON   4 P.M.

EXPENSES

Coving: A large moulding often found at the base of a column.

DAILY MINDER

√ Verify receipt of all sub and supplier payment requisitions.

√ Jobsite safety reviews performed?

√ Request/received outstanding design info?

√ Cost report info assembled?

WORK CAL			JULY
MONTH TO DATE	13	18	
MONTH REMAINING	9	13	
YEAR TO DATE	139	199	
YEAR REMAINING	115	166	THURSDAY

18

KEY EVENTS

Meetings

Schedule Updates

Cost Report Updates

Change Proposals

Material Deliveries

Special Information/Instructions

Arch./Owner Direction Received

DAILY DIARY

JOB NO. APPOINTMENTS/EVENTS/CALLS

7 A.M.

8 A.M.

9 A.M.

10 A.M.

11 A.M.

12 NOON

1 P.M.

2 P.M.

3 P.M.

4 P.M.

5 P.M.

6 P.M.

WEATHER/TEMP.   8 A.M.   12 NOON   4 P.M.

EXPENSES

	JUNE							JULY							AUGUST					
S	M	T	W	T	F	S	S	M	T	W	T	F	S	S	M	T	W	T	F	S
						1		1	2	3	4	5	6					1	2	3
2	3	4	5	6	7	8	7	8	9	10	11	12	13	4	5	6	7	8	9	10
9	10	11	12	13	14	15	14	15	16	17	18	19	20	11	12	13	14	15	16	17
16	17	18	19	20	21	22	21	22	23	24	25	26	27	18	19	20	21	22	23	24
23	24	25	26	27	28	29	28	29	30	31				25	26	27	28	29	30	31
30																				

19 JULY
FRIDAY

WORK	CAL
MONTH TO DATE	14	19
MONTH REMAINING	8	12
YEAR TO DATE	140	200
YEAR REMAINING	114	165

DAILY MINDER

√ Assemble all schedule update information.
√ Schedule update complete?
√ Job meeting minutes and reports complete?
√ Key material deliveries confirmed?

JOB NO. APPOINTMENTS/EVENTS/CALLS

7 A.M.

8 A.M.

9 A.M.

10 A.M.

11 A.M.

12 NOON

1 P.M.

2 P.M.

3 P.M.

4 P.M.

5 P.M.

6 P.M.

KEY EVENTS

Meetings

Schedule Updates

Cost Report Updates

Change Proposals

Material Deliveries

Special Information/Instructions

Arch./Owner Direction Received

DAILY DIARY

WEATHER/TEMP.   8 A.M.   12 NOON   4 P.M.

EXPENSES

Authogenous heating: A long natural process of filling and closing of cracks in the concrete or mortar of a structure.

20

JULY

SATURDAY

	WORK	CAL
MONTH TO DATE	14	20
MONTH REMAINING	8	11
YEAR TO DATE	140	201
YEAR REMAINING	114	164

	WORK	CAL
MONTH TO DATE	14	21
MONTH REMAINING	8	10
YEAR TO DATE	140	202
YEAR REMAINING	114	163

JULY

SUNDAY

21

JOB NO. APPOINTMENTS/EVENTS/CALLS

JOB NO. APPOINTMENTS/EVENTS/CALLS

DAILY DIARY

DAILY DIARY

WEEK Beginning 22 JULY
Ending 28 JULY

WEEKLY EVENT CHECKLIST

Job meetings and preparation ___	Submittals for pending work in/appr ___	All permits in place ___
Special meetings ___	All other submittals in/approved ___	Req testing/inspections arranged ___
Dinners and seminars ___	Shop drawing log up to date ___	Inspection certificates received ___
Assemble schedule information ___	All sub change proposals in ___	Safety inspections performed ___
Complete schedule updates ___	All change proposals to owner prep'd ___	Safety recommendations acted on ___
Requests out for all required information ___	Submitted change proposals appr ___	Field reports complete ___
Outstanding sub/supplier responses ___	Change order logs up to date ___	Special photos taken ___
Outstanding owner responses ___	Required bonds received for all subs ___	_____ ___
Outstanding architect/engineer responses ___	Certificates of insurance rec'd for all	_____ ___
Critical material deliveries confirmed ___	subs (proper amounts) ___	_____ ___
Shop drawings for ongoing work in/appr ___	Equipment/scaffolding release forms in ___	_____ ___

TO DO

Item	Job No.	Item	Job No.

WEEKLY MILESTONE UPDATE

	Planned Date	Actual Date	Variance

DAILY MINDER

√ Verify approval of outstanding change orders.

√ Verify receipt of all sub and supplier payment requisitions.

√ Job meeting minutes and reports complete?

√ Current schedules in-process?

WORK	CAL	
MONTH TO DATE	15	22
MONTH REMAINING	7	9
YEAR TO DATE	141	203
YEAR REMAINING	113	162

JULY

22

MONDAY

KEY EVENTS

Meetings

Schedule Updates

Cost Report Updates

Change Proposals

Material Deliveries

Special Information/Instructions

Arch./Owner Direction Received

DAILY DIARY

WEATHER/TEMP.   8A.M.   12NOON   4P.M.

EXPENSES

JOB NO. APPOINTMENTS/EVENTS/CALLS

7 A.M.

8 A.M.

9 A.M.

10 A.M.

11 A.M.

12 NOON

1 P.M.

2 P.M.

3 P.M.

4 P.M.

5 P.M.

6 P.M.

	JUNE								JULY								AUGUST					
S	M	T	W	T	F	S	S	M	T	W	T	F	S	S	M	T	W	T	F	S		
						1		1	2	3	4	5	6					1	2	3		
2	3	4	5	6	7	8	7	8	9	10	11	12	13	4	5	6	7	8	9	10		
9	10	11	12	13	14	15	14	15	16	17	18	19	20	11	12	13	14	15	16	17		
16	17	18	19	20	21	22	21	22	23	24	25	26	27	18	19	20	21	22	23	24		
23	24	25	26	27	28	29	28	29	30	31				25	26	27	28	29	30	31		
30																						

23 JULY
TUESDAY

WORK CAL		
MONTH TO DATE	16	23
MONTH REMAINING	6	8
YEAR TO DATE	142	204
YEAR REMAINING	112	161

DAILY MINDER

√ Verify approval of outstanding change orders.

√ Submit requisition(s) to owner(s).

√ Authorize/approve sub and supplier payments.

√ Key material deliveries confirmed?

JOB NO. APPOINTMENTS/EVENTS/CALLS

7 A.M.

8 A.M.

9 A.M.

10 A.M.

11 A.M.

12 NOON

1 P.M.

2 P.M.

3 P.M.

4 P.M.

5 P.M.

6 P.M.

KEY EVENTS

Meetings

Schedule Updates

Cost Report Updates

Change Proposals

Material Deliveries

Special Information/Instructions

Arch./Owner Direction Received

DAILY DIARY

WEATHER/TEMP.   8 A.M.   12 NOON   4 P.M.

EXPENSES

Rodding: In plaster work, straightening the plaster surface between the grounds and screeds.

DAILY MINDER

√ Assemble all schedule update information.

√ Schedule update complete?

√ All monthly reports and narratives complete?

√ All cost report information assembled?

KEY EVENTS

Meetings

Schedule Updates

Cost Report Updates

Change Proposals

Material Deliveries

Special Information/Instructions

Arch./Owner Direction Received

DAILY DIARY

WEATHER/TEMP.   8A.M.   12NOON   4P.M.

EXPENSES

	WORK	CAL	JULY
MONTH TO DATE	17	24	
MONTH REMAINING	5	7	**24**
YEAR TO DATE	143	205	
YEAR REMAINING	111	160	WEDNESDAY

JOB NO. APPOINTMENTS/EVENTS/CALLS

7A.M.

8A.M.

9A.M.

10A.M.

11A.M.

12NOON

1P.M.

2P.M.

3P.M.

4P.M.

5P.M.

6P.M.

JUNE							JULY							AUGUST						
S	M	T	W	T	F	S	S	M	T	W	T	F	S	S	M	T	W	T	F	S
						1		1	2	3	4	5	6					1	2	3
2	3	4	5	6	7	8	7	8	9	10	11	12	13	4	5	6	7	8	9	10
9	10	11	12	13	14	15	14	15	16	17	18	19	20	11	12	13	14	15	16	17
16	17	18	19	20	21	22	21	22	23	24	25	26	27	18	19	20	21	22	23	24
23	24	25	26	27	28	29	28	29	30	31				25	26	27	28	29	30	31
30																				

25 JULY

THURSDAY

	WORK	CAL
MONTH TO DATE	18	25
MONTH REMAINING	4	6
YEAR TO DATE	144	206
YEAR REMAINING	110	159

JOB NO. APPOINTMENTS/EVENTS/CALLS

7 A.M.

8 A.M.

9 A.M.

10 A.M.

11 A.M.

12 NOON

1 P.M.

2 P.M.

3 P.M.

4 P.M.

5 P.M.

6 P.M.

KEY EVENTS

Meetings

Schedule Updates

Cost Report Updates

Change Proposals

Material Deliveries

Special Information/Instructions

Arch./Owner Direction Received

DAILY DIARY

WEATHER/TEMP.   8 A.M.   12 NOON   4 P.M.

EXPENSES

Yoke: An architectural term describing the horizontal top member of window frame.

DAILY MINDER

√ Schedule update complete?

√ Job meeting minutes and reports complete?

√ All monthly reports and narratives complete?

√ Cost report complete?

<table>
<tr><td></td><td>WORK</td><td>CAL</td></tr>
<tr><td>MONTH TO DATE</td><td>19</td><td>26</td></tr>
<tr><td>MONTH REMAINING</td><td>3</td><td>5</td></tr>
<tr><td>YEAR TO DATE</td><td>145</td><td>207</td></tr>
<tr><td>YEAR REMAINING</td><td>109</td><td>158</td></tr>
</table>

JULY

26

FRIDAY

KEY EVENTS

Meetings

Schedule Updates

Cost Report Updates

Change Proposals

Material Deliveries

Special Information/Instructions

Arch./Owner Direction Received

DAILY DIARY

WEATHER/TEMP.   8A.M.   12NOON   4P.M.

EXPENSES

JOB NO.   APPOINTMENTS/EVENTS/CALLS

7 A.M.

8 A.M.

9 A.M.

10 A.M.

11 A.M.

12 NOON

1 P.M.

2 P.M.

3 P.M.

4 P.M.

5 P.M.

6 P.M.

JUNE							JULY							AUGUST						
S	M	T	W	T	F	S	S	M	T	W	T	F	S	S	M	T	W	T	F	S
						1		1	2	3	4	5	6					1	2	3
2	3	4	5	6	7	8	7	8	9	10	11	12	13	4	5	6	7	8	9	10
9	10	11	12	13	14	15	14	15	16	17	18	19	20	11	12	13	14	15	16	17
16	17	18	19	20	21	22	21	22	23	24	25	26	27	18	19	20	21	22	23	24
23	24	25	26	27	28	29	28	29	30	31				25	26	27	28	29	30	31
30																				

27 JULY
SATURDAY

JULY 28
SUNDAY

JOB NO. APPOINTMENTS/EVENTS/CALLS

JOB NO. APPOINTMENTS/EVENTS/CALLS

DAILY DIARY

DAILY DIARY

WEEK Beginning 29 JULY
Ending 4 AUGUST

WEEKLY EVENT CHECKLIST

Job meetings and preparation ⌐
Special meetings ⌐
Dinners and seminars ⌐
Assemble schedule information ⌐
Complete schedule updates ⌐
Requests out for all required information ⌐
Outstanding sub/supplier responses ⌐
Outstanding owner responses ⌐
Outstanding architect/engineer responses ⌐
Critical material deliveries confirmed ⌐
Shop drawings for ongoing work in/appr ⌐

Submittals for pending work in/appr ⌐
All other submittals in/approved ⌐
Shop drawing log up to date ⌐
All sub change proposals in ⌐
All change proposals to owner prep'd ⌐
Submitted change proposals appr ⌐
Change order logs up to date ⌐
Required bonds received for all subs ⌐
Certificates of insurance rec'd for all subs (proper amounts) ⌐
Equipment/scaffolding release forms in ⌐

All permits in place ⌐
Req testing/inspections arranged ⌐
Inspection certificates received ⌐
Safety inspections performed ⌐
Safety recommendations acted on ⌐
Field reports complete ⌐
Special photos taken ⌐
_____ ⌐
_____ ⌐
_____ ⌐

TO DO

Item	Job No.	Item	Job No.

WEEKLY MILESTONE UPDATE

	Planned Date	Actual Date	Variance

29 JULY
MONDAY

DAILY MINDER

√ Verify approval of outstanding change orders.

√ Submit requisition(s) to owner(s).

√ Authorize/approve sub and supplier payments.

√ Cost report complete?

JOB NO. APPOINTMENTS/EVENTS/CALLS

7 A.M.

8 A.M.

9 A.M.

10 A.M.

11 A.M.

12 NOON

1 P.M.

2 P.M.

3 P.M.

4 P.M.

5 P.M.

6 P.M.

KEY EVENTS

Meetings

Schedule Updates

Cost Report Updates

Change Proposals

Material Deliveries

Special Information/Instructions

Arch./Owner Direction Received

DAILY DIARY

WEATHER/TEMP.　　8 A.M.　　12 NOON　　4 P.M.

EXPENSES

Key Console: A console placed at the crown of an arch that is the intersection of the archivolt.

DAILY MINDER

√ Current schedules in-process?
√ Schedule update complete?
√ Reports and narrative complete?
√ Key material deliveries confirmed?

KEY EVENTS

Meetings

Schedule Updates

Cost Report Updates

Change Proposals

Material Deliveries

Special Information/Instructions

Arch./Owner Direction Received

DAILY DIARY

WEATHER/TEMP.   8A.M.   12NOON   4P.M.

EXPENSES

	WORK CAL		**JULY**
MONTH TO DATE	21	30	
MONTH REMAINING	1	1	
YEAR TO DATE	147	211	
YEAR REMAINING	107	154	**TUESDAY**

30

JOB NO.   APPOINTMENTS/EVENTS/CALLS

7A.M.

8A.M.

9A.M.

10A.M.

11A.M.

12NOON

1P.M.

2P.M.

3P.M.

4P.M.

5P.M.

6P.M.

	JUNE								JULY								AUGUST					
S	M	T	W	T	F	S	S	M	T	W	T	F	S	S	M	T	W	T	F	S
						1			1	2	3	4	5	6						1	2	3
2	3	4	5	6	7	8	7	8	9	10	11	12	13	4	5	6	7	8	9	10
9	10	11	12	13	14	15	14	15	16	17	18	19	20	11	12	13	14	15	16	17
16	17	18	19	20	21	22	21	22	23	24	25	26	27	18	19	20	21	22	23	24
23	24	25	26	27	28	29	28	29	30	31				25	26	27	28	29	30	31
30																				

31 JULY
WEDNESDAY

WORK	CAL
MONTH TO DATE	22	31
MONTH REMAINING	0	0
YEAR TO DATE	148	212
YEAR REMAINING	106	153

DAILY MINDER
√Schedule update complete?
√Reports and narratives complete?
√Progress photos taken?
√Meeting minutes received/prepared?

JOB NO.   APPOINTMENTS/EVENTS/CALLS

7 A.M.

8 A.M.

9 A.M.

10 A.M.

11 A.M.

12 NOON

1 P.M.

2 P.M.

3 P.M.

4 P.M.

5 P.M.

6 P.M.

KEY EVENTS
Meetings

Schedule Updates

Cost Report Updates

Change Proposals

Material Deliveries

Special Information/Instructions

Arch./Owner Direction Received

DAILY DIARY

WEATHER/TEMP.   8 A.M.   12 NOON   4 P.M.

EXPENSES

Slip Newel: Three-sided newel, fitting the free end of a partition wall.

AUGUST

22 Working Days

31 Calendar Days

JULY						
S	M	T	W	T	F	S
		1	2	3	4	5	6
7	8	9	10	11	12	13
14	15	16	17	18	19	20
21	22	23	24	25	26	27
28	29	30	31			

AUGUST						
S	M	T	W	T	F	S
				1	2	3
4	5	6	7	8	9	10
11	12	13	14	15	16	17
18	19	20	21	22	23	24
25	26	27	28	29	30	31

SEPTEMBER						
S	M	T	W	T	F	S
1	2	3	4	5	6	7
8	9	10	11	12	13	14
15	16	17	18	19	20	21
22	23	24	25	26	27	28
29	30					

MONTHLY KEY ACTIVITY UPDATE

Job/C.O. No.	Description	Planned Date	Actual Date	Variance	Remarks

MONTHLY SCHEDULE UPDATE SUMMARY

Job/C.O. No.	Activities	Original Duration	Days Spent	Days Remaining	Status/Remarks

MONTHLY RECAP

S	M	T	W	T	F	S
				1	2	3
4	5	6	7	8	9	10
11	12	13	14	15	16	17
18	19	20	21	22	23	24
25	26	27	28	29	30	31

AUGUST

MONTHLY EVENT CHECKLIST

Schedule updates complete ____

Requests out for all required info. ____

Outstanding sub/supplier responses rec'd ____

Outstanding owner responses rec'd ____

Outstanding arch./eng. responses rec'd ____

Critical material deliveries confirmed ____

Shop drawings for ongoing work in/appr ____

Submittals for pending work in/appr ____

All other submittals in/approved ____

All sub change proposals in ____

All change proposals to owner prepared ____

Submitted change proposals approved ____

Guarantees/warrantees rec'd ____

Inspection certificates rec'd ____

As-built drawings rec'd ____

Safety inspections performed ____

Safety reports complete ____

Narratives complete ____

Sub/supplier contract(s) rec'd ____

Requisition(s) submitted to owner(s) ____

Sub/supplier adjustments complete ____

Progress photos taken ____

Job cost report info. assembled ____

Job cost reports complete ____

Other: ____

_____ ____

_____ ____

CRITICAL ITEM COST REPORT SUMMARY

Job/CO No.	Description	(A) Budget $ Amount	(B) Cost To Date	(C) Cost Remaining	(D) Total Commitment (B + C)	(E) +/− (A − D)

CHANGE ORDER SUMMARY

Job No.	C.O. No.	Description	Submission Date Required	Submission Date Actual	Approval Date Required	Approval Date Actual	Remarks

DAILY MINDER

√Schedule update complete?
√Key material deliveries confirmed?
√Progress photos taken?
√July payments received?

KEY EVENTS

Meetings

Schedule Updates

Cost Report Updates

Change Proposals

Material Deliveries

Special Information/Instructions

Arch./Owner Direction Received

DAILY DIARY

WEATHER/TEMP.   8A.M.   12NOON   4P.M.

EXPENSES

	WORK	CAL	**AUGUST**	**1**
MONTH TO DATE	1	1		
MONTH REMAINING	21	30		
YEAR TO DATE	149	213		
YEAR REMAINING	105	150	**THURSDAY**	

JOB NO. APPOINTMENTS/EVENTS/CALLS

7A.M.

8A.M.

9A.M.

10A.M.

11A.M.

12NOON

1P.M.

2P.M.

3P.M.

4P.M.

5P.M.

6P.M.

	JULY								AUGUST								SEPTEMBER					
S	M	T	W	T	F	S	S	M	T	W	T	F	S	S	M	T	W	T	F	S
	1	2	3	4	5	6					1	2	3	1	2	3	4	5	6	7
7	8	9	10	11	12	13	4	5	6	7	8	9	10	8	9	10	11	12	13	14
14	15	16	17	18	19	20	11	12	13	14	15	16	17	15	16	17	18	19	20	21
21	22	23	24	25	26	27	18	19	20	21	22	23	24	22	23	24	25	26	27	28
28	29	30	31				25	26	27	28	29	30	31	29	30					

2 AUGUST

FRIDAY

WORK CAL		
MONTH TO DATE	2	2
MONTH REMAINING	20	29
YEAR TO DATE	150	214
YEAR REMAINING	104	149

DAILY MINDER

√ Job meeting minutes and reports complete?

√ Progress photos taken?

√ All required design info. received?

√ Next week's schedules confirmed?

JOB NO. APPOINTMENTS/EVENTS/CALLS

7 A.M.

8 A.M.

9 A.M.

10 A.M.

11 A.M.

12 NOON

1 P.M.

2 P.M.

3 P.M.

4 P.M.

5 P.M.

6 P.M.

KEY EVENTS

Meetings

Schedule Updates

Cost Report Updates

Change Proposals

Material Deliveries

Special Information/Instructions

Arch./Owner Direction Received

DAILY DIARY

WEATHER/TEMP.   8 A.M.   12 NOON   4 P.M.

EXPENSES

Cementation: The process of adhering materials together by using an additive, such as asphalt or Portland cement.

3 AUGUST
SATURDAY

	WORK	CAL
MONTH TO DATE	2	3
MONTH REMAINING	20	26
YEAR TO DATE	150	215
YEAR REMAINING	104	148

AUGUST 4
SUNDAY

	WORK	CAL
MONTH TO DATE	2	4
MONTH REMAINING	20	27
YEAR TO DATE	150	216
YEAR REMAINING	104	147

JOB NO. APPOINTMENTS/EVENTS/CALLS

JOB NO. APPOINTMENTS/EVENTS/CALLS

DAILY DIARY

DAILY DIARY

WEEK Beginning   5 AUGUST
Ending   11 AUGUST

WEEKLY EVENT CHECKLIST

Job meetings and preparation ____
Special meetings ____
Dinners and seminars ____
Assemble schedule information ____
Complete schedule updates ____
Requests out for all required information ____
Outstanding sub/supplier responses ____
Outstanding owner responses ____
Outstanding architect/engineer responses ____
Critical material deliveries confirmed ____
Shop drawings for ongoing work in/appr ____

Submittals for pending work in/appr ____
All other submittals in/approved ____
Shop drawing log up to date ____
All sub change proposals in ____
All change proposals to owner prep'd ____
Submitted change proposals appr ____
Change order logs up to date ____
Required bonds received for all subs ____
Certificates of insurance rec'd for all subs (proper amounts) ____
Equipment/scaffolding release forms in ____

All permits in place ____
Req testing/inspections arranged ____
Inspection certificates received ____
Safety inspections performed ____
Safety recommendations acted on ____
Field reports complete ____
Special photos taken ____
_____ ____
_____ ____
_____ ____

TO DO

Item	Job No.	Item	Job No.

WEEKLY MILESTONE UPDATE

	Planned Date	Actual Date	Variance

DAILY MINDER

√ Job meeting minutes and reports complete?

√ All requests for change proposals out?

√ July payments received?

√ Current schedule commitments in-process?

KEY EVENTS

Meetings

Schedule Updates

Cost Report Updates

Change Proposals

Material Deliveries

Special Information/Instructions

Arch./Owner Direction Received

DAILY DIARY

WEATHER/TEMP.   8A.M.   12NOON   4P.M.

EXPENSES

	WORK	CAL
MONTH TO DATE	3	5
MONTH REMAINING	19	27
YEAR TO DATE	151	217
YEAR REMAINING	103	146

AUGUST

5

MONDAY

JOB NO.   APPOINTMENTS/EVENTS/CALLS

7A.M.

8A.M.

9A.M.

10A.M.

11A.M.

12NOON

1P.M.

2P.M.

3P.M.

4P.M.

5P.M.

6P.M.

	JULY					
S	M	T	W	T	F	S
	1	2	3	4	5	6
7	8	9	10	11	12	13
14	15	16	17	18	19	20
21	22	23	24	25	26	27
28	29	30	31			

	AUGUST					
S	M	T	W	T	F	S
				1	2	3
4	5	6	7	8	9	10
11	12	13	14	15	16	17
18	19	20	21	22	23	24
25	26	27	28	29	30	31

	SEPTEMBER					
S	M	T	W	T	F	S
1	2	3	4	5	6	7
8	9	10	11	12	13	14
15	16	17	18	19	20	21
22	23	24	25	26	27	28
29	30					

6

AUGUST

TUESDAY

DAILY MINDER

√ Verify receipt of last month's payment.

√ All change proposals submitted?

√ Requested design info. received?

JOB NO. APPOINTMENTS/EVENTS/CALLS

7 A.M.

8 A.M.

9 A.M.

10 A.M.

11 A.M.

12 NOON

1 P.M.

2 P.M.

3 P.M.

4 P.M.

5 P.M.

6 P.M.

KEY EVENTS

Meetings

Schedule Updates

Cost Report Updates

Change Proposals

Material Deliveries

Special Information/Instructions

Arch./Owner Direction Received

DAILY DIARY

WEATHER/TEMP.   8 A.M.   12 NOON   4 P.M.

EXPENSES

Hover Effect: Frictional forces in prestressed concrete that cause tendons to regain the diameter they had before stressing.

DAILY MINDER

√ Key material deliveries confirmed?

√ Field reports up-to-date?

√ Meeting minutes received/prepared?

WORK CAL

MONTH TO DATE	5	7
MONTH REMAINING	17	24
YEAR TO DATE	153	219
YEAR REMAINING	101	144

AUGUST

WEDNESDAY

7

KEY EVENTS

Meetings

Schedule Updates

Cost Report Updates

Change Proposals

Material Deliveries

Special Information/Instructions

Arch./Owner Direction Received

DAILY DIARY

WEATHER/TEMP.   8A.M.   12NOON   4P.M.

EXPENSES

JOB NO.   APPOINTMENTS/EVENTS/CALLS

7 A.M.

8 A.M.

9 A.M.

10 A.M.

11 A.M.

12 NOON

1 P.M.

2 P.M.

3 P.M.

4 P.M.

5 P.M.

6 P.M.

8 AUGUST

THURSDAY

WORK	CAL	
MONTH TO DATE	6	8
MONTH REMAINING	16	23
YEAR TO DATE	154	220
YEAR REMAINING	100	143

DAILY MINDER

√ Jobsite safety reviews completed?

√ All required design information received?

√ Current changes prepared/submitted?

JOB NO. APPOINTMENTS/EVENTS/CALLS

7 A.M.

8 A.M.

9 A.M.

10 A.M.

11 A.M.

12 NOON

1 P.M.

2 P.M.

3 P.M.

4 P.M.

5 P.M.

6 P.M.

KEY EVENTS

Meetings

Schedule Updates

Cost Report Updates

Change Proposals

Material Deliveries

Special Information/Instructions

Arch./Owner Direction Received

DAILY DIARY

WEATHER/TEMP.   8 A.M.   12 NOON   4 P.M.

EXPENSES

Oriel: A window projecting from the outer face of a wall, particularly in upper stories, supported by brackets.

DAILY MINDER

√ Job meeting minutes and reports complete?

√ Key material deliveries confirmed?

√ July payments received?

9

KEY EVENTS

Meetings

Schedule Updates

Cost Report Updates

Change Proposals

Material Deliveries

Special Information/Instructions

Arch./Owner Direction Received

DAILY DIARY

WEATHER/TEMP.   8A.M.   12NOON   4P.M.

EXPENSES

JOB NO.   APPOINTMENTS/EVENTS/CALLS

7A.M.

8A.M.

9A.M.

10A.M.

11A.M.

12NOON

1P.M.

2P.M.

3P.M.

4P.M.

5P.M.

6P.M.

	JULY								AUGUST							SEPTEMBER					
S	M	T	W	T	F	S	S	M	T	W	T	F	S	S	M	T	W	T	F	S
	1	2	3	4	5	6					1	2	3	1	2	3	4	5	6	7
7	8	9	10	11	12	13	4	5	6	7	8	9	10	8	9	10	11	12	13	14
14	15	16	17	18	19	20	11	12	13	14	15	16	17	15	16	17	18	19	20	21
21	22	23	24	25	26	27	18	19	20	21	22	23	24	22	23	24	25	26	27	28
28	29	30	31				25	26	27	28	29	30	31	29	30					

10 AUGUST
SATURDAY

JOB NO. APPOINTMENTS/EVENTS/CALLS

DAILY DIARY

11 AUGUST
SUNDAY

JOB NO. APPOINTMENTS/EVENTS/CALLS

DAILY DIARY

WEEK Beginning 12 AUGUST
Ending 18 AUGUST

WEEKLY EVENT CHECKLIST

- Job meetings and preparation
- Special meetings
- Dinners and seminars
- Assemble schedule information
- Complete schedule updates
- Requests out for all required information
- Outstanding sub/supplier responses
- Outstanding owner responses
- Outstanding architect/engineer responses
- Critical material deliveries confirmed
- Shop drawings for ongoing work in/appr

- Submittals for pending work in/appr
- All other submittals in/approved
- Shop drawing log up to date
- All sub change proposals in
- All change proposals to owner prep'd
- Submitted change proposals appr
- Change order logs up to date
- Required bonds received for all subs
- Certificates of insurance rec'd for all subs (proper amounts)
- Equipment/scaffolding release forms in

- All permits in place
- Req testing/inspections arranged
- Inspection certificates received
- Safety inspections performed
- Safety recommendations acted on
- Field reports complete
- Special photos taken
- _____
- _____
- _____
- _____

TO DO

Item	Job No.	Item	Job No.

WEEKLY MILESTONE UPDATE

	Planned Date	Actual Date	Variance

12 AUGUST MONDAY

WORK CAL		
MONTH TO DATE	8	12
MONTH REMAINING	14	19
YEAR TO DATE	156	224
YEAR REMAINING	98	139

DAILY MINDER

√ Job meeting minutes and reports complete?
√ Submitted change order approved?
√ Current schedule commitments in-process?

JOB NO. APPOINTMENTS/EVENTS/CALLS

7 A.M.

8 A.M.

9 A.M.

10 A.M.

11 A.M.

12 NOON

1 P.M.

2 P.M.

3 P.M.

4 P.M.

5 P.M.

6 P.M.

KEY EVENTS

Meetings

Schedule Updates

Cost Report Updates

Change Proposals

Material Deliveries

Special Information/Instructions

Arch./Owner Direction Received

DAILY DIARY

WEATHER/TEMP.   8 A.M.   12 NOON   4 P.M.

EXPENSES

Quarter Round: A moulding design which presents a profile of a quarter circle.

DAILY MINDER

√ Key material deliveries confirmed?

√ All requests for change proposals out?

√ Sub change proposals received?

	WORK	CAL
MONTH TO DATE	9	13
MONTH REMAINING	13	18
YEAR TO DATE	157	225
YEAR REMAINING	97	138

AUGUST

13

TUESDAY

KEY EVENTS

Meetings

Schedule Updates

Cost Report Updates

Change Proposals

Material Deliveries

Special Information/Instructions

Arch./Owner Direction Received

DAILY DIARY

WEATHER/TEMP.   8A.M.   12NOON   4P.M.

EXPENSES

JOB NO.   APPOINTMENTS/EVENTS/CALLS

7A.M.

8A.M.

9A.M.

10A.M.

11A.M.

12NOON

1P.M.

2P.M.

3P.M.

4P.M.

5P.M.

6P.M.

JULY						
S	M	T	W	T	F	S
	1	2	3	4	5	6
7	8	9	10	11	12	13
14	15	16	17	18	19	20
21	22	23	24	25	26	27
28	29	30	31			

AUGUST						
S	M	T	W	T	F	S
				1	2	3
4	5	6	7	8	9	10
11	12	13	14	15	16	17
18	19	20	21	22	23	24
25	26	27	28	29	30	31

SEPTEMBER						
S	M	T	W	T	F	S
1	2	3	4	5	6	7
8	9	10	11	12	13	14
15	16	17	18	19	20	21
22	23	24	25	26	27	28
29	30					

14 AUGUST
WEDNESDAY

WORK	CAL		
MONTH TO DATE		10	14
MONTH REMAINING		12	17
YEAR TO DATE		158	226
YEAR REMAINING		96	137

JOB NO.   APPOINTMENTS/EVENTS/CALLS

7 A.M.

8 A.M.

9 A.M.

10 A.M.

11 A.M.

12 NOON

1 P.M.

2 P.M.

3 P.M.

4 P.M.

5 P.M.

6 P.M.

DAILY MINDER
√ Assemble all schedule update information.
√ Required submittals in/approved?
√ Sub change proposals received?

KEY EVENTS
Meetings

Schedule Updates

Cost Report Updates

Change Proposals

Material Deliveries

Special Information/Instructions

Arch./Owner Direction Received

DAILY DIARY

WEATHER/TEMP.   8 A.M.   12 NOON   4 P.M.

EXPENSES

Stopped Miter: A butt joint or miter used to join pieces of differing thicknesses.

DAILY MINDER

√ Key material deliveries confirmed?

√ All change proposals submitted?

√ Field reports current?

WORK	CAL	
MONTH TO DATE	11	15
MONTH REMAINING	11	16
YEAR TO DATE	159	227
YEAR REMAINING	95	136

AUGUST

THURSDAY

15

KEY EVENTS

Meetings

Schedule Updates

Cost Report Updates

Change Proposals

Material Deliveries

Special Information/Instructions

Arch./Owner Direction Received

DAILY DIARY

WEATHER/TEMP.   8A.M.   12NOON   4P.M.

EXPENSES

JOB NO. APPOINTMENTS/EVENTS/CALLS

7 A.M.

8 A.M.

9 A.M.

10 A.M.

11 A.M.

12 NOON

1 P.M.

2 P.M.

3 P.M.

4 P.M.

5 P.M.

6 P.M.

	JULY							AUGUST							SEPTEMBER					
S	M	T	W	T	F	S	S	M	T	W	T	F	S	S	M	T	W	T	F	S
	1	2	3	4	5	6					1	2	3	1	2	3	4	5	6	7
7	8	9	10	11	12	13	4	5	6	7	8	9	10	8	9	10	11	12	13	14
14	15	16	17	18	19	20	11	12	13	14	15	16	17	15	16	17	18	19	20	21
21	22	23	24	25	26	27	18	19	20	21	22	23	24	22	23	24	25	26	27	28
28	29	30	31				25	26	27	28	29	30	31	29	30					

16 AUGUST

FRIDAY

DAILY MINDER

√ Assemble all schedule update information.

√ Job meeting minutes and reports complete?

√ All required design info. received?

√ Next week's schedules confirmed?

JOB NO. APPOINTMENTS/EVENTS/CALLS

7 A.M.

8 A.M.

9 A.M.

10 A.M.

11 A.M.

12 NOON

1 P.M.

2 P.M.

3 P.M.

4 P.M.

5 P.M.

6 P.M.

KEY EVENTS

Meetings

Schedule Updates

Cost Report Updates

Change Proposals

Material Deliveries

Special Information/Instructions

Arch./Owner Direction Received

DAILY DIARY

WEATHER/TEMP.   8 A.M.   12 NOON   4 P.M.

EXPENSES

Waffle Slap: A concrete joist floor with reinforced ribs running in both directions, with waffle-like appearance at its underside.

17

AUGUST

SATURDAY

	WORK	CAL
MONTH TO DATE	12	17
MONTH REMAINING	10	14
YEAR TO DATE	160	229
YEAR REMAINING	94	134

	WORK	CAL
MONTH TO DATE	12	18
MONTH REMAINING	10	13
YEAR TO DATE	160	230
YEAR REMAINING	94	133

AUGUST

SUNDAY

18

JOB NO. APPOINTMENTS/EVENTS/CALLS

JOB NO. APPOINTMENTS/EVENTS/CALLS

DAILY DIARY

DAILY DIARY

WEEK Beginning 19 AUGUST
Ending 25 AUGUST

WEEKLY EVENT CHECKLIST

Job meetings and preparation	Submittals for pending work in/appr	All permits in place
Special meetings	All other submittals in/approved	Req testing/inspections arranged
Dinners and seminars	Shop drawing log up to date	Inspection certificates received
Assemble schedule information	All sub change proposals in	Safety inspections performed
Complete schedule updates	All change proposals to owner prep'd	Safety recommendations acted on
Requests out for all required information	Submitted change proposals appr	Field reports complete
Outstanding sub/supplier responses	Change order logs up to date	Special photos taken
Outstanding owner responses	Required bonds received for all subs	_____
Outstanding architect/engineer responses	Certificates of insurance rec'd for all	_____
Critical material deliveries confirmed	subs (proper amounts)	_____
Shop drawings for ongoing work in/appr	Equipment/scaffolding release forms in	_____

TO DO

Item	Job No.	Item	Job No.

WEEKLY MILESTONE UPDATE

	Planned Date	Actual Date	Variance

DAILY MINDER

√ Verify receipt of all sub and supplier payment requisitions.
√ Job meeting minutes and reports complete?
√ Current schedule commitments in-process?

WORK CAL

AUGUST

MONTH TO DATE	13	19
MONTH REMAINING	9	12
YEAR TO DATE	161	231
YEAR REMAINING	93	132

MONDAY

19

KEY EVENTS

Meetings

Schedule Updates

Cost Report Updates

Change Proposals

Material Deliveries

Special Information/Instructions

Arch./Owner Direction Received

DAILY DIARY

WEATHER/TEMP.   8A.M.   12NOON   4P.M.

EXPENSES

JOB NO. APPOINTMENTS/EVENTS/CALLS

7 A.M.

8 A.M.

9 A.M.

10 A.M.

11 A.M.

12 NOON

1 P.M.

2 P.M.

3 P.M.

4 P.M.

5 P.M.

6 P.M.

JULY							AUGUST							SEPTEMBER						
S	M	T	W	T	F	S	S	M	T	W	T	F	S	S	M	T	W	T	F	S
	1	2	3	4	5	6					1	2	3	1	2	3	4	5	6	7
7	8	9	10	11	12	13	4	5	6	7	8	9	10	8	9	10	11	12	13	14
14	15	16	17	18	19	20	11	12	13	14	15	16	17	15	16	17	18	19	20	21
21	22	23	24	25	26	27	18	19	20	21	22	23	24	22	23	24	25	26	27	28
28	29	30	31				25	26	27	28	29	30	31	29	30					

20 AUGUST TUESDAY

DAILY MINDER

√ Verify approval of outstanding change orders.
√ Verify receipt of all sub and supplier payment requisitions.
√ Submit requisition(s) to owner(s).
√ Schedule update complete

JOB NO. APPOINTMENTS/EVENTS/CALLS

7 A.M.

8 A.M.

9 A.M.

10 A.M.

11 A.M.

12 NOON

1 P.M.

2 P.M.

3 P.M.

4 P.M.

5 P.M.

6 P.M.

KEY EVENTS

Meetings

Schedule Updates

Cost Report Updates

Change Proposals

Material Deliveries

Special Information/Instructions

Arch./Owner Direction Received

DAILY DIARY

WEATHER/TEMP.   8 A.M.   12 NOON   4 P.M.

EXPENSES

Vertex: The highest point of an arch, and the point at which the keystone is placed.

DAILY MINDER

√ Authorize sub and supplier payments.
√ Assemble all schedule update information.
√ All monthly reports and narratives complete?
√ Key material deliveries confirmed?

KEY EVENTS

Meetings

Schedule Updates

Cost Report Updates

Change Proposals

Material Deliveries

Special Information/Instructions

Arch./Owner Direction Received

DAILY DIARY

WEATHER/TEMP.   8A.M.   12NOON   4P.M.

EXPENSES

	WORK	CAL
MONTH TO DATE	15	21
MONTH REMAINING	7	10
YEAR TO DATE	163	233
YEAR REMAINING	91	130

AUGUST
21
WEDNESDAY

JOB NO.   APPOINTMENTS/EVENTS/CALLS

7A.M.

8A.M.

9A.M.

10A.M.

11A.M.

12NOON

1P.M.

2P.M.

3P.M.

4P.M.

5P.M.

6P.M.

JULY							AUGUST							SEPTEMBER						
S	M	T	W	T	F	S	S	M	T	W	T	F	S	S	M	T	W	T	F	S
	1	2	3	4	5	6					1	2	3	1	2	3	4	5	6	7
7	8	9	10	11	12	13	4	5	6	7	8	9	10	8	9	10	11	12	13	14
14	15	16	17	18	19	20	11	12	13	14	15	16	17	15	16	17	18	19	20	21
21	22	23	24	25	26	27	18	19	20	21	22	23	24	22	23	24	25	26	27	28
28	29	30	31				25	26	27	28	29	30	31	29	30					

22 AUGUST
THURSDAY

WORK	CAL
MONTH TO DATE	16	22
MONTH REMAINING	6	9
YEAR TO DATE	164	234
YEAR REMAINING	90	129

DAILY MINDER

√ Verify approval of outstanding change orders.
√ Authorize/approve sub and supplier payments.
√ Schedule update complete?
√ All cost report information assembled?

JOB NO. APPOINTMENTS/EVENTS/CALLS

7 A.M.

8 A.M.

9 A.M.

10 A.M.

11 A.M.

12 NOON

1 P.M.

2 P.M.

3 P.M.

4 P.M.

5 P.M.

6 P.M.

KEY EVENTS

Meetings

Schedule Updates

Cost Report Updates

Change Proposals

Material Deliveries

Special Information/Instructions

Arch./Owner Direction Received

DAILY DIARY

WEATHER/TEMP.   8 A.M.   12 NOON   4 P.M.

EXPENSES

Plum: A large, undressed stone, which together with similar stones, is used in mass concrete to form footings, in order to reduce the amount of concrete.

DAILY MINDER

√ Assemble all schedule update information?

√ Job meeting minutes and reports complete?

√ All monthly reports and narratives complete?

√ All cost report information assembled?

KEY EVENTS

Meetings

Schedule Updates

Cost Report Updates

Change Proposals

Material Deliveries

Special Information/Instructions

Arch./Owner Direction Received

DAILY DIARY

WEATHER/TEMP. 8A.M.   12NOON   4P.M.

EXPENSES

WORK	CAL	**AUGUST**
MONTH TO DATE	17	23
MONTH REMAINING	5	8
YEAR TO DATE	165	235
YEAR REMAINING	89	128

AUGUST

23

FRIDAY

JOB NO. APPOINTMENTS/EVENTS/CALLS

7A.M.

8A.M.

9A.M.

10A.M.

11A.M.

12NOON

1P.M.

2P.M.

3P.M.

4P.M.

5P.M.

6P.M.

JULY							AUGUST							SEPTEMBER						
S	M	T	W	T	F	S	S	M	T	W	T	F	S	S	M	T	W	T	F	S
	1	2	3	4	5	6				1	2	3		1	2	3	4	5	6	7
7	8	9	10	11	12	13	4	5	6	7	8	9	10	8	9	10	11	12	13	14
14	15	16	17	18	19	20	11	12	13	14	15	16	17	15	16	17	18	19	20	21
21	22	23	24	25	26	27	18	19	20	21	22	23	24	22	23	24	25	26	27	28
28	29	30	31				25	26	27	28	29	30	31	29	30					

24 AUGUST SATURDAY

WORK CAL		
MONTH TO DATE	17	24
MONTH REMAINING	5	7
YEAR TO DATE	165	236
YEAR REMAINING	89	127

25 AUGUST SUNDAY

WORK CAL		
MONTH TO DATE	17	25
MONTH REMAINING	5	6
YEAR TO DATE	165	237
YEAR REMAINING	89	126

JOB NO. APPOINTMENTS/EVENTS/CALLS

JOB NO. APPOINTMENTS/EVENTS/CALLS

DAILY DIARY

DAILY DIARY

WEEK Beginning 26 AUGUST
Ending 1 SEPTEMBER

WEEKLY EVENT CHECKLIST

Job meetings and preparation	Submittals for pending work in/appr	All permits in place
Special meetings	All other submittals in/approved	Req testing/inspections arranged
Dinners and seminars	Shop drawing log up to date	Inspection certificates received
Assemble schedule information	All sub change proposals in	Safety inspections performed
Complete schedule updates	All change proposals to owner prep'd	Safety recommendations acted on
Requests out for all required information	Submitted change proposals appr	Field reports complete
Outstanding sub/supplier responses	Change order logs up to date	Special photos taken
Outstanding owner responses	Required bonds received for all subs	_____
Outstanding architect/engineer responses	Certificates of insurance rec'd for all	_____
Critical material deliveries confirmed	subs (proper amounts)	_____
Shop drawings for ongoing work in/appr	Equipment/scaffolding release forms in	

TO DO

Item	Job No.	Item	Job No.

WEEKLY MILESTONE UPDATE

	Planned Date	Actual Date	Variance

26 AUGUST
MONDAY

DAILY MINDER

√ Submit requisition(s) to owner(s).
√ Schedule update complete?
√ Key material deliveries confirmed?
√ Cost report complete?

JOB NO. APPOINTMENTS/EVENTS/CALLS

7 A.M.

8 A.M.

9 A.M.

10 A.M.

11 A.M.

12 NOON

1 P.M.

2 P.M.

3 P.M.

4 P.M.

5 P.M.

6 P.M.

KEY EVENTS

Meetings

Schedule Updates

Cost Report Updates

Change Proposals

Material Deliveries

Special Information/Instructions

Arch./Owner Direction Received

DAILY DIARY

WEATHER/TEMP.   8 A.M.   12 NOON   4 P.M.

EXPENSES

Rake Moulding: A gable moulding with a larger face than that of the eave moulding.

DAILY MINDER

√ Verify approval of outstanding change orders.

√ Submit requisition(s) to owner(s).

√ Authorize/approve sub and supplier payments.

√ Cost report complete?

KEY EVENTS

Meetings

Schedule Updates

Cost Report Updates

Change Proposals

Material Deliveries

Special Information/Instructions

Arch./Owner Direction Received

DAILY DIARY

WEATHER/TEMP.   8A.M.   12NOON   4P.M.

EXPENSES

	WORK	CAL	**AUGUST**
MONTH TO DATE	19	27	
MONTH REMAINING	3	4	**27**
YEAR TO DATE	167	239	
YEAR REMAINING	87	124	**TUESDAY**

JOB NO.   APPOINTMENTS/EVENTS/CALLS

7 A.M.

8 A.M.

9 A.M.

10 A.M.

11 A.M.

12 NOON

1 P.M.

2 P.M.

3 P.M.

4 P.M.

5 P.M.

6 P.M.

	JULY								AUGUST								SEPTEMBER				
S	M	T	W	T	F	S	S	M	T	W	T	F	S	S	M	T	W	T	F	S
	1	2	3	4	5	6					1	2	3	1	2	3	4	5	6	7
7	8	9	10	11	12	13	4	5	6	7	8	9	10	8	9	10	11	12	13	14
14	15	16	17	18	19	20	11	12	13	14	15	16	17	15	16	17	18	19	20	21
21	22	23	24	25	26	27	18	19	20	21	22	23	24	22	23	24	25	26	27	28
28	29	30	31				25	26	27	28	29	30	31	29	30					

28 AUGUST
WEDNESDAY

DAILY MINDER

√ This month's schedule update complete?
√ This month's reports and narratives complete?
√ Key material deliveries confirmed?
√ Current schedule commitments in-process?

JOB NO. APPOINTMENTS/EVENTS/CALLS

7 A.M.
8 A.M.
9 A.M.
10 A.M.
11 A.M.
12 NOON
1 P.M.
2 P.M.
3 P.M.
4 P.M.
5 P.M.
6 P.M.

KEY EVENTS

Meetings

Schedule Updates

Cost Report Updates

Change Proposals

Material Deliveries

Special Information/Instructions

Arch./Owner Direction Received

DAILY DIARY

WEATHER/TEMP.   8 A.M.   12 NOON   4 P.M.

EXPENSES

Squint Window: A small dormer designed as a lookout.

DAILY MINDER

√ Verify approval of outstanding change orders.
√ Submit requisition(s) to owner(s).
√ Authorize/approve sub and supplier payments.
√ Cost report complete?

	WORK	CAL	**AUGUST**
MONTH TO DATE	21	29	
MONTH REMAINING	1	2	
YEAR TO DATE	169	241	
YEAR REMAINING	85	122	**THURSDAY**

29

KEY EVENTS

Meetings

Schedule Updates

Cost Report Updates

Change Proposals

Material Deliveries

Special Information/Instructions

Arch./Owner Direction Received

DAILY DIARY

_____

_____

_____

_____

_____

_____

_____

_____

_____

_____

_____

_____

_____

_____

_____

_____

WEATHER/TEMP.   8A.M.   12NOON   4P.M.

EXPENSES

JOB NO.   APPOINTMENTS/EVENTS/CALLS

7 A.M.

8 A.M.

9 A.M.

10 A.M.

11 A.M.

12 NOON

1 P.M.

2 P.M.

3 P.M.

4 P.M.

5 P.M.

6 P.M.

	JULY							AUGUST							SEPTEMBER					
S	M	T	W	T	F	S	S	M	T	W	T	F	S	S	M	T	W	T	F	S
	1	2	3	4	5	6					1	2	3	1	2	3	4	5	6	7
7	8	9	10	11	12	13	4	5	6	7	8	9	10	8	9	10	11	12	13	14
14	15	16	17	18	19	20	11	12	13	14	15	16	17	15	16	17	18	19	20	21
21	22	23	24	25	26	27	18	19	20	21	22	23	24	22	23	24	25	26	27	28
28	29	30	31				25	26	27	28	29	30	31	29	30					

30 AUGUST FRIDAY

DAILY MINDER

√ Schedule update complete?

√ Job meeting minutes and reports complete?

√ Key material deliveries confirmed?

√ Progress photos taken?

JOB NO. APPOINTMENTS/EVENTS/CALLS

7 A.M.

8 A.M.

9 A.M.

10 A.M.

11 A.M.

12 NOON

1 P.M.

2 P.M.

3 P.M.

4 P.M.

5 P.M.

6 P.M.

KEY EVENTS

Meetings

Schedule Updates

Cost Report Updates

Change Proposals

Material Deliveries

Special Information/Instructions

Arch./Owner Direction Received

DAILY DIARY

WEATHER/TEMP.   8 A.M.   12 NOON   4 P.M.

EXPENSES

Monial: Mullion, the vertical bar between window lights.

DAILY MINDER

	WORK	CAL
MONTH TO DATE	22	31
MONTH REMAINING	0	0
YEAR TO DATE	170	243
YEAR REMAINING	84	120

AUGUST

SATURDAY

31

KEY EVENTS

Meetings

Schedule Updates

Cost Report Updates

Change Proposals

Material Deliveries

Special Information/Instructions

Arch./Owner Direction Received

DAILY DIARY

WEATHER/TEMP.   8A.M.   12NOON   4P.M.

EXPENSES

JOB NO.   APPOINTMENTS/EVENTS/CALLS

7 A.M.

8 A.M.

9 A.M.

10 A.M.

11 A.M.

12 NOON

1 P.M.

2 P.M.

3 P.M.

4 P.M.

5 P.M.

6 P.M.

		JULY								AUGUST								SEPTEMBER				
S	M	T	W	T	F	S	S	M	T	W	T	F	S	S	M	T	W	T	F	S
	1	2	3	4	5	6					1	2	3	1	2	3	4	5	6	7
7	8	9	10	11	12	13	4	5	6	7	8	9	10	8	9	10	11	12	13	14
14	15	16	17	18	19	20	11	12	13	14	15	16	17	15	16	17	18	19	20	21
21	22	23	24	25	26	27	18	19	20	21	22	23	24	22	23	24	25	26	27	28
28	29	30	31				25	26	27	28	29	30	31	29	30					

SEPTEMBER

20 Working Days

30 Calendar Days

AUGUST

S	M	T	W	T	F	S
				1	2	3
4	5	6	7	8	9	10
11	12	13	14	15	16	17
18	19	20	21	22	23	24
25	26	27	28	29	30	31

SEPTEMBER

S	M	T	W	T	F	S
1	2	3	4	5	6	7
8	9	10	11	12	13	14
15	16	17	18	19	20	21
22	23	24	25	26	27	28
29	30					

OCTOBER

S	M	T	W	T	F	S
		1	2	3	4	5
6	7	8	9	10	11	12
13	14	15	16	17	18	19
20	21	22	23	24	25	26
27	28	29	30	31		

MONTHLY KEY ACTIVITY UPDATE

Job/C.O. No.	Description	Planned Date	Actual Date	Variance	Remarks

MONTHLY SCHEDULE UPDATE SUMMARY

Job/C.O. No.	Activities	Original Duration	Days Spent	Days Remaining	Status/Remarks

MONTHLY RECAP

S	M	T	W	T	F	S
1	2	3	4	5	6	7
8	9	10	11	12	13	14
15	16	17	18	19	20	21
22	23	24	25	26	27	28
29	30					

SEPTEMBER

MONTHLY EVENT CHECKLIST

Schedule updates complete

Requests out for all required info.

Outstanding sub/supplier responses rec'd

Outstanding owner responses rec'd

Outstanding arch./eng. responses rec'd

Critical material deliveries confirmed

Shop drawings for ongoing work in/appr

Submittals for pending work in/appr

All other submittals in/approved

All sub change proposals in

All change proposals to owner prepared

Submitted change proposals approved

Guarantees/warrantees rec'd

Inspection certificates rec'd

As-built drawings rec'd

Safety inspections performed

Safety reports complete

Narratives complete

Sub/supplier contract(s) rec'd

Requisition(s) submitted to owner(s)

Sub/supplier adjustments complete

Progress photos taken

Job cost report info. assembled

Job cost reports complete

Other:

_____

_____

CRITICAL ITEM COST REPORT SUMMARY

Job/CO No.	Description	(A) Budget $ Amount	(B) Cost To Date	(C) Cost Remaining	(D) Total Commitment (B + C)	(E) +/− (A − D)

CHANGE ORDER SUMMARY

Job No.	C.O. No.	Description	Submission Date Required	Submission Date Actual	Approval Date Required	Approval Date Actual	Remarks

1

SEPTEMBER
SUNDAY

WORK CAL		
MONTH TO DATE	0	1
MONTH REMAINING	20	30
YEAR TO DATE	170	244
YEAR REMAINING	84	121

JOB NO.   APPOINTMENTS/EVENTS/CALLS

7 A.M.

8 A.M.

9 A.M.

10 A.M.

11 A.M.

12 NOON

1 P.M.

2 P.M.

3 P.M.

4 P.M.

5 P.M.

6 P.M.

DAILY MINDER

KEY EVENTS

Meetings

Schedule Updates

Cost Report Updates

Change Proposals

Material Deliveries

Special Information/Instructions

Arch./Owner Direction Received

DAILY DIARY

WEATHER/TEMP.   8 A.M.   12 NOON   4 P.M.

EXPENSES

Cord: A pile of wood measuring 4' high, 4' wide, and 4' long.

WEEK Beginning 2 SEPTEMBER
Ending   8 SEPTEMBER

WEEKLY EVENT CHECKLIST

Job meetings and preparation	Submittals for pending work in/appr	All permits in place
Special meetings	All other submittals in/approved	Req testing/inspections arranged
Dinners and seminars	Shop drawing log up to date	Inspection certificates received
Assemble schedule information	All sub change proposals in	Safety inspections performed
Complete schedule updates	All change proposals to owner prep'd	Safety recommendations acted on
Requests out for all required information	Submitted change proposals appr	Field reports complete
Outstanding sub/supplier responses	Change order logs up to date	Special photos taken
Outstanding owner responses	Required bonds received for all subs	
Outstanding architect/engineer responses	Certificates of insurance rec'd for all	
Critical material deliveries confirmed	subs (proper amounts)	
Shop drawings for ongoing work in/appr	Equipment/scaffolding release forms in	

TO DO

Item	Job No.	Item	Job No.

WEEKLY MILESTONE UPDATE

	Planned Date	Actual Date	Variance

2
SEPTEMBER
Labor
Day
MONDAY

	WORK	CAL
MONTH TO DATE	0	2
MONTH REMAINING	20	29
YEAR TO DATE	170	245
YEAR REMAINING	84	120

JOB NO. APPOINTMENTS/EVENTS/CALLS

7 A.M.

8 A.M.

9 A.M.

10 A.M.

11 A.M.

12 NOON

1 P.M.

2 P.M.

3 P.M.

4 P.M.

5 P.M.

6 P.M.

DAILY MINDER

KEY EVENTS
Meetings

Schedule Updates

Cost Report Updates

Change Proposals

Material Deliveries

Special Information/Instructions

Arch./Owner Direction Received

DAILY DIARY

WEATHER/TEMP.   8 A.M.   12 NOON   4 P.M.

EXPENSES

Scaling: Local flaking or spoiling of the outer surface of concrete or mortar.

DAILY MINDER

√ Last month's reports and narratives complete?
√ All requests for change proposals out?
√ Current schedule commitments in-process?
√ Schedule updates complete?

KEY EVENTS

Meetings

Schedule Updates

Cost Report Updates

Change Proposals

Material Deliveries

Special Information/Instructions

Arch./Owner Direction Received

DAILY DIARY

WEATHER/TEMP.   8 A.M.   12 NOON   4 P.M.

EXPENSES

WORK	CAL
MONTH TO DATE	1	3
MONTH REMAINING	19	28
YEAR TO DATE	171	246
YEAR REMAINING	83	119

SEPTEMBER
3
TUESDAY

JOB NO. APPOINTMENTS/EVENTS/CALLS

7 A.M.

8 A.M.

9 A.M.

10 A.M.

11 A.M.

12 NOON

1 P.M.

2 P.M.

3 P.M.

4 P.M.

5 P.M.

6 P.M.

AUGUST						
S	M	T	W	T	F	S
					1	2	3
4	5	6	7	8	9	10
11	12	13	14	15	16	17
18	19	20	21	22	23	24
25	26	27	28	29	30	31

SEPTEMBER						
S	M	T	W	T	F	S
1	2	3	4	5	6	7
8	9	10	11	12	13	14
15	16	17	18	19	20	21
22	23	24	25	26	27	28
29	30					

OCTOBER						
S	M	T	W	T	F	S
		1	2	3	4	5
6	7	8	9	10	11	12
13	14	15	16	17	18	19
20	21	22	23	24	25	26
27	28	29	30	31		

4

SEPTEMBER
WEDNESDAY

	WORK	CAL
MONTH TO DATE	2	4
MONTH REMAINING	18	27
YEAR TO DATE	172	247
YEAR REMAINING	82	118

JOB NO.   APPOINTMENTS/EVENTS/CALLS

7 A.M.

8 A.M.

9 A.M.

10 A.M.

11 A.M.

12 NOON

1 P.M.

2 P.M.

3 P.M.

4 P.M.

5 P.M.

6 P.M.

DAILY MINDER

√Verify receipt of last month's payment.
√Meeting minutes received/prepared?
√Sub change proposals received?
√Reports and narratives complete?

KEY EVENTS

Meetings

Schedule Updates

Cost Report Updates

Change Proposals

Material Deliveries

Special Information/Instructions

Arch./Owner Direction Received

DAILY DIARY

WEATHER/TEMP.   8 A.M.   12 NOON   4 P.M.

EXPENSES

Neat Plaster: Plaster made with sand.

DAILY MINDER

√ Key material deliveries confirmed?
√ All required design info. received?
√ Submitted change orders approved?
√ Schedule updates complete?

KEY EVENTS

Meetings

Schedule Updates

Cost Report Updates

Change Proposals

Material Deliveries

Special Information/Instructions

Arch./Owner Direction Received

DAILY DIARY

WEATHER/TEMP.   8A.M.   12NOON   4P.M.

EXPENSES

		WORK CAL	
MONTH TO DATE		3	5
MONTH REMAINING	17	27	
YEAR TO DATE		173	248
YEAR REMAINING		81	117

SEPTEMBER

5

THURSDAY

JOB NO.   APPOINTMENTS/EVENTS/CALLS

7A.M.

8A.M.

9A.M.

10A.M.

11A.M.

12NOON

1P.M.

2P.M.

3P.M.

4P.M.

5P.M.

6P.M.

AUGUST						
S	M	T	W	T	F	S
					1	2	3
4	5	6	7	8	9	10
11	12	13	14	15	16	17
18	19	20	21	22	23	24
25	26	27	28	29	30	31

SEPTEMBER						
S	M	T	W	T	F	S
1	2	3	4	5	6	7
8	9	10	11	12	13	14
15	16	17	18	19	20	21
22	23	24	25	26	27	28
29	30					

OCTOBER						
S	M	T	W	T	F	S
		1	2	3	4	5
6	7	8	9	10	11	12
13	14	15	16	17	18	19
20	21	22	23	24	25	26
27	28	29	30	31		

6

SEPTEMBER

FRIDAY

WORK CAL		
MONTH TO DATE	4	6
MONTH REMAINING	16	25
YEAR TO DATE	174	249
YEAR REMAINING	80	116

JOB NO. APPOINTMENTS/EVENTS/CALLS

7 A.M.

8 A.M.

9 A.M.

10 A.M.

11 A.M.

12 NOON

1 P.M.

2 P.M.

3 P.M.

4 P.M.

5 P.M.

6 P.M.

KEY EVENTS

Meetings

Schedule Updates

Cost Report Updates

Change Proposals

Material Deliveries

Special Information/Instructions

Arch./Owner Direction Received

DAILY DIARY

WEATHER/TEMP.   8 A.M.   12 NOON   4 P.M.

EXPENSES

Scribing: Fitting woodwork to an irregular or uneven surface.

7

SEPTEMBER

SATURDAY

	WORK	CAL
MONTH TO DATE	4	7
MONTH REMAINING	16	24
YEAR TO DATE	174	250
YEAR REMAINING	80	115

	WORK	CAL
MONTH TO DATE	4	8
MONTH REMAINING	16	23
YEAR TO DATE	174	251
YEAR REMAINING	80	114

SEPTEMBER

SUNDAY

8

JOB NO. APPOINTMENTS/EVENTS/CALLS

JOB NO. APPOINTMENTS/EVENTS/CALLS

DAILY DIARY

DAILY DIARY

WEEK Beginning   9 SEPTEMBER
Ending   15 SEPTEMBER

WEEKLY EVENT CHECKLIST

Job meetings and preparation   Submittals for pending work in/appr   All permits in place

Special meetings   All other submittals in/approved   Req testing/inspections arranged

Dinners and seminars   Shop drawing log up to date   Inspection certificates received

Assemble schedule information   All sub change proposals in   Safety inspections performed

Complete schedule updates   All change proposals to owner prep'd   Safety recommendations acted on

Requests out for all required information   Submitted change proposals appr   Field reports complete

Outstanding sub/supplier responses   Change order logs up to date   Special photos taken

Outstanding owner responses   Required bonds received for all subs

Outstanding architect/engineer responses   Certificates of insurance rec'd for all

Critical material deliveries confirmed   subs (proper amounts)

Shop drawings for ongoing work in/appr   Equipment/scaffolding release forms in

TO DO

Item	Job No.	Item	Job No.

WEEKLY MILESTONE UPDATE

	Planned Date	Actual Date	Variance

DAILY MINDER

√ Job meeting minutes and reports complete?

√ All requests for change proposals out?

√ August payment(s) received?

WORK CAL

MONTH TO DATE	5	9
MONTH REMAINING	15	22
YEAR TO DATE	175	252
YEAR REMAINING	79	113

SEPTEMBER

Rosh
Hashanah

MONDAY

9

KEY EVENTS

Meetings

Schedule Updates

Cost Report Updates

Change Proposals

Material Deliveries

Special Information/Instructions

Arch./Owner Direction Received

DAILY DIARY

WEATHER/TEMP.   8A.M.   12NOON   4P.M.

EXPENSES

JOB NO.   APPOINTMENTS/EVENTS/CALLS

7A.M.

8A.M.

9A.M.

10A.M.

11A.M.

12NOON

1P.M.

2P.M.

3P.M.

4P.M.

5P.M.

6P.M.

	AUGUST							SEPTEMBER							OCTOBER					
S	M	T	W	T	F	S	S	M	T	W	T	F	S	S	M	T	W	T	F	S
				1	2	3	1	2	3	4	5	6	7			1	2	3	4	5
4	5	6	7	8	9	10	8	9	10	11	12	13	14	6	7	8	9	10	11	12
11	12	13	14	15	16	17	15	16	17	18	19	20	21	13	14	15	16	17	18	19
18	19	20	21	22	23	24	22	23	24	25	26	27	28	20	21	22	23	24	25	26
25	26	27	28	29	30	31	29	30						27	28	29	30	31		

10

SEPTEMBER
TUESDAY

	WORK	CAL
MONTH TO DATE	6	10
MONTH REMAINING	14	21
YEAR TO DATE	176	253
YEAR REMAINING	78	112

JOB NO. APPOINTMENTS/EVENTS/CALLS

7 A.M.

8 A.M.

9 A.M.

10 A.M.

11 A.M.

12 NOON

1 P.M.

2 P.M.

3 P.M.

4 P.M.

5 P.M.

6 P.M.

DAILY MINDER

، Verify receipt of last month's payment.

، Jobsite safety reviews performed?

، Current schedule commitments in-process?

، Sub change proposals in?

KEY EVENTS

Meetings

Schedule Updates

Cost Report Updates

Change Proposals

Material Deliveries

Special Information/Instructions

Arch./Owner Direction Received

DAILY DIARY

WEATHER/TEMP.   8 A.M.   12 NOON   4 P.M.

EXPENSES

Dog's Tooth: A string course of masonry in which the bricks are laid so that one corner projects.

DAILY MINDER

√ Key material deliveries confirmed?

√ All change proposals submitted?

√ Meeting minutes received/prepared?

WORK	CAL
MONTH TO DATE	7	11
MONTH REMAINING	13	20
YEAR TO DATE	177	254
YEAR REMAINING	77	111

SEPTEMBER

11

WEDNESDAY

KEY EVENTS

Meetings

Schedule Updates

Cost Report Updates

Change Proposals

Material Deliveries

Special Information/Instructions

Arch./Owner Direction Received

DAILY DIARY

WEATHER/TEMP.   8A.M.   12NOON   4P.M.

EXPENSES

JOB NO.   APPOINTMENTS/EVENTS/CALLS

7 A.M.

8 A.M.

9 A.M.

10 A.M.

11 A.M.

12 NOON

1 P.M.

2 P.M.

3 P.M.

4 P.M.

5 P.M.

6 P.M.

	AUGUST							SEPTEMBER							OCTOBER					
S	M	T	W	T	F	S	S	M	T	W	T	F	S	S	M	T	W	T	F	S
					1	2	3	1	2	3	4	5	6	7			1	2	3	4	5
4	5	6	7	8	9	10	8	9	10	11	12	13	14	6	7	8	9	10	11	12
11	12	13	14	15	16	17	15	16	17	18	19	20	21	13	14	15	16	17	18	19
18	19	20	21	22	23	24	22	23	24	25	26	27	28	20	21	22	23	24	25	26
25	26	27	28	29	30	31	29	30						27	28	29	30	31		

12 SEPTEMBER

THURSDAY

WORK CAL		
MONTH TO DATE	8	12
MONTH REMAINING	12	19
YEAR TO DATE	178	255
YEAR REMAINING	76	110

DAILY MINDER

√ Scheduled a complete physical examination this year?

√ Required submittals in/approved?

√ Field reports up-to-date?

√ Required design info. requested/received?

JOB NO. APPOINTMENTS/EVENTS/CALLS

7 A.M.

8 A.M.

9 A.M.

10 A.M.

11 A.M.

12 NOON

1 P.M.

2 P.M.

3 P.M.

4 P.M.

5 P.M.

6 P.M.

KEY EVENTS

Meetings

Schedule Updates

Cost Report Updates

Change Proposals

Material Deliveries

Special Information/Instructions

Arch./Owner Direction Received

DAILY DIARY

WEATHER/TEMP.	8 A.M.	12 NOON	4 P.M.

EXPENSES

Concave: A curved recess hollowed out like the inner surface of a circle or sphere.

DAILY MINDER

√Assemble all schedule update information.
√Job meeting minutes and reports complete?
√Key material deliveries confirmed?
√Next week's schedules confirmed?

KEY EVENTS

Meetings

Schedule Updates

Cost Report Updates

Change Proposals

Material Deliveries

Special Information/Instructions

Arch./Owner Direction Received

DAILY DIARY

WEATHER/TEMP.   8A.M.   12NOON   4P.M.

EXPENSES

	WORK	CAL
MONTH TO DATE	9	13
MONTH REMAINING	11	18
YEAR TO DATE	179	256
YEAR REMAINING	75	109

SEPTEMBER

13

FRIDAY

JOB NO.   APPOINTMENTS/EVENTS/CALLS

7 A.M.

8 A.M.

9 A.M.

10 A.M.

11 A.M.

12 NOON

1 P.M.

2 P.M.

3 P.M.

4 P.M.

5 P.M.

6 P.M.

AUGUST						
S	M	T	W	T	F	S
					1	2	3
4	5	6	7	8	9	10
11	12	13	14	15	16	17
18	19	20	21	22	23	24
25	26	27	28	29	30	31

SEPTEMBER						
S	M	T	W	T	F	S
1	2	3	4	5	6	7
8	9	10	11	12	13	14
15	16	17	18	19	20	21
22	23	24	25	26	27	28
29	30					

OCTOBER						
S	M	T	W	T	F	S
		1	2	3	4	5
6	7	8	9	10	11	12
13	14	15	16	17	18	19
20	21	22	23	24	25	26
27	28	29	30	31		

14 SEPTEMBER

SATURDAY

JOB NO. APPOINTMENTS/EVENTS/CALLS

DAILY DIARY

SEPTEMBER 15

SUNDAY

JOB NO. APPOINTMENTS/EVENTS/CALLS

DAILY DIARY

WEEK Beginning 16 SEPTEMBER
Ending 22 SEPTEMBER

WEEKLY EVENT CHECKLIST

Job meetings and preparation
Special meetings
Dinners and seminars
Assemble schedule information
Complete schedule updates
Requests out for all required information
Outstanding sub/supplier responses
Outstanding owner responses
Outstanding architect/engineer responses
Critical material deliveries confirmed
Shop drawings for ongoing work in/appr

Submittals for pending work in/appr
All other submittals in/approved
Shop drawing log up to date
All sub change proposals in
All change proposals to owner prep'd
Submitted change proposals appr
Change order logs up to date
Required bonds received for all subs
Certificates of insurance rec'd for all subs (proper amounts)
Equipment/scaffolding release forms in

All permits in place
Req testing/inspections arranged
Inspection certificates received
Safety inspections performed
Safety recommendations acted on
Field reports complete
Special photos taken

TO DO

Item	Job No.	Item	Job No.

WEEKLY MILESTONE UPDATE

	Planned Date	Actual Date	Variance

16 SEPTEMBER

MONDAY

WORK CAL		
MONTH TO DATE	10	16
MONTH REMAINING	10	15
YEAR TO DATE	180	259
YEAR REMAINING	74	106

DAILY MINDER

√ Job meeting minutes and reports complete?

√ All required design info. received?

√ Submitted change proposals approved?

JOB NO. APPOINTMENTS/EVENTS/CALLS

7 A.M.

8 A.M.

9 A.M.

10 A.M.

11 A.M.

12 NOON

1 P.M.

2 P.M.

3 P.M.

4 P.M.

5 P.M.

6 P.M.

KEY EVENTS

Meetings

Schedule Updates

Cost Report Updates

Change Proposals

Material Deliveries

Special Information/Instructions

Arch./Owner Direction Received

DAILY DIARY

WEATHER/TEMP.   8 A.M.   12 NOON   4 P.M.

EXPENSES

Rim Latch: A door lock designed to be screwed to the face of a door (opposed to mortise lock).

DAILY MINDER

√ Verify approval of outstanding change orders.
√ Key material deliveries confirmed?
√ All submittals in and approved?
√ Current schedule commitments in-process?

WORK CAL		
MONTH TO DATE	11	17
MONTH REMAINING	9	14
YEAR TO DATE	181	260
YEAR REMAINING	73	105

SEPTEMBER 17
TUESDAY

KEY EVENTS

Meetings

Schedule Updates

Cost Report Updates

Change Proposals

Material Deliveries

Special Information/Instructions

Arch./Owner Direction Received

DAILY DIARY

WEATHER/TEMP.   8A.M.   12NOON   4P.M.

EXPENSES

JOB NO. APPOINTMENTS/EVENTS/CALLS

7 A.M.

8 A.M.

9 A.M.

10 A.M.

11 A.M.

12 NOON

1 P.M.

2 P.M.

3 P.M.

4 P.M.

5 P.M.

6 P.M.

AUGUST						
S	M	T	W	T	F	S
					1	2	3
4	5	6	7	8	9	10
11	12	13	14	15	16	17
18	19	20	21	22	23	24
25	26	27	28	29	30	31

SEPTEMBER						
S	M	T	W	T	F	S
1	2	3	4	5	6	7
8	9	10	11	12	13	14
15	16	17	18	19	20	21
22	23	24	25	26	27	28
29	30					

OCTOBER						
S	M	T	W	T	F	S
		1	2	3	4	5
6	7	8	9	10	11	12
13	14	15	16	17	18	19
20	21	22	23	24	25	26
27	28	29	30	31		

18 SEPTEMBER
Yom Kippur
WEDNESDAY

WORK CAL
MONTH TO DATE	12	18
MONTH REMAINING	8	13
YEAR TO DATE	182	261
YEAR REMAINING	72	104

JOB NO. APPOINTMENTS/EVENTS/CALLS

7 A.M.

8 A.M.

9 A.M.

10 A.M.

11 A.M.

12 NOON

1 P.M.

2 P.M.

3 P.M.

4 P.M.

5 P.M.

6 P.M.

DAILY MINDER

√ Verify receipt of all sub and supplier payment requisitions.

√ Assemble all schedule update information..

√ Quarterly report info. assembled?

√ Cost report info. assembled?

KEY EVENTS

Meetings

Schedule Updates

Cost Report Updates

Change Proposals

Material Deliveries

Special Information/Instructions

Arch./Owner Direction Received

DAILY DIARY

WEATHER/TEMP.   8 A.M.   12 NOON   4 P.M.

EXPENSES

Extension Rule: Carpenter's rule used to take measurements between surfaces.

DAILY MINDER

√ Verify receipt of all sub and supplier payment requisitions?

√ Schedule update complete?

√ Key material deliveries confirmed?

√ Request/receive outstanding design info?

	WORK	CAL
MONTH TO DATE	13	19
MONTH REMAINING	7	12
YEAR TO DATE	183	262
YEAR REMAINING	71	103

SEPTEMBER

19

THURSDAY

KEY EVENTS

Meetings

Schedule Updates

Cost Report Updates

Change Proposals

Material Deliveries

Special Information/Instructions

Arch./Owner Direction Received

DAILY DIARY

WEATHER/TEMP.   8 A.M.   12 NOON   4 P.M.

EXPENSES

JOB NO.   APPOINTMENTS/EVENTS/CALLS

7 A.M.

8 A.M.

9 A.M.

10 A.M.

11 A.M.

12 NOON

1 P.M.

2 P.M.

3 P.M.

4 P.M.

5 P.M.

6 P.M.

	AUGUST					
S	M	T	W	T	F	S
					1	2	3
4	5	6	7	8	9	10
11	12	13	14	15	16	17
18	19	20	21	22	23	24
25	26	27	28	29	30	31

	SEPTEMBER					
S	M	T	W	T	F	S
1	2	3	4	5	6	7
8	9	10	11	12	13	14
15	16	17	18	19	20	21
22	23	24	25	26	27	28
29	30					

	OCTOBER					
S	M	T	W	T	F	S
		1	2	3	4	5
6	7	8	9	10	11	12
13	14	15	16	17	18	19
20	21	22	23	24	25	26
27	28	29	30	31		

20 SEPTEMBER
FRIDAY

WORK	CAL	
MONTH TO DATE	14	20
MONTH REMAINING	6	11
YEAR TO DATE	184	263
YEAR REMAINING	70	102

JOB NO. APPOINTMENTS/EVENTS/CALLS

7 A.M.

8 A.M.

9 A.M.

10 A.M.

11 A.M.

12 NOON

1 P.M.

2 P.M.

3 P.M.

4 P.M.

5 P.M.

6 P.M.

DAILY MINDER

√ Submit requisition(s) to owner(s).

√ Authorize/approve sub and supplier payments.

√ Assemble all schedule update information.

√ All monthly reports and narratives complete?

KEY EVENTS

Meetings

Schedule Updates

Cost Report Updates

Change Proposals

Material Deliveries

Special Information/Instructions

Arch./Owner Direction Received

DAILY DIARY

WEATHER/TEMP.   8 A.M.   12 NOON   4 P.M.

EXPENSES

Adze: Cutting tool resembling an ax, with a thin arched blade set at a right angle to the handle.

21

SEPTEMBER

SATURDAY

	WORK	CAL
MONTH TO DATE	14	21
MONTH REMAINING	6	10
YEAR TO DATE	184	264
YEAR REMAINING	70	101

JOB NO. APPOINTMENTS/EVENTS/CALLS

DAILY DIARY

22

SEPTEMBER

SUNDAY

	WORK	CAL
MONTH TO DATE	14	22
MONTH REMAINING	6	9
YEAR TO DATE	184	265
YEAR REMAINING	70	100

JOB NO. APPOINTMENTS/EVENTS/CALLS

DAILY DIARY

WEEK Beginning 23 SEPTEMBER
Ending 29 SEPTEMBER

WEEKLY EVENT CHECKLIST

Job meetings and preparation ☐	Submittals for pending work in/appr ☐	All permits in place ☐
Special meetings ☐	All other submittals in/approved ☐	Req testing/inspections arranged ☐
Dinners and seminars ☐	Shop drawing log up to date ☐	Inspection certificates received ☐
Assemble schedule information ☐	All sub change proposals in ☐	Safety inspections performed ☐
Complete schedule updates ☐	All change proposals to owner prep'd ☐	Safety recommendations acted on ☐
Requests out for all required information ☐	Submitted change proposals appr ☐	Field reports complete ☐
Outstanding sub/supplier responses ☐	Change order logs up to date ☐	Special photos taken ☐
Outstanding owner responses ☐	Required bonds received for all subs ☐	_____ ☐
Outstanding architect/engineer responses ☐	Certificates of insurance rec'd for all	_____ ☐
Critical material deliveries confirmed ☐	subs (proper amounts) ☐	_____ ☐
Shop drawings for ongoing work in/appr ☐	Equipment/scaffolding release forms in ☐	_____ ☐

TO DO

Item	Job No.	Item	Job No.

WEEKLY MILESTONE UPDATE

	Planned Date	Actual Date	Variance

DAILY MINDER

√ Verify approval of outstanding change orders.
√ Verify receipt of all sub and supplier payment requisitions.
√ Job meeting minutes and reports complete?
√ All cost report information assembled?

WORK CAL		
MONTH TO DATE	15	23
MONTH REMAINING	5	8
YEAR TO DATE	185	266
YEAR REMAINING	69	99

SEPTEMBER
23
MONDAY

KEY EVENTS

Meetings

Schedule Updates

Cost Report Updates

Change Proposals

Material Deliveries

Special Information/Instructions

Arch./Owner Direction Received

DAILY DIARY

WEATHER/TEMP.   8A.M.   12NOON   4P.M.

EXPENSES

JOB NO.   APPOINTMENTS/EVENTS/CALLS

7 A.M.

8 A.M.

9 A.M.

10 A.M.

11 A.M.

12 NOON

1 P.M.

2 P.M.

3 P.M.

4 P.M.

5 P.M.

6 P.M.

	AUGUST							SEPTEMBER							OCTOBER					
S	M	T	W	T	F	S	S	M	T	W	T	F	S	S	M	T	W	T	F	S
				1	2	3	1	2	3	4	5	6	7			1	2	3	4	5
4	5	6	7	8	9	10	8	9	10	11	12	13	14	6	7	8	9	10	11	12
11	12	13	14	15	16	17	15	16	17	18	19	20	21	13	14	15	16	17	18	19
18	19	20	21	22	23	24	22	23	24	25	26	27	28	20	21	22	23	24	25	26
25	26	27	28	29	30	31	29	30						27	28	29	30	31		

24

SEPTEMBER
TUESDAY

WORK	CAL
MONTH TO DATE	16	24
MONTH REMAINING	4	7
YEAR TO DATE	186	267
YEAR REMAINING	68	98

JOB NO.   APPOINTMENTS/EVENTS/CALLS

7 A.M.

8 A.M.

9 A.M.

10 A.M.

11 A.M.

12 NOON

1 P.M.

2 P.M.

3 P.M.

4 P.M.

5 P.M.

6 P.M.

DAILY MINDER

√ Verify approval of outstanding change orders.

√ Submit requisition(s) to owner(s).

√ Authorize/approve sub and supplier payments.

√ Quarterly report info. assembled?

KEY EVENTS

Meetings

Schedule Updates

Cost Report Updates

Change Proposals

Material Deliveries

Special Information/Instructions

Arch./Owner Direction Received

DAILY DIARY

WEATHER/TEMP.   8 A.M.   12 NOON   4 P.M.

EXPENSES

Closure: Part of a brick used to close the end of a course.

DAILY MINDER

√ Submit requisition(s) to owner(s).
√ Schedule update complete?
√ Key material deliveries confirmed?
√ Cost report complete?

WORK CAL		
MONTH TO DATE	17	25
MONTH REMAINING	3	6
YEAR TO DATE	187	268
YEAR REMAINING	67	97

SEPTEMBER
25
WEDNESDAY

KEY EVENTS

Meetings

Schedule Updates

Cost Report Updates

Change Proposals

Material Deliveries

Special Information/Instructions

Arch./Owner Direction Received

DAILY DIARY

JOB NO. APPOINTMENTS/EVENTS/CALLS

7 A.M.

8 A.M.

9 A.M.

10 A.M.

11 A.M.

12 NOON

1 P.M.

2 P.M.

3 P.M.

4 P.M.

5 P.M.

6 P.M.

WEATHER/TEMP.   8A.M.   12NOON   4P.M.

EXPENSES

26

SEPTEMBER
THURSDAY

WORK	CAL
MONTH TO DATE	18	26
MONTH REMAINING	2	5
YEAR TO DATE	188	269
YEAR REMAINING	66	96

JOB NO. APPOINTMENTS/EVENTS/CALLS

7 A.M.

8 A.M.

9 A.M.

10 A.M.

11 A.M.

12 NOON

1 P.M.

2 P.M.

3 P.M.

4 P.M.

5 P.M.

6 P.M.

DAILY MINDER

√ Verify approval of outstanding change orders.

√ Submit requisition(s) to owner(s).

√ Authorize/aprove sub and supplier payments.

√ Cost report complete?

KEY EVENTS

Meetings

Schedule Updates

Cost Report Updates

Change Proposals

Material Deliveries

Special Information/Instructions

Arch./Owner Direction Received

DAILY DIARY

WEATHER/TEMP.   8 A.M.   12 NOON   4 P.M.

EXPENSES

Pailing: Form sheathing that is run vertically.

DAILY MINDER

√ This month's schedule update complete?
√ Job meeting minutes and reports complete?
√ This month's reports and narratives complete?
√ Quarterly report(s) prepared?

	WORK	CAL
MONTH TO DATE	19	27
MONTH REMAINING	1	4
YEAR TO DATE	189	270
YEAR REMAINING	65	95

SEPTEMBER

27

FRIDAY

KEY EVENTS

Meetings

Schedule Updates

Cost Report Updates

Change Proposals

Material Deliveries

Special Information/Instructions

Arch./Owner Direction Received

DAILY DIARY

WEATHER/TEMP.   8A.M.   12NOON   4P.M.

EXPENSES

JOB NO.   APPOINTMENTS/EVENTS/CALLS

7 A.M.

8 A.M.

9 A.M.

10 A.M.

11 A.M.

12 NOON

1 P.M.

2 P.M.

3 P.M.

4 P.M.

5 P.M.

6 P.M.

		AUGUST							SEPTEMBER							OCTOBER				
S	M	T	W	T	F	S	S	M	T	W	T	F	S	S	M	T	W	T	F	S
				1	2	3	1	2	3	4	5	6	7			1	2	3	4	5
4	5	6	7	8	9	10	8	9	10	11	12	13	14	6	7	8	9	10	11	12
11	12	13	14	15	16	17	15	16	17	18	19	20	21	13	14	15	16	17	18	19
18	19	20	21	22	23	24	22	23	24	25	26	27	28	20	21	22	23	24	25	26
25	26	27	28	29	30	31	29	30						27	28	29	30	31		

28
SEPTEMBER
SATURDAY

WORK	CAL	
MONTH TO DATE	19	28
MONTH REMAINING	1	3
YEAR TO DATE	189	271
YEAR REMAINING	65	94

WORK	CAL	
MONTH TO DATE	19	29
MONTH REMAINING	1	2
YEAR TO DATE	189	272
YEAR REMAINING	65	93

SEPTEMBER
SUNDAY
29

JOB NO. APPOINTMENTS/EVENTS/CALLS

JOB NO. APPOINTMENTS/EVENTS/CALLS

DAILY DIARY

DAILY DIARY

WEEK Beginning 30 SEPTEMBER
Ending 6 OCTOBER

WEEKLY EVENT CHECKLIST

Job meetings and preparation	☐ Submittals for pending work in/appr	☐ All permits in place ☐
Special meetings	☐ All other submittals in/approved	☐ Req testing/inspections arranged ☐
Dinners and seminars	☐ Shop drawing log up to date	☐ Inspection certificates received ☐
Assemble schedule information	☐ All sub change proposals in	☐ Safety inspections performed ☐
Complete schedule updates	☐ All change proposals to owner prep'd	☐ Safety recommendations acted on ☐
Requests out for all required information	☐ Submitted change proposals appr	☐ Field reports complete ☐
Outstanding sub/supplier responses	☐ Change order logs up to date	☐ Special photos taken ☐
Outstanding owner responses	☐ Required bonds received for all subs ☐	☐ _____
Outstanding architect/engineer responses	☐ Certificates of insurance rec'd for all	_____
Critical material deliveries confirmed	☐ subs (proper amounts)	_____
Shop drawings for ongoing work in/appr	☐ Equipment/scaffolding release forms in ☐	_____

TO DO

Item	Job No.	Item	Job No.

WEEKLY MILESTONE UPDATE

	Planned Date	Actual Date	Variance

30 SEPTEMBER
MONDAY

	WORK	CAL
MONTH TO DATE	20	30
MONTH REMAINING	0	1
YEAR TO DATE	190	273
YEAR REMAINING	64	92

DAILY MINDER

√ Sept. requisition(s) submitted?

√ Last month's schedule update complete?

√ Key material deliveries confirmed?

√ Progress photos taken?

JOB NO. APPOINTMENTS/EVENTS/CALLS

7 A.M.

8 A.M.

9 A.M.

10 A.M.

11 A.M.

12 NOON

1 P.M.

2 P.M.

3 P.M.

4 P.M.

5 P.M.

6 P.M.

KEY EVENTS

Meetings

Schedule Updates

Cost Report Updates

Change Proposals

Material Deliveries

Special Information/Instructions

Arch./Owner Direction Received

DAILY DIARY

WEATHER/TEMP.   8 A.M.   12 NOON   4 P.M.

EXPENSES

Gilmore Needle: Device used to determine the time of setting of hydraulic cement.

OCTOBER

23 Working Days

31 Calendar Days

SEPTEMBER

S	M	T	W	T	F	S
	1	2	3	4	5	6	7
8	9	10	11	12	13	14
15	16	17	18	19	20	21
22	23	24	25	26	27	28
29	30

OCTOBER

S	M	T	W	T	F	S
		1	2	3	4	5
6	7	8	9	10	11	12
13	14	15	16	17	18	19
20	21	22	23	24	25	26
27	28	29	30	31

NOVEMBER

S	M	T	W	T	F	S
					1	2
3	4	5	6	7	8	9
10	11	12	13	14	15	16
17	18	19	20	21	22	23
24	25	26	27	28	29	30

MONTHLY KEY ACTIVITY UPDATE

Job/C.O. No.	Description	Planned Date	Actual Date	Variance	Remarks

MONTHLY SCHEDULE UPDATE SUMMARY

Job/C.O. No.	Activities	Original Duration	Days Spent	Days Remaining	Status/Remarks

MONTHLY RECAP

S	M	T	W	T	F	S
		1	2	3	4	5
6	7	8	9	10	11	12
13	14	15	16	17	18	19
20	21	22	23	24	25	26
27	28	29	30	31		

OCTOBER

MONTHLY EVENT CHECKLIST

Schedule updates complete

Requests out for all required info.

Outstanding sub/supplier responses rec'd ☐

Outstanding owner responses rec'd

Outstanding arch./eng. responses rec'd

Critical material deliveries confirmed

Shop drawings for ongoing work in/appr

Submittals for pending work in/appr

All other submittals in/approved

☐ All sub change proposals in

☐ All change proposals to owner prepared

☐ Submitted change proposals approved

☐ Guarantees/warrantees rec'd

☐ Inspection certificates rec'd

☐ As-built drawings rec'd

☐ Safety inspections performed

☐ Safety reports complete

☐ Narratives complete

☐ Sub/supplier contract(s) rec'd ☐

☐ Requisition(s) submitted to owner(s) ☐

☐ Sub/supplier adjustments complete ☐

☐ Progress photos taken

☐ Job cost report info. assembled

☐ Job cost reports complete

☐ Other:

☐ _____

☐ _____

CRITICAL ITEM COST REPORT SUMMARY

Job/CO No.	Description	(A) Budget $ Amount	(B) Cost To Date	(C) Cost Remaining	(D) Total Commitment (B + C)	(E) +/− (A − D)

CHANGE ORDER SUMMARY

Job No.	C.O. No.	Description	Submission Date Required	Submission Date Actual	Approval Date Required	Approval Date Actual	Remarks

DAILY MINDER

√ Progress photos taken?
√ All requests for change quotations out?
√ September payment requisition(s) submitted.
√ Current schedule commitments in-process?

KEY EVENTS

Meetings

Schedule Updates

Cost Report Updates

Change Proposals

Material Deliveries

Special Information/Instructions

Arch./Owner Direction Received

DAILY DIARY

WEATHER/TEMP.   8 A.M.   12 NOON   4 P.M.

EXPENSES

		WORK	CAL
MONTH TO DATE		1	1
MONTH REMAINING		22	30
YEAR TO DATE		191	274
YEAR REMAINING		63	89

OCTOBER

TUESDAY

1

JOB NO.   APPOINTMENTS/EVENTS/CALLS

7 A.M.

8 A.M.

9 A.M.

10 A.M.

11 A.M.

12 NOON

1 P.M.

2 P.M.

3 P.M.

4 P.M.

5 P.M.

6 P.M.

SEPTEMBER						
S	M	T	W	T	F	S
1	2	3	4	5	6	7
8	9	10	11	12	13	14
15	16	17	18	19	20	21
22	23	24	25	26	27	28
29	30					

OCTOBER						
S	M	T	W	T	F	S
		1	2	3	4	5
6	7	8	9	10	11	12
13	14	15	16	17	18	19
20	21	22	23	24	25	26
27	28	29	30	31		

NOVEMBER						
S	M	T	W	T	F	S
					1	2
3	4	5	6	7	8	9
10	11	12	13	14	15	16
17	18	19	20	21	22	23
24	25	26	27	28	29	30

2 OCTOBER
WEDNESDAY

DAILY MINDER

√ Key material deliveries confirmed?
√ Field reports up-to-date?
√ Meeting minutes received/prepared?
√ Sept. cost report(s) prepared?

JOB NO. APPOINTMENTS/EVENTS/CALLS

7 A.M.

8 A.M.

9 A.M.

10 A.M.

11 A.M.

12 NOON

1 P.M.

2 P.M.

3 P.M.

4 P.M.

5 P.M.

6 P.M.

KEY EVENTS

Meetings

Schedule Updates

Cost Report Updates

Change Proposals

Material Deliveries

Special Information/Instructions

Arch./Owner Direction Received

DAILY DIARY

WEATHER/TEMP. 8A.M.   12NOON   4P.M.

EXPENSES

Couple-Close: Pair of rafters which are framed together with a tie fixed at the foot, or with a dollar beam.

DAILY MINDER

√Job meeting minutes and reports complete?
√All change proposals submitted?
√Requests for change proposals out?
√September requisitions submitted?

	WORK	CAL
MONTH TO DATE	3	3
MONTH REMAINING	20	28
YEAR TO DATE	193	276
YEAR REMAINING	61	87

OCTOBER

THURSDAY

3

KEY EVENTS

Meetings

Schedule Updates

Cost Report Updates

Change Proposals

Material Deliveries

Special Information/Instructions

Arch./Owner Direction Received

DAILY DIARY

WEATHER/TEMP.   8A.M.   12NOON   4P.M.

EXPENSES

JOB NO.   APPOINTMENTS/EVENTS/CALLS

7A.M.

8A.M.

9A.M.

10A.M.

11A.M.

12NOON

1P.M.

2P.M.

3P.M.

4P.M.

5P.M.

6P.M.

SEPTEMBER						
S	M	T	W	T	F	S
1	2	3	4	5	6	7
8	9	10	11	12	13	14
15	16	17	18	19	20	21
22	23	24	25	26	27	28
29	30					

OCTOBER						
S	M	T	W	T	F	S
		1	2	3	4	5
6	7	8	9	10	11	12
13	14	15	16	17	18	19
20	21	22	23	24	25	26
27	28	29	30	31		

NOVEMBER						
S	M	T	W	T	F	S
					1	2
3	4	5	6	7	8	9
10	11	12	13	14	15	16
17	18	19	20	21	22	23
24	25	26	27	28	29	30

4 OCTOBER FRIDAY

WORK CAL		
MONTH TO DATE	4	4
MONTH REMAINING	19	27
YEAR TO DATE	194	277
YEAR REMAINING	60	86

DAILY MINDER

√ Job meeting minutes and reports complete?
√ Change proposals in/approved?
√ Next week's schedules confirmed?
√ Payments received?

JOB NO. APPOINTMENTS/EVENTS/CALLS

7 A.M.

8 A.M.

9 A.M.

10 A.M.

11 A.M.

12 NOON

1 P.M.

2 P.M.

3 P.M.

4 P.M.

5 P.M.

6 P.M.

KEY EVENTS

Meetings

Schedule Updates

Cost Report Updates

Change Proposals

Material Deliveries

Special Information/Instructions

Arch./Owner Direction Received

DAILY DIARY

WEATHER/TEMP.   8 A.M.   12 NOON   4 P.M.

EXPENSES

Whetstone: An artificial or natural stone used for sharpening the cutting edge of tools.

5 OCTOBER

SATURDAY

OCTOBER 6

SUNDAY

JOB NO. APPOINTMENTS/EVENTS/CALLS

JOB NO. APPOINTMENTS/EVENTS/CALLS

DAILY DIARY

DAILY DIARY

WEEK Beginning 7 OCTOBER
Ending 13 OCTOBER

WEEKLY EVENT CHECKLIST

Job meetings and preparation	Submittals for pending work in/appr	All permits in place
Special meetings	All other submittals in/approved	Req testing/inspections arranged
Dinners and seminars	Shop drawing log up to date	Inspection certificates received
Assemble schedule information	All sub change proposals in	Safety inspections performed
Complete schedule updates	All change proposals to owner prep'd	Safety recommendations acted on
Requests out for all required information	Submitted change proposals appr	Field reports complete
Outstanding sub/supplier responses	Change order logs up to date	Special photos taken
Outstanding owner responses	Required bonds received for all subs	
Outstanding architect/engineer responses	Certificates of insurance rec'd for all	
Critical material deliveries confirmed	subs (proper amounts)	
Shop drawings for ongoing work in/appr	Equipment/scaffolding release forms in	

TO DO

Item	Job No.	Item	Job No.

WEEKLY MILESTONE UPDATE

	Planned Date	Actual Date	Variance

DAILY MINDER

√ Verify receipt of last month's payment?
√ All change proposals submitted?
√ Current schedule commitments in-process?

	WORK	CAL
MONTH TO DATE	5	7
MONTH REMAINING	18	24
YEAR TO DATE	195	280
YEAR REMAINING	59	83

OCTOBER

7

MONDAY

KEY EVENTS

Meetings

Schedule Updates

Cost Report Updates

Change Proposals

Material Deliveries

Special Information/Instructions

Arch./Owner Direction Received

DAILY DIARY

WEATHER/TEMP.   8A.M.   12NOON   4P.M.

EXPENSES

JOB NO. APPOINTMENTS/EVENTS/CALLS

7A.M.

8A.M.

9A.M.

10A.M.

11A.M.

12NOON

1P.M.

2P.M.

3P.M.

4P.M.

5P.M.

6P.M.

SEPTEMBER						
S	M	T	W	T	F	S
	1	2	3	4	5	6	7
8	9	10	11	12	13	14
15	16	17	18	19	20	21
22	23	24	25	26	27	28
29	30					

OCTOBER						
S	M	T	W	T	F	S
		1	2	3	4	5
6	7	8	9	10	11	12
13	14	15	16	17	18	19
20	21	22	23	24	25	26
27	28	29	30	31		

NOVEMBER						
S	M	T	W	T	F	S
					1	2
3	4	5	6	7	8	9
10	11	12	13	14	15	16
17	18	19	20	21	22	23
24	25	26	27	28	29	30

8 OCTOBER

TUESDAY

JOB NO. APPOINTMENTS/EVENTS/CALLS

7 A.M.

8 A.M.

9 A.M.

10 A.M.

11 A.M.

12 NOON

1 P.M.

2 P.M.

3 P.M.

4 P.M.

5 P.M.

6 P.M.

DAILY MINDER

√ Key material deliveries confirmed?

√ Jobsite safety reviews performed?

√ Field reports up to date?

√ Sub change proposals requested?

KEY EVENTS

Meetings

Schedule Updates

Cost Report Updates

Change Proposals

Material Deliveries

Special Information/Instructions

Arch./Owner Direction Received

DAILY DIARY

WEATHER/TEMP.   8 A.M.   12 NOON   4 P.M.

EXPENSES

Lierne: In Gothic vault design, a short connecting rib.

DAILY MINDER

√ All required design info. received?

√ September payment(s) received?

√ Change proposals submitted/approved?

WORK CAL

MONTH TO DATE	7	9
MONTH REMAINING	16	22
YEAR TO DATE	197	282
YEAR REMAINING	57	81

OCTOBER

9

WEDNESDAY

KEY EVENTS

Meetings

Schedule Updates

Cost Report Updates

Change Proposals

Material Deliveries

Special Information/Instructions

Arch./Owner Direction Received

DAILY DIARY

WEATHER/TEMP.   8A.M.   12NOON   4P.M.

EXPENSES

JOB NO.   APPOINTMENTS/EVENTS/CALLS

7A.M.

8A.M.

9A.M.

10A.M.

11A.M.

12NOON

1P.M.

2P.M.

3P.M.

4P.M.

5P.M.

6P.M.

SEPTEMBER							OCTOBER							NOVEMBER						
S	M	T	W	T	F	S	S	M	T	W	T	F	S	S	M	T	W	T	F	S
1	2	3	4	5	6	7			1	2	3	4	5						1	2
8	9	10	11	12	13	14	6	7	8	9	10	11	12	3	4	5	6	7	8	9
15	16	17	18	19	20	21	13	14	15	16	17	18	19	10	11	12	13	14	15	16
22	23	24	25	26	27	28	20	21	22	23	24	25	26	17	18	19	20	21	22	23
29	30						27	28	29	30	31			24	25	26	27	28	29	30

10 OCTOBER

THURSDAY

WORK	CAL		
MONTH TO DATE	8	10
MONTH REMAINING	15	21
YEAR TO DATE	198	283
YEAR REMAINING	56	80

DAILY MINDER

√ Job meeting minutes and reports complete?
√ Key material deliveries confirmed?
√ Required submittals in/approved?
√ Outstanding design info. requested/received?

JOB NO. APPOINTMENTS/EVENTS/CALLS

7 A.M.

8 A.M.

9 A.M.

10 A.M.

11 A.M.

12 NOON

1 P.M.

2 P.M.

3 P.M.

4 P.M.

5 P.M.

6 P.M.

KEY EVENTS

Meetings

Schedule Updates

Cost Report Updates

Change Proposals

Material Deliveries

Special Information/Instructions

Arch./Owner Direction Received

DAILY DIARY

WEATHER/TEMP.   8 A.M.   12 NOON   4 P.M.

EXPENSES

Corbel: A short piece of stone or wood projecting from the face of a walk to form a support for a timber or other weight.

DAILY MINDER

√ Job meeting minutes and reports complete?

√ All requests for change proposals out?

√ September payment(s) received?

√ Next week's schedules confirmed?

	WORK	CAL
MONTH TO DATE	9	11
MONTH REMAINING	14	20
YEAR TO DATE	199	284
YEAR REMAINING	55	79

OCTOBER

FRIDAY

11

KEY EVENTS

Meetings

Schedule Updates

Cost Report Updates

Change Proposals

Material Deliveries

Special Information/Instructions

Arch./Owner Direction Received

DAILY DIARY

WEATHER/TEMP.   8 A.M.   12 NOON   4 P.M.

EXPENSES

JOB NO. APPOINTMENTS/EVENTS/CALLS

7 A.M.

8 A.M.

9 A.M.

10 A.M.

11 A.M.

12 NOON

1 P.M.

2 P.M.

3 P.M.

4 P.M.

5 P.M.

6 P.M.

SEPTEMBER

S	M	T	W	T	F	S
1	2	3	4	5	6	7
8	9	10	11	12	13	14
15	16	17	18	19	20	21
22	23	24	25	26	27	28
29	30					

OCTOBER

S	M	T	W	T	F	S
		1	2	3	4	5
6	7	8	9	10	11	12
13	14	15	16	17	18	19
20	21	22	23	24	25	26
27	28	29	30	31		

NOVEMBER

S	M	T	W	T	F	S
					1	2
3	4	5	6	7	8	9
10	11	12	13	14	15	16
17	18	19	20	21	22	23
24	25	26	27	28	29	30

12

OCTOBER

SATURDAY

	WORK	CAL
MONTH TO DATE	9	12
MONTH REMAINING	14	19
YEAR TO DATE	199	285
YEAR REMAINING	55	78

JOB NO.   APPOINTMENTS/EVENTS/CALLS

DAILY DIARY

13

OCTOBER

SUNDAY

	WORK	CAL
MONTH TO DATE	9	13
MONTH REMAINING	14	18
YEAR TO DATE	199	286
YEAR REMAINING	55	77

JOB NO.   APPOINTMENTS/EVENTS/CALLS

DAILY DIARY

WEEK Beginning 14 OCTOBER
Ending 20 OCTOBER

WEEKLY EVENT CHECKLIST

Job meetings and preparation ☐   ☐ Submittals for pending work in/appr   ☐ All permits in place ☐
Special meetings ☐   ☐ All other submittals in/approved   ☐ Req testing/inspections arranged ☐
Dinners and seminars ☐   ☐ Shop drawing log up to date   ☐ Inspection certificates received ☐
Assemble schedule information ☐   ☐ All sub change proposals in   ☐ Safety inspections performed ☐
Complete schedule updates ☐   ☐ All change proposals to owner prep'd   ☐ Safety recommendations acted on ☐
Requests out for all required information ☐   ☐ Submitted change proposals appr   ☐ Field reports complete ☐
Outstanding sub/supplier responses ☐   ☐ Change order logs up to date   ☐ Special photos taken ☐
Outstanding owner responses ☐   ☐ Required bonds received for all subs ☐   _____ ☐
Outstanding architect/engineer responses ☐   ☐ Certificates of insurance rec'd for all   _____ ☐
Critical material deliveries confirmed ☐   ☐ subs (proper amounts) ☐   _____ ☐
Shop drawings for ongoing work in/appr ☐   ☐ Equipment/scaffolding release forms in ☐   _____ ☐

TO DO

	Item	Job No.	Item	Job No.

WEEKLY MILESTONE UPDATE

	Planned Date	Actual Date	Variance

14 OCTOBER

14 OCTOBER
Columbus
Day Obsvd.
MONDAY

	WORK	CAL
MONTH TO DATE	10	14
MONTH REMAINING	13	17
YEAR TO DATE	200	287
YEAR REMAINING	54	76

DAILY MINDER

√ Verify approval of outstanding orders.
√ Key material deliveries confirmed?
√ Current schedule commitments in-process?

JOB NO. APPOINTMENTS/EVENTS/CALLS

7 A.M.

8 A.M.

9 A.M.

10 A.M.

11 A.M.

12 NOON

1 P.M.

2 P.M.

3 P.M.

4 P.M.

5 P.M.

6 P.M.

KEY EVENTS

Meetings

Schedule Updates

Cost Report Updates

Change Proposals

Material Deliveries

Special Information/Instructions

Arch./Owner Direction Received

DAILY DIARY

WEATHER/TEMP.   8 A.M.   12 NOON   4 P.M.

EXPENSES

Avoirdupois Weight: A commonly used system of weights for weighing all commodities except precious metals and stones.

DAILY MINDER

√ Assemble all schedule update infomation?

√ Sub change proposals received?

√ Field reports up-to-date?

WORK CAL			OCTOBER
MONTH TO DATE	11	15	
MONTH REMAINING	12	16	
YEAR TO DATE	201	288	
YEAR REMAINING	53	75	TUESDAY

15

KEY EVENTS

Meetings

Schedule Updates

Cost Report Updates

Change Proposals

Material Deliveries

Special Information/Instructions

Arch./Owner Direction Received

DAILY DIARY

WEATHER/TEMP.   8A.M.   12NOON   4P.M.

EXPENSES

JOB NO. APPOINTMENTS/EVENTS/CALLS

7A.M.

8A.M.

9A.M.

10A.M.

11A.M.

12NOON

1P.M.

2P.M.

3P.M.

4P.M.

5P.M.

6P.M.

SEPTEMBER							OCTOBER							NOVEMBER						
S	M	T	W	T	F	S	S	M	T	W	T	F	S	S	M	T	W	T	F	S
1	2	3	4	5	6	7			1	2	3	4	5						1	2
8	9	10	11	12	13	14	6	7	8	9	10	11	12	3	4	5	6	7	8	9
15	16	17	18	19	20	21	13	14	15	16	17	18	19	10	11	12	13	14	15	16
22	23	24	25	26	27	28	20	21	22	23	24	25	26	17	18	19	20	21	22	23
29	30						27	28	29	30	31			24	25	26	27	28	29	30

16 OCTOBER
WEDNESDAY

WORK CAL		
MONTH TO DATE	12	16
MONTH REMAINING	11	15
YEAR TO DATE	202	289
YEAR REMAINING	52	74

DAILY MINDER

√ Verify receipt of all sub and supplier payment requisitions.
√ Key material deliveries confirmed?
√ Submitted change proposals approval?

JOB NO. APPOINTMENTS/EVENTS/CALLS

7 A.M.

8 A.M.

9 A.M.

10 A.M.

11 A.M.

12 NOON

1 P.M.

2 P.M.

3 P.M.

4 P.M.

5 P.M.

6 P.M.

KEY EVENTS

Meetings

Schedule Updates

Cost Report Updates

Change Proposals

Material Deliveries

Special Information/Instructions

Arch./Owner Direction Received

DAILY DIARY

WEATHER/TEMP.   8 A.M.   12 NOON   4 P.M.

EXPENSES

Fenestral: A window opening closed with transparent paper or cloth instead of glass.

DAILY MINDER

√ Schedule update complete?
√ Job meeting minutes and reports complete?
√ Assemble cost report information?

	WORK	CAL
MONTH TO DATE	13	17
MONTH REMAINING	10	14
YEAR TO DATE	203	290
YEAR REMAINING	51	73

OCTOBER

THURSDAY

17

KEY EVENTS

Meetings

Schedule Updates

Cost Report Updates

Change Proposals

Material Deliveries

Special Information/Instructions

Arch./Owner Direction Received

DAILY DIARY

WEATHER/TEMP.   8A.M.   12NOON   4P.M.

EXPENSES

JOB NO.   APPOINTMENTS/EVENTS/CALLS

7A.M.

8A.M.

9A.M.

10A.M.

11A.M.

12NOON

1P.M.

2P.M.

3P.M.

4P.M.

5P.M.

6P.M.

SEPTEMBER							OCTOBER							NOVEMBER						
S	M	T	W	T	F	S	S	M	T	W	T	F	S	S	M	T	W	T	F	S
1	2	3	4	5	6	7			1	2	3	4	5						1	2
8	9	10	11	12	13	14	6	7	8	9	10	11	12	3	4	5	6	7	8	9
15	16	17	18	19	20	21	13	14	15	16	17	18	19	10	11	12	13	14	15	16
22	23	24	25	26	27	28	20	21	22	23	24	25	26	17	18	19	20	21	22	23
29	30						27	28	29	30	31			24	25	26	27	28	29	30

18 OCTOBER
FRIDAY

WORK	CAL
MONTH TO DATE	14	18
MONTH REMAINING	9	13
YEAR TO DATE	204	291
YEAR REMAINING	50	72

DAILY MINDER

√ Verify approval of outstanding change orders.
√ Verify receipt of all sub and supplier payment requisitions.
√ Job meeting minutes and reports complete?
√ Next week's schedules confirmed?

JOB NO. APPOINTMENTS/EVENTS/CALLS

7 A.M.

8 A.M.

9 A.M.

10 A.M.

11 A.M.

12 NOON

1 P.M.

2 P.M.

3 P.M.

4 P.M.

5 P.M.

6 P.M.

KEY EVENTS

Meetings

Schedule Updates

Cost Report Updates

Change Proposals

Material Deliveries

Special Information/Instructions

Arch./Owner Direction Received

DAILY DIARY

WEATHER/TEMP.	8 A.M.	12 NOON	4 P.M.

EXPENSES

Mock Rafter: In the construction of an open cornice, a short piece of timber used to give the appearance of a real rafter.

19

OCTOBER

SATURDAY

WORK	CAL	
MONTH TO DATE	14	19
MONTH REMAINING	9	12
YEAR TO DATE	204	292
YEAR REMAINING	50	71

JOB NO. APPOINTMENTS/EVENTS/CALLS

DAILY DIARY

20

OCTOBER

SUNDAY

WORK	CAL	
MONTH TO DATE	14	20
MONTH REMAINING	9	11
YEAR TO DATE	204	293
YEAR REMAINING	50	70

JOB NO. APPOINTMENTS/EVENTS/CALLS

DAILY DIARY

WEEK Beginning 21 OCTOBER
Ending 27 OCTOBER

WEEKLY EVENT CHECKLIST

Job meetings and preparation ___
Special meetings ___
Dinners and seminars ___
Assemble schedule information ___
Complete schedule updates ___
Requests out for all required information ___
Outstanding sub/supplier responses ___
Outstanding owner responses ___
Outstanding architect/engineer responses ___
Critical material deliveries confirmed ___
Shop drawings for ongoing work in/appr ___

Submittals for pending work in/appr ___
All other submittals in/approved ___
Shop drawing log up to date ___
All sub change proposals in ___
All change proposals to owner prep'd ___
Submitted change proposals appr ___
Change order logs up to date ___
Required bonds received for all subs ___
Certificates of insurance rec'd for all subs (proper amounts) ___
Equipment/scaffolding release forms in ___

All permits in place ___
Req testing/inspections arranged ___
Inspection certificates received ___
Safety inspections performed ___
Safety recommendations acted on ___
Field reports complete ___
Special photos taken ___
_____ ___
_____ ___
_____ ___
_____ ___

TO DO

Item	Job No.	Item	Job No.

WEEKLY MILESTONE UPDATE

	Planned Date	Actual Date	Variance

DAILY MINDER

√ Verify approval of outstanding change orders.

√ Submit requisition(s) to owner(s).

√ Authorize/approve sub and supplier payments.

√ All cost report information assembled?

WORK	CAL
MONTH TO DATE	15	21
MONTH REMAINING	8	10
YEAR TO DATE	205	294
YEAR REMAINING	49	69

OCTOBER

21

MONDAY

KEY EVENTS

Meetings

Schedule Updates

Cost Report Updates

Change Proposals

Material Deliveries

Special Information/Instructions

Arch./Owner Direction Received

DAILY DIARY

WEATHER/TEMP.   8A.M.   12NOON   4P.M.

EXPENSES

JOB NO.   APPOINTMENTS/EVENTS/CALLS

7 A.M.

8 A.M.

9 A.M.

10 A.M.

11 A.M.

12 NOON

1 P.M.

2 P.M.

3 P.M.

4 P.M.

5 P.M.

6 P.M.

	SEPTEMBER							OCTOBER							NOVEMBER					
S	M	T	W	T	F	S	S	M	T	W	T	F	S	S	M	T	W	T	F	S
1	2	3	4	5	6	7			1	2	3	4	5						1	2
8	9	10	11	12	13	14	6	7	8	9	10	11	12	3	4	5	6	7	8	9
15	16	17	18	19	20	21	13	14	15	16	17	18	19	10	11	12	13	14	15	16
22	23	24	25	26	27	28	20	21	22	23	24	25	26	17	18	19	20	21	22	23
29	30						27	28	29	30	31			24	25	26	27	28	29	30

22 OCTOBER
TUESDAY

DAILY MINDER

√ Assemble all schedule update information.
√ All monthly reports and narratives complete?
√ Key material deliveries confirmed?
√ All cost report information assembled?

JOB NO. APPOINTMENTS/EVENTS/CALLS

7 A.M.

8 A.M.

9 A.M.

10 A.M.

11 A.M.

12 NOON

1 P.M.

2 P.M.

3 P.M.

4 P.M.

5 P.M.

6 P.M.

KEY EVENTS

Meetings

Schedule Updates

Cost Report Updates

Change Proposals

Material Deliveries

Special Information/Instructions

Arch./Owner Direction Received

DAILY DIARY

WEATHER/TEMP.   8 A.M.   12 NOON   4 P.M.

EXPENSES

Bossing: A plumbing process that shaped lead or other soft metal to conform to the irregularities of a surface that it is covering.

DAILY MINDER

√ Verify approval of outstanding change orders.

√ Submit requisition(s) to owner(s).

√ Authorize/approve sub and supplier payments for September?

√ Verify receipt of sub/supplier requisitions?

KEY EVENTS

Meetings

Schedule Updates

Cost Report Updates

Change Proposals

Material Deliveries

Special Information/Instructions

Arch./Owner Direction Received

DAILY DIARY

WEATHER/TEMP.   8 A.M.   12 NOON   4 P.M.

EXPENSES

	WORK	CAL
MONTH TO DATE	17	23
MONTH REMAINING	6	8
YEAR TO DATE	207	296
YEAR REMAINING	47	67

OCTOBER
WEDNESDAY **23**

JOB NO. APPOINTMENTS/EVENTS/CALLS

7 A.M.

8 A.M.

9 A.M.

10 A.M.

11 A.M.

12 NOON

1 P.M.

2 P.M.

3 P.M.

4 P.M.

5 P.M.

6 P.M.

SEPTEMBER						
S	M	T	W	T	F	S
1	2	3	4	5	6	7
8	9	10	11	12	13	14
15	16	17	18	19	20	21
22	23	24	25	26	27	28
29	30					

OCTOBER						
S	M	T	W	T	F	S
		1	2	3	4	5
6	7	8	9	10	11	12
13	14	15	16	17	18	19
20	21	22	23	24	25	26
27	28	29	30	31		

NOVEMBER						
S	M	T	W	T	F	S
					1	2
3	4	5	6	7	8	9
10	11	12	13	14	15	16
17	18	19	20	21	22	23
24	25	26	27	28	29	30

24 OCTOBER
THURSDAY

WORK	CAL
MONTH TO DATE	18	24
MONTH REMAINING	5	7
YEAR TO DATE	208	297
YEAR REMAINING	46	66

JOB NO. APPOINTMENTS/EVENTS/CALLS

7 A.M.

8 A.M.

9 A.M.

10 A.M.

11 A.M.

12 NOON

1 P.M.

2 P.M.

3 P.M.

4 P.M.

5 P.M.

6 P.M.

DAILY MINDER

√ Submit requisition(s) to owner(s)?

√ Schedule update complete?

√ All monthly reports and narratives complete?

√ Cost report complete?

KEY EVENTS

Meetings

Schedule Updates

Cost Report Updates

Change Proposals

Material Deliveries

Special Information/Instructions

Arch./Owner Direction Received

DAILY DIARY

WEATHER/TEMP.   8 A.M.   12 NOON   4 P.M.

EXPENSES

Four-way Switch: Used in house wiring when lights are to be operated from more than two locations.

DAILY MINDER

√ Verify approval of outstanding change orders.
√ Submit requisition(s) to owner(s).
√ Job meeting minutes and reports complete?
√ Cost report complete?

KEY EVENTS

Meetings

Schedule Updates

Cost Report Updates

Change Proposals

Material Deliveries

Special Information/Instructions

Arch./Owner Direction Received

DAILY DIARY

WEATHER/TEMP.   8 A.M.   12 NOON   4 P.M.

EXPENSES

WORK CAL

OCTOBER

MONTH TO DATE   19   25
MONTH REMAINING   4   6
YEAR TO DATE   207   298
YEAR REMAINING   45   65

FRIDAY

25

JOB NO. APPOINTMENTS/EVENTS/CALLS

7 A.M.

8 A.M.

9 A.M.

10 A.M.

11 A.M.

12 NOON

1 P.M.

2 P.M.

3 P.M.

4 P.M.

5 P.M.

6 P.M.

SEPTEMBER							OCTOBER							NOVEMBER						
S	M	T	W	T	F	S	S	M	T	W	T	F	S	S	M	T	W	T	F	S
1	2	3	4	5	6	7			1	2	3	4	5						1	2
8	9	10	11	12	13	14	6	7	8	9	10	11	12	3	4	5	6	7	8	9
15	16	17	18	19	20	21	13	14	15	16	17	18	19	10	11	12	13	14	15	16
22	23	24	25	26	27	28	20	21	22	23	24	25	26	17	18	19	20	21	22	23
29	30						27	28	29	30	31			24	25	26	27	28	29	30

26 OCTOBER

SATURDAY

	WORK	CAL
MONTH TO DATE	19	26
MONTH REMAINING	4	5
YEAR TO DATE	209	299
YEAR REMAINING	45	64

JOB NO. APPOINTMENTS/EVENTS/CALLS

DAILY DIARY

OCTOBER 27

SUNDAY

	WORK	CAL
MONTH TO DATE	19	27
MONTH REMAINING	4	4
YEAR TO DATE	209	300
YEAR REMAINING	45	63

JOB NO. APPOINTMENTS/EVENTS/CALLS

DAILY DIARY

WEEK Beginning 28 OCTOBER
Ending 3 NOVEMBER

WEEKLY EVENT CHECKLIST

Job meetings and preparation

Special meetings

Dinners and seminars

Assemble schedule information

Complete schedule updates

Requests out for all required information

Outstanding sub/supplier responses

Outstanding owner responses

Outstanding architect/engineer responses

Critical material deliveries confirmed

Shop drawings for ongoing work in/appr

Submittals for pending work in/appr

All other submittals in/approved

Shop drawing log up to date

All sub change proposals in

All change proposals to owner prep'd

Submitted change proposals appr

Change order logs up to date

Required bonds received for all subs

Certificates of insurance rec'd for all subs (proper amounts)

Equipment/scaffolding release forms in

All permits in place

Req testing/inspections arranged

Inspection certificates received

Safety inspections performed

Safety recommendations acted on

Field reports complete

Special photos taken

TO DO

Item	Job No.	Item	Job No.

WEEKLY MILESTONE UPDATE

	Planned Date	Actual Date	Variance

28 OCTOBER / MONDAY

JOB NO. APPOINTMENTS/EVENTS/CALLS

7 A.M.

8 A.M.

9 A.M.

10 A.M.

11 A.M.

12 NOON

1 P.M.

2 P.M.

3 P.M.

4 P.M.

5 P.M.

6 P.M.

DAILY MINDER

√ This month's schedule update complete?

√ Key material deliveries confirmed?

√ Progress photos taken?

√ Invoices submitted to owner(s)?

KEY EVENTS

Meetings

Schedule Updates

Cost Report Updates

Change Proposals

Material Deliveries

Special Information/Instructions

Arch./Owner Direction Received

DAILY DIARY

WEATHER/TEMP.   8 A.M.   12 NOON   4 P.M.

EXPENSES

Meros: A design term referring to the plain surfaces between the channels of a triglyph.

DAILY MINDER

√ This month's schedule update complete?
√ Key material deliveries confirmed?
√ Progress photos taken?
√ Current schedule commitments in-process?

WORK CAL

MONTH TO DATE	21	29
MONTH REMAINING	2	2
YEAR TO DATE	211	302
YEAR REMAINING	43	61

OCTOBER
29
TUESDAY

KEY EVENTS

Meetings

Schedule Updates

Cost Report Updates

Change Proposals

Material Deliveries

Special Information/Instructions

Arch./Owner Direction Received

DAILY DIARY

JOB NO. APPOINTMENTS/EVENTS/CALLS

7A.M.

8A.M.

9A.M.

10A.M.

11A.M.

12NOON

1P.M.

2P.M.

3P.M.

4P.M.

5P.M.

6P.M.

WEATHER/TEMP.   8A.M.   12NOON   4P.M.

EXPENSES

	SEPTEMBER							OCTOBER							NOVEMBER					
S	M	T	W	T	F	S	S	M	T	W	T	F	S	S	M	T	W	T	F	S
	1	2	3	4	5	6			1	2	3	4	5						1	2
7	8	9	10	11	12	13	6	7	8	9	10	11	12	3	4	5	6	7	8	9
14	15	16	17	18	19	20	13	14	15	16	17	18	19	10	11	12	13	14	15	16
21	22	23	24	25	26	27	20	21	22	23	24	25	26	17	18	19	20	21	22	23
28	29	30					27	28	29	30	31			24	25	26	27	28	29	30

30 OCTOBER
WEDNESDAY

WORK CAL		
MONTH TO DATE	22	30
MONTH REMAINING	1	1
YEAR TO DATE	212	303
YEAR REMAINING	42	60

JOB NO. APPOINTMENTS/EVENTS/CALLS

7 A.M.

8 A.M.

9 A.M.

10 A.M.

11 A.M.

12 NOON

1 P.M.

2 P.M.

3 P.M.

4 P.M.

5 P.M.

6 P.M.

KEY EVENTS
Meetings

Schedule Updates

Cost Report Updates

Change Proposals

Material Deliveries

Special Information/Instructions

Arch./Owner Direction Received

DAILY DIARY

WEATHER/TEMP.   8 A.M.   12 NOON   4 P.M.

EXPENSES

Knuckle: Portion of a hinge or butt that enclosed the pin.

DAILY MINDER

√ Job meeting minutes and reports complete?

√ Key material deliveries confirmed?

√ Progress photos taken?

√ October requisition(s) submitted?

	WORK	CAL
MONTH TO DATE	23	31
MONTH REMAINING	0	0
YEAR TO DATE	213	304
YEAR REMAINING	41	59

OCTOBER
Halloween

THURSDAY

31

KEY EVENTS

Meetings

Schedule Updates

Cost Report Updates

Change Proposals

Material Deliveries

Special Information/Instructions

Arch./Owner Direction Received

DAILY DIARY

JOB NO. APPOINTMENTS/EVENTS/CALLS

7 A.M.

8 A.M.

9 A.M.

10 A.M.

11 A.M.

12 NOON

1 P.M.

2 P.M.

3 P.M.

4 P.M.

5 P.M.

6 P.M.

WEATHER/TEMP.   8 A.M.   12 NOON   4 P.M.

EXPENSES

	SEPTEMBER								OCTOBER								NOVEMBER					
S	M	T	W	T	F	S		S	M	T	W	T	F	S		S	M	T	W	T	F	S
1	2	3	4	5	6	7				1	2	3	4	5							1	2
8	9	10	11	12	13	14		6	7	8	9	10	11	12		3	4	5	6	7	8	9
15	16	17	18	19	20	21		13	14	15	16	17	18	19		10	11	12	13	14	15	16
22	23	24	25	26	27	28		20	21	22	23	24	25	26		17	18	19	20	21	22	23
29	30							27	28	29	30	31				24	25	26	27	28	29	30

NOVEMBER

20 Working Days

30 Calendar Days

OCTOBER

S	M	T	W	T	F	S
		1	2	3	4	5
6	7	8	9	10	11	12
13	14	15	16	17	18	19
20	21	22	23	24	25	26
27	28	29	30	31		

NOVEMBER

S	M	T	W	T	F	S
					1	2
3	4	5	6	7	8	9
10	11	12	13	14	15	16
17	18	19	20	21	22	23
24	25	26	27	28	29	30

DECEMBER

S	M	T	W	T	F	S
1	2	3	4	5	6	7
8	9	10	11	12	13	14
15	16	17	18	19	20	21
22	23	24	25	26	27	28
29	30	31				

MONTHLY KEY ACTIVITY UPDATE

Job/C.O. No.	Description	Planned Date	Actual Date	Variance	Remarks

MONTHLY SCHEDULE UPDATE SUMMARY

Job/C.O. No.	Activities	Original Duration	Days Spent	Days Remaining	Status/Remarks

MONTHLY RECAP

	S	M	T	W	T	F	S
						1	2
	3	4	5	6	7	8	9
	10	11	12	13	14	15	16
	17	18	19	20	21	22	23
	24	25	26	27	28	29	30

NOVEMBER

MONTHLY EVENT CHECKLIST

Schedule updates complete	☐ All sub change proposals in	☐ Sub/supplier contract(s) rec'd ☐
Requests out for all required info.	☐ All change proposals to owner prepared	☐ Requisition(s) submitted to owner(s) ☐
Outstanding sub/supplier responses rec'd ☐	Submitted change proposals approved	☐ Sub/supplier adjustments complete ☐
Outstanding owner responses rec'd ☐	Guarantees/warrantees rec'd	☐ Progress photos taken ☐
Outstanding arch./eng. responses rec'd ☐	Inspection certificates rec'd	☐ Job cost report info. assembled ☐
Critical material deliveries confirmed ☐	As-built drawings rec'd	☐ Job cost reports complete ☐
Shop drawings for ongoing work in/appr ☐	Safety inspections performed	☐ Other: ☐
Submittals for pending work in/appr ☐	Safety reports complete	☐ _____ ☐
All other submittals in/approved ☐	Narratives complete	☐ _____ ☐

CRITICAL ITEM COST REPORT SUMMARY

Job/CO No.	Description	(A) Budget $ Amount	(B) Cost To Date	(C) Cost Remaining	(D) Total Commitment (B + C)	(E) +/− (A − D)

CHANGE ORDER SUMMARY

Job No.	C.O. No.	Description	Submission Date Required	Actual	Approval Date Required	Actual	Remarks

1

NOVEMBER
FRIDAY

WORK	CAL
MONTH TO DATE	1	1
MONTH REMAINING	19	30
YEAR TO DATE	214	305
YEAR REMAINING	40	58

DAILY MINDER

√ Job meeting minutes and reports complete?

√ All requests for change proposals out?

√ Next week's schedules confirmed?

√ Attend any professional development seminars?

JOB NO. APPOINTMENTS/EVENTS/CALLS

7 A.M.

8 A.M.

9 A.M.

10 A.M.

11 A.M.

12 NOON

1 P.M.

2 P.M.

3 P.M.

4 P.M.

5 P.M.

6 P.M.

KEY EVENTS

Meetings

Schedule Updates

Cost Report Updates

Change Proposals

Material Deliveries

Special Information/Instructions

Arch./Owner Direction Received

DAILY DIARY

WEATHER/TEMP.   8 A.M.   12 NOON   4 P.M.

EXPENSES

Ripsaw: Saw having chisel-shaped, coarse teeth, used to cut wood in the direction of the grain.

2
NOVEMBER
SATURDAY

	WORK	CAL
MONTH TO DATE	1	2
MONTH REMAINING	19	29
YEAR TO DATE	214	306
YEAR REMAINING	40	57

JOB NO. APPOINTMENTS/EVENTS/CALLS

DAILY DIARY

3
NOVEMBER
SUNDAY

	WORK	CAL
MONTH TO DATE	1	3
MONTH REMAINING	19	28
YEAR TO DATE	214	307
YEAR REMAINING	40	56

JOB NO. APPOINTMENTS/EVENTS/CALLS

DAILY DIARY

WEEK Beginning 4 NOVEMBER
Ending 10 NOVEMBER

WEEKLY EVENT CHECKLIST

Job meetings and preparation	Submittals for pending work in/appr	All permits in place
Special meetings	All other submittals in/approved	Req testing/inspections arranged
Dinners and seminars	Shop drawing log up to date	Inspection certificates received
Assemble schedule information	All sub change proposals in	Safety inspections performed
Complete schedule updates	All change proposals to owner prep'd	Safety recommendations acted on
Requests out for all required information	Submitted change proposals appr	Field reports complete
Outstanding sub/supplier responses	Change order logs up to date	Special photos taken
Outstanding owner responses	Required bonds received for all subs	
Outstanding architect/engineer responses	Certificates of insurance rec'd for all subs (proper amounts)	
Critical material deliveries confirmed		
Shop drawings for ongoing work in/appr	Equipment/scaffolding release forms in	

TO DO

Item	Job No.	Item	Job No.

WEEKLY MILESTONE UPDATE

	Planned Date	Actual Date	Variance

DAILY MINDER

√ Verify receipt of last month's payment.
√ Key material deliveries confirmed?
√ Current schedules in-process?
√ Sub change proposals received?

KEY EVENTS

Meetings

Schedule Updates

Cost Report Updates

Change Proposals

Material Deliveries

Special Information/Instructions

Arch./Owner Direction Received

DAILY DIARY

WEATHER/TEMP.   8A.M.   12NOON   4P.M.

EXPENSES

	WORK	CAL
MONTH TO DATE	2	4
MONTH REMAINING	18	27
YEAR TO DATE	215	308
YEAR REMAINING	38	55

NOVEMBER

4

MONDAY

JOB NO.   APPOINTMENTS/EVENTS/CALLS

7A.M.

8A.M.

9A.M.

10A.M.

11A.M.

12NOON

1P.M.

2P.M.

3P.M.

4P.M.

5P.M.

6P.M.

OCTOBER						
S	M	T	W	T	F	S
		1	2	3	4	5
6	7	8	9	10	11	12
13	14	15	16	17	18	19
20	21	22	23	24	25	26
27	28	29	30	31		

NOVEMBER						
S	M	T	W	T	F	S
					1	2
3	4	5	6	7	8	9
10	11	12	13	14	15	16
17	18	19	20	21	22	23
24	25	26	27	28	29	30

DECEMBER						
S	M	T	W	T	F	S
1	2	3	4	5	6	7
8	9	10	11	12	13	14
15	16	17	18	19	20	21
22	23	24	25	26	27	28
29	30	31				

5 NOVEMBER
Election Day
TUESDAY

WORK	CAL
MONTH TO DATE	3	5
MONTH REMAINING	17	27
YEAR TO DATE	216	309
YEAR REMAINING	38	54

DAILY MINDER
√All requests for change quotations out?
√All required design info. received?
√Submitted change proposals approved?
√All requisitions submitted?

JOB NO. APPOINTMENTS/EVENTS/CALLS

7 A.M.

8 A.M.

9 A.M.

10 A.M.

11 A.M.

12 NOON

1 P.M.

2 P.M.

3 P.M.

4 P.M.

5 P.M.

6 P.M.

KEY EVENTS
Meetings

Schedule Updates

Cost Report Updates

Change Proposals

Material Deliveries

Special Information/Instructions

Arch./Owner Direction Received

DAILY DIARY

WEATHER/TEMP. 8 A.M.   12 NOON   4 P.M.

EXPENSES

Invert: The lowest point of the inside surface of any drain pipe or conduit that is not vertical.

DAILY MINDER

√ Key material deliveries confirmed?

√ Scheduled a complete physical examination this year?

√ Field reports up-to-date?

√ Current changes submitted/approved?

WORK CAL

MONTH TO DATE	4	6
MONTH REMAINING	16	25
YEAR TO DATE	217	310
YEAR REMAINING	37	53

NOVEMBER

WEDNESDAY

6

KEY EVENTS

Meetings

Schedule Updates

Cost Report Updates

Change Proposals

Material Deliveries

Special Information/Instructions

Arch./Owner Direction Received

DAILY DIARY

WEATHER/TEMP.   8 A.M.   12 NOON   4 P.M.

EXPENSES

JOB NO.   APPOINTMENTS/EVENTS/CALLS

7 A.M.

8 A.M.

9 A.M.

10 A.M.

11 A.M.

12 NOON

1 P.M.

2 P.M.

3 P.M.

4 P.M.

5 P.M.

6 P.M.

OCTOBER						
S	M	T	W	T	F	S
		1	2	3	4	5
6	7	8	9	10	11	12
13	14	15	16	17	18	19
20	21	22	23	24	25	26
27	28	29	30	31		

NOVEMBER						
S	M	T	W	T	F	S
					1	2
3	4	5	6	7	8	9
10	11	12	13	14	15	16
17	18	19	20	21	22	23
24	25	26	27	28	29	30

DECEMBER						
S	M	T	W	T	F	S
1	2	3	4	5	6	7
8	9	10	11	12	13	14
15	16	17	18	19	20	21
22	23	24	25	26	27	28
29	30	31				

7

NOVEMBER
THURSDAY

WORK CAL		
MONTH TO DATE	5	7
MONTH REMAINING	15	24
YEAR TO DATE	218	311
YEAR REMAINING	26	52

DAILY MINDER

√ Job meeting minutes and reports complete?
√ Jobsite safety review performed?
√ Requested/received outstanding design info?

JOB NO. APPOINTMENTS/EVENTS/CALLS

7 A.M.

8 A.M.

9 A.M.

10 A.M.

11 A.M.

12 NOON

1 P.M.

2 P.M.

3 P.M.

4 P.M.

5 P.M.

6 P.M.

KEY EVENTS

Meetings

Schedule Updates

Cost Report Updates

Change Proposals

Material Deliveries

Special Information/Instructions

Arch./Owner Direction Received

DAILY DIARY

WEATHER/TEMP.   8 A.M.   12 NOON   4 P.M.

EXPENSES

Slamming Stile: Vertical side of a door opening against which the door touches when closed.

DAILY MINDER

√ Job meeting minutes and reports complete?
√ All change order proposals submitted?
√ Next week's schedules confirmed?
√ Dinner reservations made for the weekend?

KEY EVENTS

Meetings

Schedule Updates

Cost Report Updates

Change Proposals

Material Deliveries

Special Information/Instructions

Arch./Owner Direction Received

DAILY DIARY

WEATHER/TEMP.   8A.M.   12NOON   4P.M.

EXPENSES

	WORK	CAL
MONTH TO DATE	6	8
MONTH REMAINING	14	23
YEAR TO DATE	219	312
YEAR REMAINING	35	51

NOVEMBER
8
FRIDAY

JOB NO.   APPOINTMENTS/EVENTS/CALLS

7A.M.

8A.M.

9A.M.

10A.M.

11A.M.

12NOON

1P.M.

2P.M.

3P.M.

4P.M.

5P.M.

6P.M.

OCTOBER						
S	M	T	W	T	F	S
		1	2	3	4	5
6	7	8	9	10	11	12
13	14	15	16	17	18	19
20	21	22	23	24	25	26
27	28	29	30	31		

NOVEMBER						
S	M	T	W	T	F	S
					1	2
3	4	5	6	7	8	9
10	11	12	13	14	15	16
17	18	19	20	21	22	23
24	25	26	27	28	29	30

DECEMBER						
S	M	T	W	T	F	S
1	2	3	4	5	6	7
8	9	10	11	12	13	14
15	16	17	18	19	20	21
22	23	24	25	26	27	28
29	30	31				

9
NOVEMBER
SATURDAY

	WORK	CAL
MONTH TO DATE	6	9
MONTH REMAINING	14	22
YEAR TO DATE	219	313
YEAR REMAINING	35	50

	WORK	CAL
MONTH TO DATE	6	10
MONTH REMAINING	14	21
YEAR TO DATE	219	314
YEAR REMAINING	35	49

NOVEMBER
SUNDAY
10

JOB NO. APPOINTMENTS/EVENTS/CALLS

JOB NO. APPOINTMENTS/EVENTS/CALLS

DAILY DIARY

DAILY DIARY

WEEK Beginning 11 NOVEMBER
Ending 17 NOVEMBER

WEEKLY EVENT CHECKLIST

Job meetings and preparation
Special meetings
Dinners and seminars
Assemble schedule information
Complete schedule updates
Requests out for all required information
Outstanding sub/supplier responses
Outstanding owner responses
Outstanding architect/engineer responses
Critical material deliveries confirmed
Shop drawings for ongoing work in/appr

Submittals for pending work in/appr
All other submittals in/approved
Shop drawing log up to date
All sub change proposals in
All change proposals to owner prep'd
Submitted change proposals appr
Change order logs up to date
Required bonds received for all subs
Certificates of insurance rec'd for all subs (proper amounts)
Equipment/scaffolding release forms in

All permits in place
Req testing/inspections arranged
Inspection certificates received
Safety inspections performed
Safety recommendations acted on
Field reports complete
Special photos taken

TO DO

Item	Job No.	Item	Job No.

WEEKLY MILESTONE UPDATE

	Planned Date	Actual Date	Variance

11

NOVEMBER
Veteran's
Day
MONDAY

DAILY MINDER
√ Begin considering winter preparations.
√ All required design info. received?
√ October payments received?
√ Current schedule commitments in-process?

JOB NO. APPOINTMENTS/EVENTS/CALLS

7 A.M.

8 A.M.

9 A.M.

10 A.M.

11 A.M.

12 NOON

1 P.M.

2 P.M.

3 P.M.

4 P.M.

5 P.M.

6 P.M.

KEY EVENTS
Meetings

Schedule Updates

Cost Report Updates

Change Proposals

Material Deliveries

Special Information/Instructions

Arch./Owner Direction Received

DAILY DIARY

WEATHER/TEMP.   8 A.M.   12 NOON   4 P.M.

EXPENSES

Marquee: A hood projecting over an entrance to a building not supported by columns or posts.

DAILY MINDER

√ Assemble all schedule update information.
√ Key material deliveries confirmed?
√ Sub change proposals received?

WORK	CAL
MONTH TO DATE	8	12
MONTH REMAINING	12	19
YEAR TO DATE	221	316
YEAR REMAINING	33	47

NOVEMBER 12

TUESDAY

KEY EVENTS

Meetings

Schedule Updates

Cost Report Updates

Change Proposals

Material Deliveries

Special Information/Instructions

Arch./Owner Direction Received

DAILY DIARY

WEATHER/TEMP.   8A.M.   12NOON   4P.M.

EXPENSES

JOB NO.   APPOINTMENTS/EVENTS/CALLS

7 A.M.

8 A.M.

9 A.M.

10 A.M.

11 A.M.

12 NOON

1 P.M.

2 P.M.

3 P.M.

4 P.M.

5 P.M.

6 P.M.

	OCTOBER							NOVEMBER							DECEMBER					
S	M	T	W	T	F	S	S	M	T	W	T	F	S	S	M	T	W	T	F	S
		1	2	3	4	5						1	2			1	2	3	4	5	6	7
6	7	8	9	10	11	12	3	4	5	6	7	8	9	8	9	10	11	12	13	14
13	14	15	16	17	18	19	10	11	12	13	14	15	16	15	16	17	18	19	20	21
20	21	22	23	24	25	26	17	18	19	20	21	22	23	22	23	24	25	26	27	28
27	28	29	30	31			24	25	26	27	28	29	30	29	30	31				

13

NOVEMBER
WEDNESDAY

WORK CAL		
MONTH TO DATE	9	13
MONTH REMAINING	11	18
YEAR TO DATE	222	317
YEAR REMAINING	32	46

DAILY MINDER

√ All change order proposals submitted?
√ Field reports up-to-date?
√ Required submittals in/approved?

JOB NO.   APPOINTMENTS/EVENTS/CALLS

7 A.M.

8 A.M.

9 A.M.

10 A.M.

11 A.M.

12 NOON

1 P.M.

2 P.M.

3 P.M.

4 P.M.

5 P.M.

6 P.M.

KEY EVENTS

Meetings

Schedule Updates

Cost Report Updates

Change Proposals

Material Deliveries

Special Information/Instructions

Arch./Owner Direction Received

DAILY DIARY

WEATHER/TEMP.	8 A.M.	12 NOON	4 P.M.

EXPENSES

Carriage: Wood or steel supports for the steps of a wooden stairway.

DAILY MINDER

√ Job meeting minutes and reports complete?

√ Key material deliveries confirmed?

√ October payments received?

WORK	CAL
MONTH TO DATE	10	14
MONTH REMAINING	10	17
YEAR TO DATE	223	318
YEAR REMAINING	31	45

NOVEMBER

14

THURSDAY

KEY EVENTS

Meetings

Schedule Updates

Cost Report Updates

Change Proposals

Material Deliveries

Special Information/Instructions

Arch./Owner Direction Received

DAILY DIARY

WEATHER/TEMP.   8 A.M.   12 NOON   4 P.M.

EXPENSES

JOB NO.   APPOINTMENTS/EVENTS/CALLS

7 A.M.

8 A.M.

9 A.M.

10 A.M.

11 A.M.

12 NOON

1 P.M.

2 P.M.

3 P.M.

4 P.M.

5 P.M.

6 P.M.

OCTOBER							NOVEMBER							DECEMBER						
S	M	T	W	T	F	S	S	M	T	W	T	F	S	S	M	T	W	T	F	S
	1	2	3	4	5							1	2	1	2	3	4	5	6	7
6	7	8	9	10	11	12	3	4	5	6	7	8	9	8	9	10	11	12	13	14
13	14	15	16	17	18	19	10	11	12	13	14	15	16	15	16	17	18	19	20	21
20	21	22	23	24	25	26	17	18	19	20	21	22	23	22	23	24	25	26	27	28
27	28	29	30	31			24	25	26	27	28	29	30	29	30	31				

15 NOVEMBER
FRIDAY

WORK	CAL
MONTH TO DATE	11	15
MONTH REMAINING	9	16
YEAR TO DATE	224	319
YEAR REMAINING	30	44

JOB NO. APPOINTMENTS/EVENTS/CALLS

7 A.M.

8 A.M.

9 A.M.

10 A.M.

11 A.M.

12 NOON

1 P.M.

2 P.M.

3 P.M.

4 P.M.

5 P.M.

6 P.M.

DAILY MINDER

√ Assemble all schedule update information.

√ Job meeting minutes and reports complete?

√ Next week's schedules confirmed?

√ Field reports up-to-date?

KEY EVENTS

Meetings

Schedule Updates

Cost Report Updates

Change Proposals

Material Deliveries

Special Information/Instructions

Arch./Owner Direction Received

DAILY DIARY

WEATHER/TEMP.   8 A.M.   12 NOON   4 P.M.

EXPENSES

Deadman: Any kind of anchoring device set into the ground to anchor the lower end of a guy wire.

16 NOVEMBER

SATURDAY

	WORK	CAL
MONTH TO DATE	11	16
MONTH REMAINING	9	15
YEAR TO DATE	224	320
YEAR REMAINING	30	43

JOB NO. APPOINTMENTS/EVENTS/CALLS

DAILY DIARY

NOVEMBER 17

SUNDAY

	WORK	CAL
MONTH TO DATE	11	17
MONTH REMAINING	9	14
YEAR TO DATE	224	321
YEAR REMAINING	30	42

JOB NO. APPOINTMENTS/EVENTS/CALLS

DAILY DIARY

WEEK Beginning 18 NOVEMBER
Ending 24 NOVEMBER

WEEKLY EVENT CHECKLIST

Job meetings and preparation ⌐	Submittals for pending work in/appr ⌐	All permits in place ⌐
Special meetings ⌐	All other submittals in/approved ⌐	Req testing/inspections arranged ⌐
Dinners and seminars ⌐	Shop drawing log up to date ⌐	Inspection certificates received ⌐
Assemble schedule information ⌐	All sub change proposals in ⌐	Safety inspections performed ⌐
Complete schedule updates ⌐	All change proposals to owner prep'd ⌐	Safety recommendations acted on ⌐
Requests out for all required information ⌐	Submitted change proposals appr ⌐	Field reports complete ⌐
Outstanding sub/supplier responses ⌐	Change order logs up to date ⌐	Special photos taken ⌐
Outstanding owner responses ⌐	Required bonds received for all subs ⌐	_____ ⌐
Outstanding architect/engineer responses ⌐	Certificates of insurance rec'd for all subs (proper amounts) ⌐	_____ ⌐
Critical material deliveries confirmed ⌐		_____ ⌐
Shop drawings for ongoing work in/appr ⌐	Equipment/scaffolding release forms in ⌐	_____ ⌐

TO DO

Item	Job No.	Item	Job No.

WEEKLY MILESTONE UPDATE

	Planned Date	Actual Date	Variance

DAILY MINDER

√ Verify approval of outstanding change orders.
√ Submit requisition(s) to owner(s).
√ Authorize/approve sub and supplier payments.
√ Key material deliveries confirmed?

WORK	CAL

		WORK	CAL
MONTH TO DATE		12	18
MONTH REMAINING		8	13
YEAR TO DATE		225	322
YEAR REMAINING		29	41

NOVEMBER **18**

MONDAY

KEY EVENTS

Meetings

Schedule Updates

Cost Report Updates

Change Proposals

Material Deliveries

Special Information/Instructions

Arch./Owner Direction Received

DAILY DIARY

JOB NO. APPOINTMENTS/EVENTS/CALLS

7 A.M.

8 A.M.

9 A.M.

10 A.M.

11 A.M.

12 NOON

1 P.M.

2 P.M.

3 P.M.

4 P.M.

5 P.M.

6 P.M.

WEATHER/TEMP. 8 A.M. 12 NOON 4 P.M.

EXPENSES

OCTOBER							NOVEMBER							DECEMBER						
S	M	T	W	T	F	S	S	M	T	W	T	F	S	S	M	T	W	T	F	S
		1	2	3	4	5						1	2	1	2	3	4	5	6	7
6	7	8	9	10	11	12	3	4	5	6	7	8	9	8	9	10	11	12	13	14
13	14	15	16	17	18	19	10	11	12	13	14	15	16	15	16	17	18	19	20	21
20	21	22	23	24	25	26	17	18	19	20	21	22	23	22	23	24	25	26	27	28
27	28	29	30	31			24	25	26	27	28	29	30	29	30	31				

19

NOVEMBER

TUESDAY

MONTH TO DATE	13	19
MONTH REMAINING	7	12
YEAR TO DATE	226	323
YEAR REMAINING	28	40

DAILY MINDER

√ Verify receipt of all sub and supplier payment requisitions.

√ Authorize/approve sub and supplier payments.

√ Assemble all schedule update information.

√ All cost report information assembled?

JOB NO. APPOINTMENTS/EVENTS/CALLS

7 A.M.

8 A.M.

9 A.M.

10 A.M.

11 A.M.

12 NOON

1 P.M.

2 P.M.

3 P.M.

4 P.M.

5 P.M.

6 P.M.

KEY EVENTS

Meetings

Schedule Updates

Cost Report Updates

Change Proposals

Material Deliveries

Special Information/Instructions

Arch./Owner Direction Received

DAILY DIARY

WEATHER/TEMP.   8A.M.   12NOON   4P.M.

EXPENSES

Web: That portion of a beam or girder between the flanges.

DAILY MINDER

√ Verify approval of outstanding change orders.

√ Submit requisition(s) to owner(s).

√ Schedule update complete?

√ Key material deliveries confirmed?

WORK	CAL	
MONTH TO DATE	14	20
MONTH REMAINING	6	11
YEAR TO DATE	227	324
YEAR REMAINING	27	39

NOVEMBER
20
WEDNESDAY

KEY EVENTS

Meetings

Schedule Updates

Cost Report Updates

Change Proposals

Material Deliveries

Special Information/Instructions

Arch./Owner Direction Received

DAILY DIARY

WEATHER/TEMP.   8A.M.   12NOON   4P.M.

EXPENSES

JOB NO.   APPOINTMENTS/EVENTS/CALLS

7 A.M.

8 A.M.

9 A.M.

10 A.M.

11 A.M.

12 NOON

1 P.M.

2 P.M.

3 P.M.

4 P.M.

5 P.M.

6 P.M.

OCTOBER								NOVEMBER								DECEMBER						
S	M	T	W	T	F	S		S	M	T	W	T	F	S		S	M	T	W	T	F	S
		1	2	3	4	5							1	2		1	2	3	4	5	6	7
6	7	8	9	10	11	12		3	4	5	6	7	8	9		8	9	10	11	12	13	14
13	14	15	16	17	18	19		10	11	12	13	14	15	16		15	16	17	18	19	20	21
20	21	22	23	24	25	26		17	18	19	20	21	22	23		22	23	24	25	26	27	28
27	28	29	30	31				24	25	26	27	28	29	30		29	30	31				

21

NOVEMBER
THURSDAY

WORK	CAL
MONTH TO DATE	15	21
MONTH REMAINING	5	10
YEAR TO DATE	228	325
YEAR REMAINING	26	38

DAILY MINDER

√ Is the turkey big enough?

JOB NO. APPOINTMENTS/EVENTS/CALLS

7 A.M.

8 A.M.

9 A.M.

10 A.M.

11 A.M.

12 NOON

1 P.M.

2 P.M.

3 P.M.

4 P.M.

5 P.M.

6 P.M.

KEY EVENTS

Meetings

Schedule Updates

Cost Report Updates

Change Proposals

Material Deliveries

Special Information/Instructions

Arch./Owner Direction Received

DAILY DIARY

WEATHER/TEMP.   8 A.M.   12 NOON   4 P.M.

EXPENSES

Zenith: A point directly overhead, the upward extension of a plumb line.

DAILY MINDER

√ Prepare requisition(s) to owner(s).

√ Schedule update complete?

√ All monthly reports and narratives complete?

√ Cost report complete?

KEY EVENTS

Meetings

Schedule Updates

Cost Report Updates

Change Proposals

Material Deliveries

Special Information/Instructions

Arch./Owner Direction Received

DAILY DIARY

WEATHER/TEMP.   8A.M.   12NOON   4P.M.

EXPENSES

	WORK	CAL
MONTH TO DATE	16	22
MONTH REMAINING	4	9
YEAR TO DATE	229	326
YEAR REMAINING	25	37

NOVEMBER
22
FRIDAY

JOB NO.   APPOINTMENTS/EVENTS/CALLS

7A.M.

8A.M.

9A.M.

10A.M.

11A.M.

12NOON

1P.M.

2P.M.

3P.M.

4P.M.

5P.M.

6P.M.

OCTOBER						
S	M	T	W	T	F	S
		1	2	3	4	5
6	7	8	9	10	11	12
13	14	15	16	17	18	19
20	21	22	23	24	25	26
27	28	29	30	31		

NOVEMBER						
S	M	T	W	T	F	S
					1	2
3	4	5	6	7	8	9
10	11	12	13	14	15	16
17	18	19	20	21	22	23
24	25	26	27	28	29	30

DECEMBER						
S	M	T	W	T	F	S
1	2	3	4	5	6	7
8	9	10	11	12	13	14
15	16	17	18	19	20	21
22	23	24	25	26	27	28
29	30	31				

23

NOVEMBER

SATURDAY

	WORK	CAL
MONTH TO DATE	16	23
MONTH REMAINING	4	8
YEAR TO DATE	229	327
YEAR REMAINING	25	36

	WORK	CAL
MONTH TO DATE	16	24
MONTH REMAINING	4	7
YEAR TO DATE	229	328
YEAR REMAINING	25	35

NOVEMBER

SUNDAY

24

JOB NO. APPOINTMENTS/EVENTS/CALLS

JOB NO. APPOINTMENTS/EVENTS/CALLS

DAILY DIARY

DAILY DIARY

WEEK Beginning 25 NOVEMBER
Ending   1 DECEMBER

WEEKLY EVENT CHECKLIST

Job meetings and preparation   Submittals for pending work in/appr   All permits in place

Special meetings   All other submittals in/approved   Req testing/inspections arranged

Dinners and seminars   Shop drawing log up to date   Inspection certificates received

Assemble schedule information   All sub change proposals in   Safety inspections performed

Complete schedule updates   All change proposals to owner prep'd   Safety recommendations acted on

Requests out for all required information   Submitted change proposals appr   Field reports complete

Outstanding sub/supplier responses   Change order logs up to date   Special photos taken

Outstanding owner responses   Required bonds received for all subs

Outstanding architect/engineer responses   Certificates of insurance rec'd for all

Critical material deliveries confirmed   subs (proper amounts)

Shop drawings for ongoing work in/appr   Equipment/scaffolding release forms in

TO DO

Item	Job No.	Item	Job No.

WEEKLY MILESTONE UPDATE

	Planned Date	Actual Date	Variance

25

NOVEMBER
MONDAY

WORK CAL		
MONTH TO DATE	17	25
MONTH REMAINING	3	6
YEAR TO DATE	230	329
YEAR REMAINING	24	34

DAILY MINDER

√ Submit requisition(s) to owner(s).

√ Authorize/approve sub and supplier payments.

√ Job meeting minutes and reports complete.

√ Cost report complete?

JOB NO. APPOINTMENTS/EVENTS/CALLS

7 A.M.

8 A.M.

9 A.M.

10 A.M.

11 A.M.

12 NOON

1 P.M.

2 P.M.

3 P.M.

4 P.M.

5 P.M.

6 P.M.

KEY EVENTS

Meetings

Schedule Updates

Cost Report Updates

Change Proposals

Material Deliveries

Special Information/Instructions

Arch./Owner Direction Received

DAILY DIARY

WEATHER/TEMP.	8 A.M.	12 NOON	4 P.M.

EXPENSES

Pike Pole: A tool with a sharp metal point used to hold telephone or other poles in an upright position while installing or removing them.

DAILY MINDER

√ All required design info. received?
√ All required submittals in and approved?
√ Current schedule commitments in-process?
√ Request/receive outstanding design info?

KEY EVENTS

Meetings

Schedule Updates

Cost Report Updates

Change Proposals

Material Deliveries

Special Information/Instructions

Arch./Owner Direction Received

DAILY DIARY

WEATHER/TEMP.   8A.M.   12NOON   4P.M.

EXPENSES

WORK CAL
NOVEMBER
26
MONTH TO DATE	18	26
MONTH REMAINING	2	5
YEAR TO DATE	231	330
YEAR REMAINING	23	33

TUESDAY

JOB NO. APPOINTMENTS/EVENTS/CALLS

7A.M.

8A.M.

9A.M.

10A.M.

11A.M.

12NOON

1P.M.

2P.M.

3P.M.

4P.M.

5P.M.

6P.M.

OCTOBER						
S	M	T W T	F	S		
		1	2	3	4	5
6	7	8	9	10	11	12
13	14	15	16	17	18	19
20	21	22	23	24	25	26
27	28	29	30	31		

NOVEMBER						
S	M	T W T	F	S		
					1	2
3	4	5	6	7	8	9
10	11	12	13	14	15	16
17	18	19	20	21	22	23
24	25	26	27	28	29	30

DECEMBER						
S	M	T W T	F	S		
1	2	3	4	5	6	7
8	9	10	11	12	13	14
15	16	17	18	19	20	21
22	23	24	25	26	27	28
29	30	31				

27

NOVEMBER
WEDNESDAY

WORK CAL		
MONTH TO DATE	19	27
MONTH REMAINING	1	4
YEAR TO DATE	232	331
YEAR REMAINING	22	32

JOB NO. APPOINTMENTS/EVENTS/CALLS

7 A.M.

8 A.M.

9 A.M.

10 A.M.

11 A.M.

12 NOON

1 P.M.

2 P.M.

3 P.M.

4 P.M.

5 P.M.

6 P.M.

DAILY MINDER

√ This month's schedule update complete?
√ Key material deliveries confirmed?
√ Requisition(s) submitted to owner(s)?
√ Cost reports prepared?

KEY EVENTS

Meetings

Schedule Updates

Cost Report Updates

Change Proposals

Material Deliveries

Special Information/Instructions

Arch./Owner Direction Received

DAILY DIARY

WEATHER/TEMP.   8 A.M.   12 NOON   4 P.M.

EXPENSES

Bradawl: A short, straight awl with a chisel or cutting edge at the end, non-tapering.

DAILY MINDER

√ Schedule update complete?

√ Job meeting minutes and reports complete?

√ Reports and narratives complete?

√ Progress photos taken?

	WORK	CAL
MONTH TO DATE	19	28
MONTH REMAINING	1	3
YEAR TO DATE	232	332
YEAR REMAINING	22	31

NOVEMBER
Thanksgiving

28

THURSDAY

KEY EVENTS

Meetings

Schedule Updates

Cost Report Updates

Change Proposals

Material Deliveries

Special Information/Instructions

Arch./Owner Direction Received

DAILY DIARY

WEATHER/TEMP.   8A.M.   12NOON   4P.M.

EXPENSES

JOB NO.   APPOINTMENTS/EVENTS/CALLS

7 A.M.

8 A.M.

9 A.M.

10 A.M.

11 A.M.

12 NOON

1 P.M.

2 P.M.

3 P.M.

4 P.M.

5 P.M.

6 P.M.

OCTOBER						
S	M	T	W	T	F	S
		1	2	3	4	5
6	7	8	9	10	11	12
13	14	15	16	17	18	19
20	21	22	23	24	25	26
27	28	29	30	31		

NOVEMBER						
S	M	T	W	T	F	S
					1	2
3	4	5	6	7	8	9
10	11	12	13	14	15	16
17	18	19	20	21	22	23
24	25	26	27	28	29	30

DECEMBER						
S	M	T	W	T	F	S
1	2	3	4	5	6	7
8	9	10	11	12	13	14
15	16	17	18	19	20	21
22	23	24	25	26	27	28
29	30	31				

29

NOVEMBER
FRIDAY

WORK	CAL
MONTH TO DATE	20	29
MONTH REMAINING	0	2
YEAR TO DATE	233	333
YEAR REMAINING	21	30

JOB NO. APPOINTMENTS/EVENTS/CALLS

7 A.M.

8 A.M.

9 A.M.

10 A.M.

11 A.M.

12 NOON

1 P.M.

2 P.M.

3 P.M.

4 P.M.

5 P.M.

6 P.M.

DAILY MINDER

√ Minutes and reports complete?
√ Progress photos taken?
√ Requisition(s) submitted to owner(s)?
√ Next week's schedules confirmed?

KEY EVENTS

Meetings

Schedule Updates

Cost Report Updates

Change Proposals

Material Deliveries

Special Information/Instructions

Arch./Owner Direction Received

DAILY DIARY

WEATHER/TEMP.   8 A.M.   12 NOON   4 P.M.

EXPENSES

Chequer: An ornamental arrangement used in furniture making consisting of squares.

DAILY MINDER

WORK CAL
MONTH TO DATE   20   30
MONTH REMAINING   0   1
YEAR TO DATE   233 334
YEAR REMAINING   21   29

NOVEMBER
30
SATURDAY

KEY EVENTS

Meetings

Schedule Updates

Cost Report Updates

Change Proposals

Material Deliveries

Special Information/Instructions

Arch./Owner Direction Received

DAILY DIARY

WEATHER/TEMP.   8A.M.   12NOON   4P.M.

EXPENSES

JOB NO. APPOINTMENTS/EVENTS/CALLS

7 A.M.

8 A.M.

9 A.M.

10 A.M.

11 A.M.

12 NOON

1 P.M.

2 P.M.

3 P.M.

4 P.M.

5 P.M.

6 P.M.

OCTOBER						
S	M	T	W	T	F	S
		1	2	3	4	5
6	7	8	9	10	11	12
13	14	15	16	17	18	19
20	21	22	23	24	25	26
27	28	29	30	31		

NOVEMBER						
S	M	T	W	T	F	S
					1	2
3	4	5	6	7	8	9
10	11	12	13	14	15	16
17	18	19	20	21	22	23
24	25	26	27	28	29	30

DECEMBER						
S	M	T	W	T	F	S
1	2	3	4	5	6	7
8	9	10	11	12	13	14
15	16	17	18	19	20	21
22	23	24	25	26	27	28
29	30	31				

DECEMBER

21 Working Days

31 Calendar Days

NOVEMBER						
S	M	T	W	T	F	S
					1	2
3	4	5	6	7	8	9
10	11	12	13	14	15	16
17	18	19	20	21	22	23
24	25	26	27	28	29	30

DECEMBER						
S	M	T	W	T	F	S
1	2	3	4	5	6	7
8	9	10	11	12	13	14
15	16	17	18	19	20	21
22	23	24	25	26	27	28
29	30	31				

JANUARY						
S	M	T	W	T	F	S
			1	2	3	4
5	6	7	8	9	10	11
12	13	14	15	16	17	18
19	20	21	22	23	24	25
26	27	28	29	30	31	

MONTHLY KEY ACTIVITY UPDATE

Job/C.O. No.	Description	Planned Date	Actual Date	Variance	Remarks

MONTHLY SCHEDULE UPDATE SUMMARY

Job/C.O. No.	Activities	Original Duration	Days Spent	Days Remaining	Status/Remarks

MONTHLY RECAP

S	M	T	W	T	F	S
1	2	3	4	5	6	7
8	9	10	11	12	13	14
15	16	17	18	19	20	21
22	23	24	25	26	27	28
29	30	31				

DECEMBER

MONTHLY EVENT CHECKLIST

Schedule updates complete

Requests out for all required info.

Outstanding sub/supplier responses rec'd

Outstanding owner responses rec'd

Outstanding arch./eng. responses rec'd

Critical material deliveries confirmed

Shop drawings for ongoing work in/appr

Submittals for pending work in/appr

All other submittals in/approved

All sub change proposals in

All change proposals to owner prepared

Submitted change proposals approved

Guarantees/warrantees rec'd

Inspection certificates rec'd

As-built drawings rec'd

Safety inspections performed

Safety reports complete

Narratives complete

Sub/supplier contract(s) rec'd

Requisition(s) submitted to owner(s)

Sub/supplier adjustments complete

Progress photos taken

Job cost report info. assembled

Job cost reports complete

Other:

_____

_____

CRITICAL ITEM COST REPORT SUMMARY

Job/CO No.	Description	(A) Budget $ Amount	(B) Cost To Date	(C) Cost Remaining	(D) Total Commitment (B + C)	(E) +/− (A − D)

CHANGE ORDER SUMMARY

Job No.	C.O. No.	Description	Submission Date Required	Actual	Approval Date Required	Actual	Remarks

1 DECEMBER
SUNDAY

DAILY MINDER

JOB NO. APPOINTMENTS/EVENTS/CALLS

7 A.M.

8 A.M.

9 A.M.

10 A.M.

11 A.M.

12 NOON

1 P.M.

2 P.M.

3 P.M.

4 P.M.

5 P.M.

6 P.M.

KEY EVENTS
Meetings

Schedule Updates

Cost Report Updates

Change Proposals

Material Deliveries

Special Information/Instructions

Arch./Owner Direction Received

DAILY DIARY

WEATHER/TEMP.	8 A.M.	12 NOON	4 P.M.

EXPENSES

Deal: Plank or board cut to standard size, 11" wide x 12" long x 2 1/2" thick.

WEEK Beginning 2 DECEMBER
Ending   8 DECEMBER

WEEKLY EVENT CHECKLIST

Job meetings and preparation	Submittals for pending work in/appr	All permits in place
Special meetings	All other submittals in/approved	Req testing/inspections arranged
Dinners and seminars	Shop drawing log up to date	Inspection certificates received
Assemble schedule information	All sub change proposals in	Safety inspections performed
Complete schedule updates	All change proposals to owner prep'd	Safety recommendations acted on
Requests out for all required information	Submitted change proposals appr	Field reports complete
Outstanding sub/supplier responses	Change order logs up to date	Special photos taken
Outstanding owner responses	Required bonds received for all subs	_____
Outstanding architect/engineer responses	Certificates of insurance rec'd for all subs (proper amounts)	_____
Critical material deliveries confirmed		_____
Shop drawings for ongoing work in/appr	Equipment/scaffolding release forms in	_____

TO DO

Item	Job No.	Item	Job No.

WEEKLY MILESTONE UPDATE

	Planned Date	Actual Date	Variance

2 DECEMBER

MONDAY

JOB NO. APPOINTMENTS/EVENTS/CALLS

7 A.M.

8 A.M.

9 A.M.

10 A.M.

11 A.M.

12 NOON

1 P.M.

2 P.M.

3 P.M.

4 P.M.

5 P.M.

6 P.M.

DAILY MINDER

√November requisition(s) submitted?

√Nov. cost reports complete?

√Required submittals in/approved?

√Requisitions submitted?

KEY EVENTS

Meetings

Schedule Updates

Cost Report Updates

Change Proposals

Material Deliveries

Special Information/Instructions

Arch./Owner Direction Received

DAILY DIARY

WEATHER/TEMP.   8 A.M.   12 NOON   4 P.M.

EXPENSES

Entablature: In classic architecture the cornice, frieze, and architrave, resting horizontally upon the columns.

DAILY MINDER

√ Key material deliveries confirmed?
√ Preparations made for winter protection?
√ Current schedule commitments in-process?
√ Schedule updates complete?

WORK CAL

	MONTH TO DATE	2	3
	MONTH REMAINING	19	28
	YEAR TO DATE	235	337
	YEAR REMAINING	19	28

DECEMBER

3

TUESDAY

KEY EVENTS

Meetings

Schedule Updates

Cost Report Updates

Change Proposals

Material Deliveries

Special Information/Instructions

Arch./Owner Direction Received

DAILY DIARY

JOB NO.   APPOINTMENTS/EVENTS/CALLS

7 A.M.

8 A.M.

9 A.M.

10 A.M.

11 A.M.

12 NOON

1 P.M.

2 P.M.

3 P.M.

WEATHER/TEMP.   8 A.M.   12 NOON   4 P.M.

4 P.M.

EXPENSES

5 P.M.

6 P.M.

NOVEMBER						
S	M	T	W	T	F	S
						1 2
3	4	5	6	7	8	9
10	11	12	13	14	15	16
17	18	19	20	21	22	23
24	25	26	27	28	29	30

DECEMBER						
S	M	T	W	T	F	S
1	2	3	4	5	6	7
8	9	10	11	12	13	14
15	16	17	18	19	20	21
22	23	24	25	26	27	28
29	30	31				

JANUARY						
S	M	T	W	T	F	S
			1	2	3	4
5	6	7	8	9	10	11
12	13	14	15	16	17	18
19	20	21	22	23	24	25
26	27	28	29	30	31	

4

DECEMBER
WEDNESDAY

WORK	CAL
MONTH TO DATE	3	4
MONTH REMAINING	18	27
YEAR TO DATE	236	338
YEAR REMAINING	18	27

DAILY MINDER

√All required design info. received?
√All change order proposals submitted?
√Verify receipt of last month's payments.

JOB NO. APPOINTMENTS/EVENTS/CALLS

7 A.M.

8 A.M.

9 A.M.

10 A.M.

11 A.M.

12 NOON

1 P.M.

2 P.M.

3 P.M.

4 P.M.

5 P.M.

6 P.M.

KEY EVENTS

Meetings

Schedule Updates

Cost Report Updates

Change Proposals

Material Deliveries

Special Information/Instructions

Arch./Owner Direction Received

DAILY DIARY

WEATHER/TEMP.   8 A.M.   12 NOON   4 P.M.

EXPENSES

Upset: The buckling of wood fibers due to crushing of a piece of timber.

DAILY MINDER

√ Job meeting minutes and reports complete?
√ Key material deliveries confirmed?
√ Next week's schedules confirmed?

WORK CAL
MONTH TO DATE   4   5
MONTH REMAINING   17   27
YEAR TO DATE   237   339
YEAR REMAINING   17   26

DECEMBER

5

THURSDAY

KEY EVENTS

Meetings

Schedule Updates

Cost Report Updates

Change Proposals

Material Deliveries

Special Information/Instructions

Arch./Owner Direction Received

DAILY DIARY

WEATHER/TEMP.   8A.M.   12NOON   4P.M.

EXPENSES

JOB NO.   APPOINTMENTS/EVENTS/CALLS

7A.M.

8A.M.

9A.M.

10A.M.

11A.M.

12NOON

1P.M.

2P.M.

3P.M.

4P.M.

5P.M.

6P.M.

NOVEMBER							DECEMBER							JANUARY						
S	M	T	W	T	F	S	S	M	T	W	T	F	S	S	M	T	W	T	F	S
					1	2	1	2	3	4	5	6	7				1	2	3	4
3	4	5	6	7	8	9	8	9	10	11	12	13	14	5	6	7	8	9	10	11
10	11	12	13	14	15	16	15	16	17	18	19	20	21	12	13	14	15	16	17	18
17	18	19	20	21	22	23	22	23	24	25	26	27	28	19	20	21	22	23	24	25
24	25	26	27	28	29	30	29	30	31					26	27	28	29	30	31	

6 DECEMBER

FRIDAY

WORK	CAL
MONTH TO DATE	5	6
MONTH REMAINING	16	25
YEAR TO DATE	238	340
YEAR REMAINING	16	25

JOB NO. APPOINTMENTS/EVENTS/CALLS

7 A.M.

8 A.M.

9 A.M.

10 A.M.

11 A.M.

12 NOON

1 P.M.

2 P.M.

3 P.M.

4 P.M.

5 P.M.

6 P.M.

DAILY MINDER

√ Job meeting minutes and reports complete?

√ Jobsite safety reviews performed?

√ Winter precautions taken?

√ Dinner reservations made for the weekend?

KEY EVENTS

Meetings

Schedule Updates

Cost Report Updates

Change Proposals

Material Deliveries

Special Information/Instructions

Arch./Owner Direction Received

DAILY DIARY

WEATHER/TEMP.   8A.M.   12NOON   4P.M.

EXPENSES

Couple-close: Pair of rafters which are framed together with a tie fixed at the foot, or with a dollar beam.

7

DECEMBER

SATURDAY

	WORK	CAL
MONTH TO DATE	5	7
MONTH REMAINING	16	24
YEAR TO DATE	238	341
YEAR REMAINING	16	24

DECEMBER

SUNDAY

8

	WORK	CAL
MONTH TO DATE	5	8
MONTH REMAINING	16	23
YEAR TO DATE	238	342
YEAR REMAINING	16	23

JOB NO. APPOINTMENTS/EVENTS/CALLS

JOB NO. APPOINTMENTS/EVENTS/CALLS

DAILY DIARY

DAILY DIARY

WEEK Beginning 9 DECEMBER
Ending 15 DECEMBER

WEEKLY EVENT CHECKLIST

Job meetings and preparation	Submittals for pending work in/appr	All permits in place
Special meetings	All other submittals in/approved	Req testing/inspections arranged
Dinners and seminars	Shop drawing log up to date	Inspection certificates received
Assemble schedule information	All sub change proposals in	Safety inspections performed
Complete schedule updates	All change proposals to owner prep'd	Safety recommendations acted on
Requests out for all required information	Submitted change proposals appr	Field reports complete
Outstanding sub/supplier responses	Change order logs up to date	Special photos taken
Outstanding owner responses	Required bonds received for all subs	
Outstanding architect/engineer responses	Certificates of insurance rec'd for all	
Critical material deliveries confirmed	subs (proper amounts)	
Shop drawings for ongoing work in/appr	Equipment/scaffolding release forms in	

TO DO

Item	Job No.	Item	Job No.

WEEKLY MILESTONE UPDATE

	Planned Date	Actual Date	Variance

DAILY MINDER

√Verify receipt of last month's payment.
√Key material deliveries confirmed?
√Current schedule commitments in-process?
√Current changes submitted/approved?

KEY EVENTS

Meetings

Schedule Updates

Cost Report Updates

Change Proposals

Material Deliveries

Special Information/Instructions

Arch./Owner Direction Received

DAILY DIARY

WEATHER/TEMP.　8A.M.　12NOON　4P.M.

EXPENSES

	WORK	CAL
MONTH TO DATE	6	9
MONTH REMAINING	15	22
YEAR TO DATE	239	343
YEAR REMAINING	15	22

DECEMBER

9

MONDAY

JOB NO.　APPOINTMENTS/EVENTS/CALLS

7A.M.

8A.M.

9A.M.

10A.M.

11A.M.

12NOON

1P.M.

2P.M.

3P.M.

4P.M.

5P.M.

6P.M.

NOVEMBER						
S	M	T	W	T	F	S
					1	2
3	4	5	6	7	8	9
10	11	12	13	14	15	16
17	18	19	20	21	22	23
24	25	26	27	28	29	30

DECEMBER						
S	M	T	W	T	F	S
1	2	3	4	5	6	7
8	9	10	11	12	13	14
15	16	17	18	19	20	21
22	23	24	25	26	27	28
29	30	31				

JANUARY						
S	M	T	W	T	F	S
			1	2	3	4
5	6	7	8	9	10	11
12	13	14	15	16	17	18
19	20	21	22	23	24	25
26	27	28	29	30	31	

10 DECEMBER

TUESDAY

WORK	CAL
MONTH TO DATE	7	10
MONTH REMAINING	14	21
YEAR TO DATE	240	344
YEAR REMAINING	14	21

DAILY MINDER

√ All requests for change proposals out?
√ Field reports up-to-date?
√ Required submittals in/approved?

JOB NO. APPOINTMENTS/EVENTS/CALLS

7 A.M.

8 A.M.

9 A.M.

10 A.M.

11 A.M.

12 NOON

1 P.M.

2 P.M.

3 P.M.

4 P.M.

5 P.M.

6 P.M.

KEY EVENTS

Meetings

Schedule Updates

Cost Report Updates

Change Proposals

Material Deliveries

Special Information/Instructions

Arch./Owner Direction Received

DAILY DIARY

WEATHER/TEMP.   8 A.M.   12 NOON   4 P.M.

EXPENSES

Ancon: A projection left on a block of masonry to serve as a bracket or console.

DAILY MINDER

√ Key material deliveries confirmed?

√ Meeting minutes received/prepared?

√ Change proposals submitted/approval?

WORK CAL

MONTH TO DATE	8	11
MONTH REMAINING	13	20
YEAR TO DATE	241	345
YEAR REMAINING	13	20

DECEMBER

11

WEDNESDAY

KEY EVENTS

Meetings

Schedule Updates

Cost Report Updates

Change Proposals

Material Deliveries

Special Information/Instructions

Arch./Owner Direction Received

DAILY DIARY

JOB NO. APPOINTMENTS/EVENTS/CALLS

7 A.M.

8 A.M.

9 A.M.

10 A.M.

11 A.M.

12 NOON

1 P.M.

2 P.M.

3 P.M.

4 P.M.

5 P.M.

6 P.M.

WEATHER/TEMP. 8 A.M. 12 NOON 4 P.M.

EXPENSES

	NOVEMBER							DECEMBER							JANUARY					
S	M	T	W	T	F	S	S	M	T	W	T	F	S	S	M	T	W	T	F	S
					1	2	1	2	3	4	5	6	7				1	2	3	4
3	4	5	6	7	8	9	8	9	10	11	12	13	14	5	6	7	8	9	10	11
10	11	12	13	14	15	16	15	16	17	18	19	20	21	12	13	14	15	16	17	18
17	18	19	20	21	22	23	22	23	24	25	26	27	28	19	20	21	22	23	24	25
24	25	26	27	28	29	30	29	30	31					26	27	28	29	30	31	

12

DECEMBER
Hanukkah

THURSDAY

	WORK	CAL
MONTH TO DATE	9	12
MONTH REMAINING	12	19
YEAR TO DATE	242	346
YEAR REMAINING	12	19

DAILY MINDER

√ Assemble all schedule update information.

√ Job meeting minutes and reports complete?

√ November payments received?

JOB NO.   APPOINTMENTS/EVENTS/CALLS

7 A.M.

8 A.M.

9 A.M.

10 A.M.

11 A.M.

12 NOON

1 P.M.

2 P.M.

3 P.M.

4 P.M.

5 P.M.

6 P.M.

KEY EVENTS

Meetings

Schedule Updates

Cost Report Updates

Change Proposals

Material Deliveries

Special Information/Instructions

Arch./Owner Direction Received

DAILY DIARY

WEATHER/TEMP.   8 A.M.   12 NOON   4 P.M.

EXPENSES

Lacing: Horizontal bracing between sharing members.

DAILY MINDER

√ All required design information received?

√ Preparations made for winter protection?

√ Next week's schedules confirmed?

WORK CAL

MONTH TO DATE	10	13
MONTH REMAINING	11	18
YEAR TO DATE	243	347
YEAR REMAINING	11	18

DECEMBER

13

FRIDAY

KEY EVENTS

Meetings

Schedule Updates

Cost Report Updates

Change Proposals

Material Deliveries

Special Information/Instructions

Arch./Owner Direction Received

DAILY DIARY

WEATHER/TEMP.　8 A.M.　　12 NOON　　4 P.M.

EXPENSES

JOB NO.　APPOINTMENTS/EVENTS/CALLS

7 A.M.

8 A.M.

9 A.M.

10 A.M.

11 A.M.

12 NOON

1 P.M.

2 P.M.

3 P.M.

4 P.M.

5 P.M.

6 P.M.

NOVEMBER							DECEMBER							JANUARY						
S	M	T	W	T	F	S	S	M	T	W	T	F	S	S	M	T	W	T	F	S
					1	2	1	2	3	4	5	6	7				1	2	3	4
3	4	5	6	7	8	9	8	9	10	11	12	13	14	5	6	7	8	9	10	11
10	11	12	13	14	15	16	15	16	17	18	19	20	21	12	13	14	15	16	17	18
17	18	19	20	21	22	23	22	23	24	25	26	27	28	19	20	21	22	23	24	25
24	25	26	27	28	29	30	29	30	31					26	27	28	29	30	31	

14 DECEMBER
SATURDAY

JOB NO.   APPOINTMENTS/EVENTS/CALLS

DAILY DIARY

DECEMBER 15
SUNDAY

JOB NO.   APPOINTMENTS/EVENTS/CALLS

DAILY DIARY

WEEK Beginning 16 DECEMBER
Ending 22 DECEMBER

WEEKLY EVENT CHECKLIST

Job meetings and preparation	Submittals for pending work in/appr ☐	All permits in place ☐
Special meetings	All other submittals in/approved ☐	Req testing/inspections arranged ☐
Dinners and seminars	Shop drawing log up to date ☐	Inspection certificates received ☐
Assemble schedule information ☐	All sub change proposals in ☐	Safety inspections performed ☐
Complete schedule updates	All change proposals to owner prep'd ☐	Safety recommendations acted on ☐
Requests out for all required information ☐	Submitted change proposals appr ☐	Field reports complete ☐
Outstanding sub/supplier responses	Change order logs up to date ☐	Special photos taken ☐
Outstanding owner responses	Required bonds received for all subs ☐	_____ ☐
Outstanding architect/engineer responses ☐	Certificates of insurance rec'd for all	_____
Critical material deliveries confirmed	subs (proper amounts) ☐	_____ ☐
Shop drawings for ongoing work in/appr ☐	Equipment/scaffolding release forms in ☐	

TO DO

Item	Job No.	Item	Job No.

WEEKLY MILESTONE UPDATE

	Planned Date	Actual Date	Variance

16

DECEMBER

MONDAY

DAILY MINDER

√ Verify approval of outstanding change orders?

√ Current schedule commitments in-process?

√ Change proposals submitted/approved?

JOB NO. APPOINTMENTS/EVENTS/CALLS

7 A.M.

8 A.M.

9 A.M.

10 A.M.

11 A.M.

12 NOON

1 P.M.

2 P.M.

3 P.M.

4 P.M.

5 P.M.

6 P.M.

KEY EVENTS

Meetings

Schedule Updates

Cost Report Updates

Change Proposals

Material Deliveries

Special Information/Instructions

Arch./Owner Direction Received

DAILY DIARY

WEATHER/TEMP.   8 A.M.   12 NOON   4 P.M.

EXPENSES

Corbie: Series of step-like projections on the sloping sides of a gable.

DAILY MINDER

√ Verify receipt of all sub and supplier payment requisitions?
√ Assemble all schedule update information?
√ Key material deliveries confirmed?
√ Sub change proposals requested/received?

KEY EVENTS

Meetings

Schedule Updates

Cost Report Updates

Change Proposals

Material Deliveries

Special Information/Instructions

Arch./Owner Direction Received

DAILY DIARY

WEATHER/TEMP.   8A.M.   12NOON   4P.M.

EXPENSES

WORK CAL

MONTH TO DATE	12	17
MONTH REMAINING	9	14
YEAR TO DATE	245	351
YEAR REMAINING	9	14

DECEMBER

17

TUESDAY

JOB NO. APPOINTMENTS/EVENTS/CALLS

7A.M.

8A.M.

9A.M.

10A.M.

11A.M.

12NOON

1P.M.

2P.M.

3P.M.

4P.M.

5P.M.

6P.M.

NOVEMBER								DECEMBER								JANUARY						
S	M	T	W	T	F	S		S	M	T	W	T	F	S		S	M	T	W	T	F	S
					1	2		1	2	3	4	5	6	7					1	2	3	4
3	4	5	6	7	8	9		8	9	10	11	12	13	14		5	6	7	8	9	10	11
10	11	12	13	14	15	16		15	16	17	18	19	20	21		12	13	14	15	16	17	18
17	18	19	20	21	22	23		22	23	24	25	26	27	28		19	20	21	22	23	24	25
24	25	26	27	28	29	30		29	30	31						26	27	28	29	30	31	

18 DECEMBER
WEDNESDAY

WORK	CAL
MONTH TO DATE	13	18
MONTH REMAINING	8	13
YEAR TO DATE	246	352
YEAR REMAINING	8	13

JOB NO. APPOINTMENTS/EVENTS/CALLS

7 A.M.

8 A.M.

9 A.M.

10 A.M.

11 A.M.

12 NOON

1 P.M.

2 P.M.

3 P.M.

4 P.M.

5 P.M.

6 P.M.

DAILY MINDER

√ Verify approval of outstanding change orders.

√ Schedule update complete?

√ Request/receive outstanding design info.?

√ Order your 1992 Construction Manager yet?

KEY EVENTS

Meetings

Schedule Updates

Cost Report Updates

Change Proposals

Material Deliveries

Special Information/Instructions

Arch./Owner Direction Received

DAILY DIARY

WEATHER/TEMP.   8A.M.   12NOON   4P.M.

EXPENSES

Lancet window: A narrow, high window, terminating with a lancet arch at the top.

DAILY MINDER

√ Verify receipt of all sub and supplier payment requisitions.
√ Assemble all schedule update information.
√ Job meeting minutes and reports complete?
√ Key material deliveries confirmed?

KEY EVENTS

Meetings

Schedule Updates

Cost Report Updates

Change Proposals

Material Deliveries

Special Information/Instructions

Arch./Owner Direction Received

DAILY DIARY

WEATHER/TEMP.   8A.M.   12NOON   4P.M.

EXPENSES

WORK CAL		
MONTH TO DATE	14	19
MONTH REMAINING	7	12
YEAR TO DATE	247	353
YEAR REMAINING	7	12

DECEMBER

19

THURSDAY

JOB NO. APPOINTMENTS/EVENTS/CALLS

7 A.M.

8 A.M.

9 A.M.

10 A.M.

11 A.M.

12 NOON

1 P.M.

2 P.M.

3 P.M.

4 P.M.

5 P.M.

6 P.M.

NOVEMBER						
S	M	T	W	T	F	S
					1	2
3	4	5	6	7	8	9
10	11	12	13	14	15	16
17	18	19	20	21	22	23
24	25	26	27	28	29	30

DECEMBER						
S	M	T	W	T	F	S
1	2	3	4	5	6	7
8	9	10	11	12	13	14
15	16	17	18	19	20	21
22	23	24	25	26	27	28
29	30	31				

JANUARY						
S	M	T	W	T	F	S
			1	2	3	4
5	6	7	8	9	10	11
12	13	14	15	16	17	18
19	20	21	22	23	24	25
26	27	28	29	30	31	

20

DECEMBER

FRIDAY

	WORK	CAL
MONTH TO DATE	15	20
MONTH REMAINING	6	11
YEAR TO DATE	248	354
YEAR REMAINING	6	11

DAILY MINDER

√ Three more shopping days.

√ Take the afternoon off.

JOB NO. APPOINTMENTS/EVENTS/CALLS

7 A.M.

8 A.M.

9 A.M.

10 A.M.

11 A.M.

12 NOON

1 P.M.

2 P.M.

3 P.M.

4 P.M.

5 P.M.

6 P.M.

KEY EVENTS

Meetings

Schedule Updates

Cost Report Updates

Change Proposals

Material Deliveries

Special Information/Instructions

Arch./Owner Direction Received

DAILY DIARY

WEATHER/TEMP.   8 A.M.   12 NOON   4 P.M.

EXPENSES

Quick Sweep: A term describing a circular work with a relatively small radius.

21

DECEMBER

SATURDAY

	WORK	CAL
MONTH TO DATE	15	21
MONTH REMAINING	6	10
YEAR TO DATE	248	355
YEAR REMAINING	6	10

JOB NO. APPOINTMENTS/EVENTS/CALLS

DAILY DIARY

22

DECEMBER

SUNDAY

	WORK	CAL
MONTH TO DATE	15	22
MONTH REMAINING	6	9
YEAR TO DATE	248	356
YEAR REMAINING	6	9

JOB NO. APPOINTMENTS/EVENTS/CALLS

DAILY DIARY

WEEK Beginning 23 DECEMBER
Ending 29 DECEMBER

WEEKLY EVENT CHECKLIST

Job meetings and preparation ___
Special meetings ___
Dinners and seminars ___
Assemble schedule information ___
Complete schedule updates ___
Requests out for all required information ___
Outstanding sub/supplier responses ___
Outstanding owner responses ___
Outstanding architect/engineer responses ___
Critical material deliveries confirmed ___
Shop drawings for ongoing work in/appr ___

Submittals for pending work in/appr ___
All other submittals in/approved ___
Shop drawing log up to date ___
All sub change proposals in ___
All change proposals to owner prep'd ___
Submitted change proposals appr ___
Change order logs up to date ___
Required bonds received for all subs ___
Certificates of insurance rec'd for all subs (proper amounts) ___
Equipment/scaffolding release forms in ___

All permits in place ___
Req testing/inspections arranged ___
Inspection certificates received ___
Safety inspections performed ___
Safety recommendations acted on ___
Field reports complete ___
Special photos taken ___
_____ ___
_____ ___
_____ ___

TO DO

Item	Job No.	Item	Job No.

WEEKLY MILESTONE UPDATE

	Planned Date	Actual Date	Variance

DAILY MINDER

√Verify approval of outstanding change orders.

√Submit requisition(s) to owner(s).

√Schedule update complete?

√All cost report information assembled?

WORK	CAL
MONTH TO DATE	16	23
MONTH REMAINING	5	8
YEAR TO DATE	249	357
YEAR REMAINING	5	8

DECEMBER

23

MONDAY

KEY EVENTS

Meetings

Schedule Updates

Cost Report Updates

Change Proposals

Material Deliveries

Special Information/Instructions

Arch./Owner Direction Received

DAILY DIARY

WEATHER/TEMP.   8A.M.   12NOON   4P.M.

EXPENSES

JOB NO.   APPOINTMENTS/EVENTS/CALLS

7A.M.

8A.M.

9A.M.

10A.M.

11A.M.

12NOON

1P.M.

2P.M.

3P.M.

4P.M.

5P.M.

6P.M.

| NOVEMBER | | | | | | | DECEMBER | | | | | | | JANUARY | | | | | | |
S	M	T	W	T	F	S	S	M	T	W	T	F	S	S	M	T	W	T	F	S
					1	2	1	2	3	4	5	6	7				1	2	3	4
3	4	5	6	7	8	9	8	9	10	11	12	13	14	5	6	7	8	9	10	11
10	11	12	13	14	15	16	15	16	17	18	19	20	21	12	13	14	15	16	17	18
17	18	19	20	21	22	23	22	23	24	25	26	27	28	19	20	21	22	23	24	25
24	25	26	27	28	29	30	29	30	31					26	27	28	29	30	31	

24 DECEMBER
TUESDAY

DAILY MINDER

√ Hope you were good this year.

JOB NO. APPOINTMENTS/EVENTS/CALLS

7 A.M.

8 A.M.

9 A.M.

10 A.M.

11 A.M.

12 NOON

1 P.M.

2 P.M.

3 P.M.

4 P.M.

5 P.M.

6 P.M.

KEY EVENTS

Meetings

Schedule Updates

Cost Report Updates

Change Proposals

Material Deliveries

Special Information/Instructions

Arch./Owner Direction Received

DAILY DIARY

WEATHER/TEMP.   8 A.M.   12 NOON   4 P.M.

EXPENSES

Transom: Any small window over a door or other window.

DAILY MINDER

√ Only people in construction work today.

WORK CAL

MONTH TO DATE	17	25
MONTH REMAINING	4	6
YEAR TO DATE	250	359
YEAR REMAINING	4	6

DECEMBER
Christmas
Day
WEDNESDAY
25

KEY EVENTS

Meetings

Schedule Updates

Cost Report Updates

Change Proposals

Material Deliveries

Special Information/Instructions

Arch./Owner Direction Received

DAILY DIARY

WEATHER/TEMP.   8A.M.   12NOON   4P.M.

EXPENSES

JOB NO.   APPOINTMENTS/EVENTS/CALLS

7A.M.

8A.M.

9A.M.

10A.M.

11A.M.

12NOON

1P.M.

2P.M.

3P.M.

4P.M.

5P.M.

6P.M.

26 DECEMBER
THURSDAY

WORK CAL		
MONTH TO DATE	18	26
MONTH REMAINING	3	5
YEAR TO DATE	251	360
YEAR REMAINING	2	5

JOB NO. APPOINTMENTS/EVENTS/CALLS

7 A.M.

8 A.M.

9 A.M.

10 A.M.

11 A.M.

12 NOON

1 P.M.

2 P.M.

3 P.M.

4 P.M.

5 P.M.

6 P.M.

DAILY MINDER

√ Submit requisition(s) to owner(s).

√ Authorize/approve sub and supplier payments.

√ Job meeting minutes and reports complete?

√ Cost report complete?

KEY EVENTS

Meetings

Schedule Updates

Cost Report Updates

Change Proposals

Material Deliveries

Special Information/Instructions

Arch./Owner Direction Received

DAILY DIARY

WEATHER/TEMP.   8 A.M.   12 NOON   4 P.M.

EXPENSES

Closure: Part of a brick used to close the end of a course.

DAILY MINDER

√ Submit requisition(s) to owner(s).
√ Authorize/approve sub and supplier payments.
√ Job meeting minutes and reports complete?
√ Cost report complete?

	WORK	CAL
MONTH TO DATE	19	27
MONTH REMAINING	2	4
YEAR TO DATE	252	361
YEAR REMAINING	2	4

DECEMBER
27
FRIDAY

KEY EVENTS

Meetings

Schedule Updates

Cost Report Updates

Change Proposals

Material Deliveries

Special Information/Instructions

Arch./Owner Direction Received

DAILY DIARY

WEATHER/TEMP.   8A.M.   12NOON   4P.M.

EXPENSES

JOB NO. APPOINTMENTS/EVENTS/CALLS

7A.M.

8A.M.

9A.M.

10A.M.

11A.M.

12NOON

1P.M.

2P.M.

3P.M.

4P.M.

5P.M.

6P.M.

	NOVEMBER								DECEMBER								JANUARY					
S	M	T	W	T	F	S		S	M	T	W	T	F	S		S	M	T	W	T	F	S
					1	2		1	2	3	4	5	6	7					1	2	3	4
3	4	5	6	7	8	9		8	9	10	11	12	13	14		5	6	7	8	9	10	11
10	11	12	13	14	15	16		15	16	17	18	19	20	21		12	13	14	15	16	17	18
17	18	19	20	21	22	23		22	23	24	25	26	27	28		19	20	21	22	23	24	25
24	25	26	27	28	29	30		29	30	31						26	27	28	29	30	31	

28

DECEMBER

SATURDAY

	WORK	CAL
MONTH TO DATE	19	28
MONTH REMAINING	2	3
YEAR TO DATE	252	362
YEAR REMAINING	2	3

JOB NO. APPOINTMENTS/EVENTS/CALLS

DAILY DIARY

	WORK	CAL
MONTH TO DATE	19	29
MONTH REMAINING	2	2
YEAR TO DATE	252	363
YEAR REMAINING	2	2

DECEMBER

29

SUNDAY

JOB NO. APPOINTMENTS/EVENTS/CALLS

DAILY DIARY

DAILY MINDER

√ Submit requisition(s) to owner(s).

√ Cost report complete?

√ Quarterly report info. assembled?

WORK	CAL
MONTH TO DATE	20	30
MONTH REMAINING	1	1
YEAR TO DATE	253	364
YEAR REMAINING	1	1

DECEMBER
30
MONDAY

KEY EVENTS

Meetings

Schedule Updates

Cost Report Updates

Change Proposals

Material Deliveries

Special Information/Instructions

Arch./Owner Direction Received

DAILY DIARY

WEATHER/TEMP.   8A.M.   12NOON   4P.M.

EXPENSES

JOB NO.   APPOINTMENTS/EVENTS/CALLS

7 A.M.

8 A.M.

9 A.M.

10 A.M.

11 A.M.

12 NOON

1 P.M.

2 P.M.

3 P.M.

4 P.M.

5 P.M.

6 P.M.

NOVEMBER						
S	M	T	W	T	F	S
						1	2
3	4	5	6	7	8	9
10	11	12	13	14	15	16
17	18	19	20	21	22	23
24	25	26	27	28	29	30

DECEMBER						
S	M	T	W	T	F	S
1	2	3	4	5	6	7
8	9	10	11	12	13	14
15	16	17	18	19	20	21
22	23	24	25	26	27	28
29	30	31				

JANUARY						
S	M	T	W	T	F	S
				1	2	3	4
5	6	7	8	9	10	11
12	13	14	15	16	17	18
19	20	21	22	23	24	25
26	27	28	29	30	31	

31 DECEMBER

TUESDAY

WORK CAL		
MONTH TO DATE	21	31
MONTH REMAINING	0	0
YEAR TO DATE	254	365
YEAR REMAINING	0	0

DAILY MINDER

√Verify approval of outstanding change orders.

√Submit requisition(s) to owner(s).

√Schedule update complete?

√Have a good time tonight; you deserve it.

JOB NO. APPOINTMENTS/EVENTS/CALLS

7 A.M.

8 A.M.

9 A.M.

10 A.M.

11 A.M.

12 NOON

1 P.M.

2 P.M.

3 P.M.

4 P.M.

5 P.M.

6 P.M.

KEY EVENTS

Meetings

Schedule Updates

Cost Report Updates

Change Proposals

Material Deliveries

Special Information/Instructions

Arch./Owner Direction Received

DAILY DIARY

WEATHER/TEMP.   8 A.M.   12 NOON   4 P.M.

EXPENSES

Beakhead: A drip moulding on the lowermost edge of the lowest point of a cornice.

1990

JANUARY
```
S  M  T  W  T  F  S
      1  2  3  4  5  6
 7  8  9 10 11 12 13
14 15 16 17 18 19 20
21 22 23 24 25 26 27
28 29 30 31
```

JULY
```
S  M  T  W  T  F  S
 1  2  3  4  5  6  7
 8  9 10 11 12 13 14
15 16 17 18 19 20 21
22 23 24 25 26 27 28
29 30 31
```

FEBRUARY
```
S  M  T  W  T  F  S
            1  2  3
 4  5  6  7  8  9 10
11 12 13 14 15 16 17
18 19 20 21 22 23 24
25 26 27 28
```

AUGUST
```
S  M  T  W  T  F  S
         1  2  3  4
 5  6  7  8  9 10 11
12 13 14 15 16 17 18
19 20 21 22 23 24 25
26 27 28 29 30 31
```

MARCH
```
S  M  T  W  T  F  S
            1  2  3
 4  5  6  7  8  9 10
11 12 13 14 15 16 17
18 19 20 21 22 23 24
25 26 27 28 29 30 31
```

SEPTEMBER
```
S  M  T  W  T  F  S
                  1
 2  3  4  5  6  7  8
 9 10 11 12 13 14 15
16 17 18 19 20 21 22
23 24 25 26 27 28 29
30
```

APRIL
```
S  M  T  W  T  F  S
 1  2  3  4  5  6  7
 8  9 10 11 12 13 14
15 16 17 18 19 20 21
22 23 24 25 26 27 28
29 30
```

OCTOBER
```
S  M  T  W  T  F  S
    1  2  3  4  5  6
 7  8  9 10 11 12 13
14 15 16 17 18 19 20
21 22 23 24 25 26 27
28 29 30 31
```

MAY
```
S  M  T  W  T  F  S
       1  2  3  4  5
 6  7  8  9 10 11 12
13 14 15 16 17 18 19
20 21 22 23 24 25 26
27 28 29 30 31
```

NOVEMBER
```
S  M  T  W  T  F  S
             1  2  3
 4  5  6  7  8  9 10
11 12 13 14 15 16 17
18 19 20 21 22 23 24
25 26 27 28 29 30
```

JUNE
```
S  M  T  W  T  F  S
                1  2
 3  4  5  6  7  8  9
10 11 12 13 14 15 16
17 18 19 20 21 22 23
24 25 26 27 28 29 30
```

DECEMBER
```
S  M  T  W  T  F  S
                   1
 2  3  4  5  6  7  8
 9 10 11 12 13 14 15
16 17 18 19 20 21 22
23 24 25 26 27 28 29
30 31
```

1991

JANUARY
```
S  M  T  W  T  F  S
       1  2  3  4  5
 6  7  8  9 10 11 12
13 14 15 16 17 18 19
20 21 22 23 24 25 26
27 28 29 30 31
```

JULY
```
S  M  T  W  T  F  S
    1  2  3  4  5  6
 7  8  9 10 11 12 13
14 15 16 17 18 19 20
21 22 23 24 25 26 27
28 29 30 31
```

FEBRUARY
```
S  M  T  W  T  F  S
                1  2
 3  4  5  6  7  8  9
10 11 12 13 14 15 16
17 18 19 20 21 22 23
24 25 26 27 28
```

AUGUST
```
S  M  T  W  T  F  S
             1  2  3
 4  5  6  7  8  9 10
11 12 13 14 15 16 17
18 19 20 21 22 23 24
25 26 27 28 29 30 31
```

MARCH
```
S  M  T  W  T  F  S
                1  2
 3  4  5  6  7  8  9
10 11 12 13 14 15 16
17 18 19 20 21 22 23
24 25 26 27 28 29 30
31
```

SEPTEMBER
```
S  M  T  W  T  F  S
 1  2  3  4  5  6  7
 8  9 10 11 12 13 14
15 16 17 18 19 20 21
22 23 24 25 26 27 28
29 30
```

APRIL
```
S  M  T  W  T  F  S
    1  2  3  4  5  6
 7  8  9 10 11 12 13
14 15 16 17 18 19 20
21 22 23 24 25 26 27
28 29 30
```

OCTOBER
```
S  M  T  W  T  F  S
       1  2  3  4  5
 6  7  8  9 10 11 12
13 14 15 16 17 18 19
20 21 22 23 24 25 26
27 28 29 30 31
```

MAY
```
S  M  T  W  T  F  S
          1  2  3  4
 5  6  7  8  9 10 11
12 13 14 15 16 17 18
19 20 21 22 23 24 25
26 27 28 29 30 31
```

NOVEMBER
```
S  M  T  W  T  F  S
                1  2
 3  4  5  6  7  8  9
10 11 12 13 14 15 16
17 18 19 20 21 22 23
24 25 26 27 28 29 30
```

JUNE
```
S  M  T  W  T  F  S
                   1
 2  3  4  5  6  7  8
 9 10 11 12 13 14 15
16 17 18 19 20 21 22
23 24 25 26 27 28 29
30
```

DECEMBER
```
S  M  T  W  T  F  S
 1  2  3  4  5  6  7
 8  9 10 11 12 13 14
15 16 17 18 19 20 21
22 23 24 25 26 27 28
29 30 31
```

1992

JANUARY
```
S  M  T  W  T  F  S
          1  2  3  4
 5  6  7  8  9 10 11
12 13 14 15 16 17 18
19 20 21 22 23 24 25
26 27 28 29 30 31
```

JULY
```
S  M  T  W  T  F  S
          1  2  3  4
 5  6  7  8  9 10 11
12 13 14 15 16 17 18
19 20 21 22 23 24 25
26 27 28 29 30 31
```

FEBRUARY
```
S  M  T  W  T  F  S
                   1
 2  3  4  5  6  7  8
 9 10 11 12 13 14 15
16 17 18 19 20 21 22
23 24 25 26 27 28 29
```

AUGUST
```
S  M  T  W  T  F  S
                   1
 2  3  4  5  6  7  8
 9 10 11 12 13 14 15
16 17 18 19 20 21 22
23 24 25 26 27 28 29
30 31
```

MARCH
```
S  M  T  W  T  F  S
 1  2  3  4  5  6  7
 8  9 10 11 12 13 14
15 16 17 18 19 20 21
22 23 24 25 26 27 28
29 30 31
```

SEPTEMBER
```
S  M  T  W  T  F  S
       1  2  3  4  5
 6  7  8  9 10 11 12
13 14 15 16 17 18 19
20 21 22 23 24 25 26
27 28 29 30
```

APRIL
```
S  M  T  W  T  F  S
          1  2  3  4
 5  6  7  8  9 10 11
12 13 14 15 16 17 18
19 20 21 22 23 24 25
26 27 28 29 30
```

OCTOBER
```
S  M  T  W  T  F  S
                1  2  3
 4  5  6  7  8  9 10
11 12 13 14 15 16 17
18 19 20 21 22 23 24
25 26 27 28 29 30 31
```

MAY
```
S  M  T  W  T  F  S
                1  2
 3  4  5  6  7  8  9
10 11 12 13 14 15 16
17 18 19 20 21 22 23
24 25 26 27 28 29 30
31
```

NOVEMBER
```
S  M  T  W  T  F  S
 1  2  3  4  5  6  7
 8  9 10 11 12 13 14
15 16 17 18 19 20 21
22 23 24 25 26 27 28
29 30
```

JUNE
```
S  M  T  W  T  F  S
    1  2  3  4  5  6
 7  8  9 10 11 12 13
14 15 16 17 18 19 20
21 22 23 24 25 26 27
28 29 30
```

DECEMBER
```
S  M  T  W  T  F  S
       1  2  3  4  5
 6  7  8  9 10 11 12
13 14 15 16 17 18 19
20 21 22 23 24 25 26
27 28 29 30 31
```

IMPORTANT DATES

1991		1992	
Jan. 1	NEW YEAR'S DAY	Jan. 1	NEW YEAR'S DAY
Jan. 21	MARTIN LUTHER KING, JR. DAY	Jan. 20	MARTIN LUTHER KING, JR. DAY
Feb. 12	LINCOLN'S BIRTHDAY	Feb. 12	LINCOLN'S BIRTHDAY
Feb. 13	ASH WEDNESDAY	March 4	ASH WEDNESDAY
Feb. 14	VALENTINE'S DAY	Feb. 14	VALENTINE'S DAY
Feb. 18	WASHINGTON'S BIRTHDAY (observed)	Feb. 17	WASHINGTON'S BIRTHDAY (observed)
Feb. 22	WASHINGTON'S BIRTHDAY	Feb. 22	WASHINGTON'S BIRTHDAY
March 17	ST. PATRICK'S DAY	March 17	ST. PATRICK'S DAY
March 29	GOOD FRIDAY	April 17	GOOD FRIDAY
March 30	PASSOVER	April 18	PASSOVER
March 31	EASTER SUNDAY	April 19	EASTER SUNDAY
May 12	MOTHER'S DAY	May 10	MOTHER'S DAY
May 27	MEMORIAL DAY (observed)	May 25	MEMORIAL DAY (observed)
June 14	FLAG DAY	June 14	FLAG DAY
June 16	FATHER'S DAY	June 21	FATHER'S DAY
July 4	INDEPENDENCE DAY	July 4	INDEPENDENCE DAY
Sept. 2	LABOR DAY	Sept. 7	LABOR DAY
Sept. 9	ROSH HASHANAH	Sept. 28	ROSH HASHANAH
Sept. 18	YOM KIPPUR	Oct. 7	YOM KIPPUR
Oct. 14	COLUMBUS DAY (observed)	Oct. 12	COLUMBUS DAY (observed)
Oct. 31	HALLOWEEN	Oct. 31	HALLOWEEN
Nov. 5	ELECTION DAY	Nov. 3	ELECTION DAY
Nov. 11	VETERANS DAY	Nov. 11	VETERANS DAY
Nov. 28	THANKSGIVING	Nov. 26	THANKSGIVING DAY
Dec. 2	HANUKKAH	Dec. 20	HANUKKAH
Dec. 25	CHRISTMAS DAY	Dec. 25	CHRISTMAS DAY

HOW TO USE THIS CALENDAR

Look for the year you want in the reference key. The letter opposite each year is the letter of the calendar to use for that year.

REFERENCE KEY

Year		Year		Year		Year	
1900	B	1926	F	1951	B	1976	L
1901	C	1927	G	1952	J	1977	G
1902	D	1928	H	1953	E	1978	A
1903	E	1929	C	1954	F	1979	B
1904	M	1930	D	1955	G	1980	J
1905	A	1931	E	1956	H	1981	E
1906	B	1932	M	1957	C	1982	F
1907	C	1933	A	1958	D	1983	G
1908	K	1934	B	1959	E	1984	H
1909	F	1935	C	1960	M	1985	C
1910	G	1936	K	1961	A	1986	D
1911	A	1937	F	1962	B	1987	E
1912	I	1938	G	1963	C	1988	M
1913	D	1939	A	1964	K	1989	A
1914	E	1940	I	1965	F	1990	B
1915	F	1941	D	1966	G	1991	C
1916	N	1942	E	1967	A	1992	K
1917	B	1943	F	1968	I	1993	F
1918	C	1944	N	1969	D	1994	G
1919	D	1945	B	1970	E	1995	A
1920	L	1946	C	1971	F	1996	I
1921	G	1947	D	1972	N	1997	D
1922	A	1948	L	1973	B	1998	E
1923	B	1949	G	1974	C	1999	F
1924	J	1950	A	1975	D	2000	N
1925	E						

A

B

C

D

E

F

JANUARY	MAY	SEPTEMBER
FEBRUARY	JUNE	OCTOBER
MARCH	JULY	NOVEMBER
APRIL	AUGUST	DECEMBER

G

JANUARY	MAY	SEPTEMBER
FEBRUARY	JUNE	OCTOBER
MARCH	JULY	NOVEMBER
APRIL	AUGUST	DECEMBER

H

JANUARY	MAY	SEPTEMBER
FEBRUARY	JUNE	OCTOBER
MARCH	JULY	NOVEMBER
APRIL	AUGUST	DECEMBER

I

JANUARY	MAY	SEPTEMBER
FEBRUARY	JUNE	OCTOBER
MARCH	JULY	NOVEMBER
APRIL	AUGUST	DECEMBER

J

JANUARY	MAY	SEPTEMBER
FEBRUARY	JUNE	OCTOBER
MARCH	JULY	NOVEMBER
APRIL	AUGUST	DECEMBER

K

JANUARY	MAY	SEPTEMBER
FEBRUARY	JUNE	OCTOBER
MARCH	JULY	NOVEMBER
APRIL	AUGUST	DECEMBER

L

JANUARY	MAY	SEPTEMBER
FEBRUARY	JUNE	OCTOBER
MARCH	JULY	NOVEMBER
APRIL	AUGUST	DECEMBER

M

JANUARY	MAY	SEPTEMBER
FEBRUARY	JUNE	OCTOBER
MARCH	JULY	NOVEMBER
APRIL	AUGUST	DECEMBER

N

JANUARY	MAY	SEPTEMBER
FEBRUARY	JUNE	OCTOBER
MARCH	JULY	NOVEMBER
APRIL	AUGUST	DECEMBER

LUMBER CONVERTED TO BOARD FOOT MEASURE

One board foot = one lineal foot of 1" x 12" board. Therefore, at one lineal foot, a 2" x 4" would equal 2x4 12 or 0.667 board feet.

Lumber size inches	Board Ft. per L.F.	Board Feet Per Length						
		8 FT.	10 FT.	12 FT.	14 FT.	16 FT.	18 FT.	20 FT.
1x2	0.166	1.33	1.67	2.00	2.33	2.67	3.00	3.33
1x3	0.250	2.00	2.50	3.00	3.50	4.00	4.50	5.00
1x4; 2x2	0.333	2.67	3.33	4.00	4.67	5.33	6.00	6.67
1x6; 2x3	0.500	4.00	5.00	6.00	7.00	8.00	9.00	10.00
1x8; 2x4	0.667	5.34	6.67	8.00	9.34	10.67	12.00	13.34
1x12; 2x6; 3x4	1.000	8.00	10.00	12.00	14.00	16.00	18.00	20.00
2x8; 4x4	1.333	10.66	13.33	16.00	18.66	21.33	24.00	26.66
2x10	1.667	13.22	16.67	20.00	23.34	26.67	30.00	33.34
2x12; 3x8; 4x6	2.000	16.00	20.00	24.00	28.00	32.00	36.00	40.00
2x14	2.333	18.66	23.33	28.00	32.66	37.33	42.00	46.66
3x10	2.500	20.00	25.00	30.00	35.00	40.00	45.00	50.00
4x10	3.333	26.66	33.33	40.00	46.62	53.33	60.00	66.66
3x6	1.500	12.00	15.00	18.00	21.00	24.00	27.00	30.00
3x12; 6x6	3.00	24.00	30.00	36.00	42.00	48.00	54.00	60.00
3x14	3.500	28.00	35.00	42.00	49.00	56.00	63.00	70.00
3x16; 4x12; 6x8	4.000	32.00	40.00	48.00	56.00	64.00	72.00	80.00
4x8	2.667	21.34	26.67	32.00	37.34	42.67	48.00	53.34
4x14	4.667	37.34	46.67	56.00	65.34	74.67	84.00	93.34
4x16; 8x8	5.333	42.66	53.33	64.00	74.66	85.33	96.00	106.66
6x10	5.000	40.00	50.00	60.00	70.00	80.00	90.00	100.00
8x10	6.667	53.34	66.67	80.00	93.34	106.67	120.00	133.34

NAILS

Size	Length, inches	TYPE		
		Common	Casing	Finishing
		Approximate number per lb.		
2d	1	830		1,351
3d	1¼	528		807
4d	1½	316	473	584
5d	1¾	271		500
6d	2	168	236	309
7d	2¼	150	210	
8d	2½	106	145	189
9d	2¾	96		
10d	3	69	94	121
12d	3¼	63		
16d	3½	49	71	90
20d	4	31	52	62
30d	4½	24		
40d	5	18		
50d	5½	14		
60d	6	11		

U.S. GALLONS IN ROUND TANKS
For One Foot in Depth

Dia. of tank Ft.	In.	No. U.S. gals.	Cu. Ft.	Dia. of tank Ft.	In.	No. U.S. gals.	Cu. Ft.
1		5.87	.785	3	1	55.86	7.467
1	1	6.89	.922	3	2	58.92	7.876
1	2	8	1.069	3	3	62.06	8.296
1	3	9.18	1.227	3	4	65.28	8.727
1	4	10.44	1.396	3	5	68.58	9.168
1	5	11.79	1.576	3	6	71.97	9.621
1	6	13.22	1.767	3	7	75.44	10.085
1	7	14.73	1.969	3	8	78.99	10.559
1	8	16.32	2.182	3	9	82.62	11.045
1	9	17.99	2.405	3	10	86.33	11.541
1	10	19.75	2.640	3	11	90.13	12.048
1	11	21.58	2.885	4		94	12.566
2		23.50	3.142	4	1	97.96	13.095
2	1	25.50	3.409	4	2	102	13.635
2	2	27.58	3.687	4	3	106.12	14.186
2	3	29.74	3.976	4	4	110.32	14.748
2	4	31.99	4.276	4	5	114.61	15.321
2	5	34.31	4.587	4	6	118.97	15.90
2	6	36.72	4.909	4	7	123.42	16.50
2	7	39.21	5.241	4	8	127.95	17.10
2	8	41.78	5.585	4	9	132.56	17.72
2	9	44.43	5.940	4	10	137.25	18.35
2	10	47.16	6.305	4	11	142.02	18.99
2	11	49.98	6.681	5		146.88	19.63
3		52.88	7.069	8	6	424.48	56.75
5	1	151.82	20.29	8	9	449.82	60.13
5	2	156.83	20.97	9		475.89	63.62
5	3	161.93	21.65	9	3	502.70	67.20
5	4	167.12	22.34	9	6	530.24	70.88
5	5	172.38	23.04	9	9	558.51	74.66
5	6	177.72	23.76	10		587.52	78.54
5	7	183.15	24.48				
5	8	188.66	25.22				
5	9	194.25	25.97				
5	10	199.92	26.73				
5	11	205.67	27.49				
6		211.51	28.27				
6	3	229.50	30.68				
6	6	248.23	33.18				
6	9	267.69	35.78				
7		287.88	38.48				
7	3	308.81	41.28				
7	6	330.48	44.18				
7	9	352.88	47.17				
8		376.01	50.27				
8	3	399.88	53.46				

WEIGHTS AND MEASURES—UNITED STATES

Linear Measure

1 mile = 8 furlongs; 80 chains; 320 rods; 1760 yards; 5280 feet
1 furlong = 10 chains; 220 yards
1 station = 33.3 yards; 100 feet
1 chain = 4 rods; 22 yards; 66 feet; 100 links
1 rod = 5.5 yards; 16.5 feet
1 yard = 3 feet; 36 inches
1 foot = 12 inches

Surveyor's Chain Measure

1 link = 7.92 inches
1 statute mile = 80 chains

Land Measure

1 township = 36 sections; 36 square miles
1 square mile = 1 section; 640 acres
1 acre = 4840 sq. yards; 43,560 sq. feet; 160 sq. rods
1 square rod = 272¼ sq. feet; 30¼ sq. yards
1 square yard = 1,296 sq. inches; 9 sq. feet
1 square foot = 144 sq. inches

Cubic Measure

1 cubic yard = 27 cubic feet
1 cord wood = 4x4x8 feet; 128 cu. ft.
1 ton (shipping) = 40 cu. ft.
1 cubic foot = 1728 cu. in.
1 bushel = 2150.42 cubic in.
1 gallon = 231 cu. in.

Weights Commercial

1 long ton = 2240 lbs.
1 short ton = 2000 lbs.
1 pound = 16 ounces
1 ounce = 16 drams

Troy Weight for Gold and Silver

1 pound = 12 ounces; 5760 grains
1 pennyweight = 24 grains
1 ounce = 20 pennyweights
1 ounce = 480 grains

Dry Measure

1 quart = 2 pints; 67.20 cu. in.
1 peck = 16 pints; 537.605 cu. in.
1 bushel = 4 pecks; 32 quarts; 2150.42 cu. in.

Mariner's Measure

1 fathom = 6 feet
1 cable length = 120 fathoms
1 statute mile = 7-1/3 cable lengths; 5,280 feet
1 marine league = 3 marine miles
1 nautical mile = 6,080 feet.

Measures of Power

1 BTU per minute = .0236 HP; 17.6 watts; .0176 kilowatts; 778 ft. lbs./min.
1 ft. lb./min. = .0226 watts; .001285 BTU per minute
1 horsepower = 746 watts; 33,000 ft. lbs./min.; 42.4 BTU/min.
1 watt = .00134 HP; .001 kilowatts; 44.2 ft. lbs./min.; .0568 BTU/min.
1 kilowatt = 1.341 HP; 1000 watts; 44,250 ft. lbs./min.; 56.8 BTU/min.

Liquid Measure

1 pint = 4 gills; 28.875 cu. in.
1 quart = 2 pints; 57.75 cu. in.
1 hogshead = 63 gallons
1 barrel = 31½ gallons
1 gallon = 4 quarts; 8 pints; 32 gills; 231 cu. in.; 8-1/3 lbs. @ 62 degrees F.
1 cu. ft. water = 7.48 gals.; 1728 cu. in.; 62½ lbs. @ 62 degrees F.

METRIC—U.S. CONVERSION FACTORS

(based on National Bureau of Standards)

Area

Sq. cm. X 0.1550 = sq. ins.
Sq. m. X 10.7639 = sq. ft.
1 are = 100 square meters
Ares X 1076.39 = sq. ft.
Sq. m. X 1.1960 = sq. yds.
Hectare X 2.4710 = acres
Sq. km. X 0.3861 = sq. miles
Sq. ins. X 6.4516 = sq. cm.
Sq. ft. X 0.0929 = sq. m.
Sq. ft. X 0.00093 = ares
Sq. yds. X 0.8361 = sq. m.
Acre X 0.4047 = hectares
Sq. miles X 2.5900 = sq. km.

Length

Centimeters X 0.3937 = inches
Meters X 3.2808 = feet
Meters X 1.0936 = yards
Kilometers X 0.6214 = statute miles
Kilometers X 0.53959 = nautical miles
Inches X 2.5400 = centimeters
Feet X 0.3048 = meters
Yards X 0.9144 = meters
Miles X 1.6093 = kilometers
Miles X 1.85325 = kilometers

Volume

Cu. cm. X 0.0610 = cu. ins.
Cu. m. X 35.3145 = cu. ft.
Cu. m. X 1.3079 = cu. yds.
Cu. ins. X 16.3872 = cu. cm.
Cu. ft. X 0.0283 = cu. m.
Cu. yds. X 0.7646 = cu. m.

Weight

Grams X 15.4324 = grains
Grams X 0.0353 = oz.
Grams X 0.0022 = lbs.
Kgs. X 2.2046 = lbs.
Kgs. X 0.0011 = tons (short)
Kgs. X 0.00098 = tons (long)
Metric Tons X 1.1023 = tons (short)
Metric Tons X 2204.62 = lbs.
Grains X 0.0648 = g.
Oz. X 28.3495 = g.
Lbs. X 453.592 = g.
Lbs. X 0.4536 = kg.
Lbs. X 0.0004536 = tons metric
Tons (short) X 907.1848 = kg.
Tons (short) X 0.9072 = metric tons
Tons (long) X 1016.05 = kg.

Capacity

Liters X 61.0250 = cu. in.
Liters X 0.0353 = cu. ft.
Liters X 0.2642 = gals. (U.S.)
Liters X 0.0284 = bushels (U.S.)
Liters X 1000.027 = cu. cm.
Liters X 1.0567 = qt. (liquid) or 0.9081 = qt. (dry)
Liters X 2.2046 = lb. of pure water at 4 C = 1 kg.
Cu. ins. X 0.0164 = liters
Cu. ft. X 28.3162 = liters
Gallons X 3.7853 = liters
Bushels X 35.2383 = liters

Pressure

Kgs. per sq. cm. X 14.223 = lbs. per sq. in.
Lbs. per sq. in. X 0.0703 = kgs. per sq. cm.
Kgs. per sq. in. X 0.2048 = lbs. per sq. ft.
Kgs. per sq. m. X 0.204817 = lbs. per sq. ft.
Lbs. per sq. ft. X 4.8824 = kgs. per sq. m.
Kgs. per sq. m. X 0.00009144 = tons (long) per sq. ft.
Tons long per sq. ft. X 0.0001094 = kg. per sq. m.
Kgs. per sq. mm. X 0.634973 = tons (long) per sq. in.
Tons (long) per sq. in. X 0.0001094 = kg. per sq. m.
Kgs. per cu. m. X 0.062428 = lbs. per cu. ft.
Lbs. per cu. ft. X 16.0184 = kgs. per cu. m.
Kgs. per m. X 0.671972 = lbs. per ft.
Lbs. per ft. X 1.48816 = kgs. per m.
Kg.-m. X 7.233 = ft.-lbs.
Ft.-lbs. X 0.13826 = kg.-m.

Power

Metric horsepower X .98632 = U.S. horsepower
U.S. horsepower X 1.01387 = metric horsepower

CONVERSION TABLE

Inches		Centimeters	Centimeters		Inches
1	=	2.54001	1	=	0.39370
2	=	5.08001	2	=	0.78740
3	=	7.62002	3	=	1.1811
4	=	10.16002	4	=	1.5748
5	=	12.70003	5	=	1.9685
6	=	15.24003	6	=	2.3622
7	=	17.78004	7	=	2.7559
8	=	20.32004	8	=	3.1496
9	=	22.86005	9	=	3.5433

Feet		Meters	Meters		Feet
1	=	0.304801	1	=	3.28083
2	=	0.609601	2	=	6.56167
3	=	0.914402	3	=	9.84250
4	=	1.219202	4	=	13.12333
5	=	1.524003	5	=	16.40417
6	=	1.828804	6	=	19.68500
7	=	2.133604	7	=	22.96583
8	=	2.438405	8	=	26.24666
9	=	2.743205	9	=	29.52750

Yards		Meters	Meters		Yards
1	=	0.914402	1	=	1.093611
2	=	1.828804	2	=	2.187222
3	=	2.743205	3	=	3.280833
4	=	3.657607	4	=	4.374444
5	=	4.572009	5	=	5.468056
6	=	5.486411	6	=	6.561667
7	=	6.400813	7	=	7.655278
8	=	7.315215	8	=	8.748889
9	=	8.229616	9	=	9.842500

Miles		Kilometers	Kilometers		Miles
1	=	1.60935	1	=	0.62137
2	=	3.21869	2	=	1.24274
3	=	4.82804	3	=	1.86411
4	=	6.43739	4	=	2.48548
5	=	8.04674	5	=	3.10685
6	=	9.65608	6	=	3.72822
7	=	11.26543	7	=	4.34959
8	=	12.87478	8	=	4.97096
9	=	14.48412	9	=	5.59233

Pounds Av.		Kilograms	Kilograms		Pounds Av.
1	=	0.45359	1	=	2.20462
2	=	0.90718	2	=	4.40924
3	=	1.36078	3	=	6.61387
4	=	1.81437	4	=	8.81849
5	=	2.26796	5	=	11.02311
6	=	2.72155	6	=	13.22773
7	=	3.17514	7	=	15.43236
8	=	3.62874	8	=	17.63698
9	=	4.08233	9	=	19.84160

DECIMALS OF AN INCH

Fraction	64ths	Decimal	Fraction	64ths	Decimal
—	1	.015625	½	32	.500
1/32	2	.03125	—	33	.515625
—	3	.046875	17/32	34	.53125
1/16	4	.0625	—	35	.546875
—	5	.078125	9/16	36	.5625
3/32	6	.09375	—	37	.578125
—	7	.109375	19/32	38	.59375
			—	39	.609375
1/8	8	.125	5/8	40	.625
—	9	.140625	—	41	.640625
5/32	10	.15625	21/32	42	.65625
—	11	.171875	—	43	.671875
3/16	12	.1875	11/16	44	.6875
—	13	.203125	—	45	.703125
7/32	14	.21875	23/32	46	.71875
—	15	.234375	—	47	.734375
1/4	16	.250	3/4	48	.750
—	17	.265625	—	49	.765625
9/32	18	.28125	25/32	50	.78125
—	19	.296875	—	51	.796875
5/16	20	.3125	13/16	52	.8125
—	21	.328125	—	53	.828125
11/32	22	.34375	27/32	54	.84375
—	23	.359375	—	55	.859375
3/8	24	.375	7/8	56	.875
—	25	.390625	—	57	.890625
13/32	26	.40625	29/32	58	.90625
—	27	.421875	—	59	.921875
7/16	28	.4375	15/16	60	.9375
—	29	.453125	—	61	.953125
15/32	30	.46875	31/32	62	.96875
—	31	.484375	—	63	.984375

DECIMALS OF A FOOT

Fraction	0"	1"	2"	3"
	.0000	.0833	.166667	.2500
1/16	.0052	.0885	.171875	.2552
1/8	.0104	.09375	.1771	.2604
3/16	.015625	.0990	.1823	.265625
1/4	.0208	.1042	.1875	.2708
5/16	.0260	.109375	.1927	.2760
3/8	.03125	.1146	.1979	.28125
7/16	.0365	.1198	.203125	.2865
1/2	.0417	.1250	.2083	.2917
9/16	.046875	.1302	.2135	.296875
5/8	.0521	.1354	.21875	.3021
11/16	.0573	.140625	.2240	.3073
3/4	.0625	.1458	.2292	.3125
13/16	.0677	.1510	.234375	.3177
7/8	.0729	.15625	.2396	.3229
15/16	.078125	.1615	.2448	.328125

Fraction	4"	5"	6"	7"
	.3333	.416667	.5000	.5833
1/16	.3385	.421875	.5052	.5885
1/8	.34375	.4271	.5104	.59375
3/16	.3490	.4323	.515625	.5990
1/4	.3542	.4375	.5208	.6042
5/16	.359375	.4427	.5260	.6093
3/8	.3646	.4479	.53125	.6146
7/16	.3698	.453125	.5365	.6198
1/2	.3750	.4583	.5417	.6250
9/16	.3802	.4635	.546875	.6302
5/8	.3854	.46875	.5521	.6354
11/16	.390625	.4740	.5573	.640625
3/4	.3958	.4792	.5625	.6458
13/16	.4010	.484375	.5677	.6510
7/8	.40625	.4896	.5729	.65625
15/16	.4115	.4948	.578125	.6615

Fraction	8"	9"	10"	11"
	.666667	.7500	.8333	.916667
1/16	.671875	.7552	.8385	.921875
1/8	.6771	.7604	.84375	.9271
3/16	.6823	.765625	.8490	.9323
1/4	.6875	.7708	.8542	.9375
5/16	.6927	.7760	.859375	.9427
3/8	.6979	.78125	.8646	.9479
7/16	.703125	.7865	.8698	.953125
1/2	.7083	.7917	.8750	.9583
9/16	.7135	.796875	.8802	.9635
5/8	.71875	.8021	.8854	.96875
11/16	.7240	.8073	.890625	.9740
3/4	.7292	.8125	.8958	.9792
13/16	.734375	.8177	.9010	.984375
7/8	.7396	.8229	.90625	.9896
15/16	.7448	.828125	.9115	.9948

SIMPLE AND COMPOUND INTEREST RATE TABLES

These tables give you the amount accumulated after a specified period at various simple interest rates.

How to Use These Tables
1. First find the column headed by the interest rate on the investment in question.
2. Then scan down to the appropriate number of years. At that intersection you will find a factor.
3. Multiply that factor by the principal. The result is the amount accumulated within that period.

Example: Lester Mannington has $600 in a savings account at Federal Bank and Trust Company that is earning 7% simple interest per year. He wants to know how much he will have in the bank at the end of 10 years.
1. Across from 10 years and under the 7% column, you will find the factor 1.70.
2. Multiply this factor (1.70) by the $600 to get $1,020, the value of the account after 10 years at simple interest.

COMPOUND INTEREST RATE

Number of Years	7%	8%	9%	10%	11%	12%	13%	14%	15%	20%
1	1.0700	1.0800	1.0900	1.1000	1.1100	1.1200	1.1300	1.1400	1.1500	1.2000
2	1.1449	1.1664	1.1881	1.2100	1.2321	1.2544	1.2769	1.2996	1.3225	1.4400
3	1.2250	1.2597	1.2950	1.3310	1.3576	1.4049	1.4428	1.4815	1.5208	1.7280
4	1.3107	1.3604	1.4115	1.4647	1.5180	1.5735	1.6304	1.6389	1.7409	2.0736
5	1.4025	1.4693	1.5386	1.6105	1.6350	1.7623	1.8424	1.9254	2.0113	2.4883
6	1.5007	1.5868	1.6771	1.7715	1.8704	1.9738	2.0819	2.1949	2.3130	2.9859
7	1.6057	1.7138	1.8230	1.9487	2.0761	2.2106	2.3526	2.5022	2.6600	3.5831
8	1.7181	1.8509	1.9925	2.1435	2.3045	2.4759	2.6584	2.8525	3.0590	4.2998
9	1.8384	1.9990	2.1718	2.3579	2.5580	2.7730	3.0040	3.2519	3.5178	5.1597
10	1.9671	2.1589	2.3673	2.5937	2.8394	3.1058	3.3945	3.7072	4.0455	6.1917
11	2.1048	2.3316	2.5804	2.8531	3.1517	3.4785	3.8358	4.2262	4.6523	7.4300
12	2.2521	2.5181	2.8126	3.1384	3.4984	3.8959	4.3345	4.8179	5.3502	8.9161
13	2.4098	2.7196	3.0658	3.4522	3.8832	4.3634	4.8980	5.4924	6.1527	10.6993
14	2.5785	2.9371	3.3417	3.7974	4.3104	4.8871	5.5347	6.2613	7.0757	12.8391
15	2.7590	3.1721	3.6424	4.1772	4.7845	5.4735	6.2542	7.1379	8.1370	15.4270
16	2.9521	3.4259	3.9703	4.5949	5.3108	6.1303	7.0673	8.1372	9.3576	18.4884
17	3.1588	3.7000	4.3276	5.0544	5.8950	6.8660	7.9860	9.2764	10.6712	22.1861
18	3.3799	3.9960	4.7171	5.5599	6.5435	7.6899	9.0242	10.5751	12.3754	26.6233
19	3.6165	4.3157	5.1416	6.1159	7.2633	8.6127	10.1974	12.0556	14.2317	31.9479
20	3.8696	4.6609	5.6044	6.7274	8.0623	9.6462	11.5230	13.7434	16.3665	38.3375
21	4.1405	5.0338	6.1088	7.4002	8.9491	10.8038	13.0210	15.6675	18.8215	46.0051
22	4.4304	5.4365	6.6586	8.1402	9.9335	12.1003	14.7138	17.8610	21.6447	55.2061
23	4.7405	5.8714	7.2578	8.9543	11.0262	13.5523	16.6266	20.3615	24.8914	66.2473
24	5.0723	6.3411	7.9110	9.8497	12.2391	15.1786	18.7880	23.2122	28.6251	79.4968
25	5.4274	6.8484	8.6230	10.8347	13.5854	17.0000	21.2305	26.4619	32.9189	95.3962
26	5.8073	7.3963	9.3991	11.9181	15.0793	19.0400	23.9905	30.1665	37.8567	114.4754
27	6.2138	7.9880	10.2450	13.1099	16.7386	21.3248	27.1092	34.3899	43.5353	137.3705
28	6.6488	8.6271	11.1671	14.4209	18.5799	23.8838	30.6334	39.2044	50.0656	164.8446
29	7.1142	9.3172	12.1721	15.8630	20.6236	26.7499	34.6158	44.6931	57.5754	197.8135
30	7.6122	10.0582	13.2676	17.4494	22.8922	29.9599	39.1158-	50.9501	66.2117	237.3763
31	8.1451	10.8676	14.4617	19.1943	25.4104	33.5551	44.2009	58.0831	76.1435	284.8515
32	8.7152	11.7370	15.7633	21.1137	28.2055	37.5817	49.9470	66.2148	87.5650	341.8218
33	9.3253	12.6760	17.1820	23.2251	31.3082	42.0915	56.4402	75.4849	100.6998	410.1862
34	9.9781	13.6901	18.7284	25.5476	34.7521	47.1425	63.7774	86.0527	115.8048	492.2235
35	10.6765	14.7853	20.4139	28.1024	38.5748	52.7996	72.0685	98.1001	133.1755	590.6682
36	11.4239	15.9681	22.2512	30.9128	42.8180	59.1355	81.4374	111.8342	153.1518	708.8018
37	12.2236	17.2456	24.2538	34.0039	47.5280	66.2318	92.0242	127.4909	176.1246	850.5622
38	13.0792	18.6252	26.4366	37.4048	52.7561	74.1796	103.9874	145.3397	202.5433	1020.6746
39	13.9948	20.1152	28.8159	41.1447	58.5593	83.0812	117.5057	165.6872	232.9248	1224.8096
40	14.9744	21.7245	31.4094	45.2592	65.0008	93.0509	132.7815	188.8835	267.6635	1469.7715

SIMPLE INTEREST RATE

Number of Years	7%	8%	9%	10%	11%	12%	13%	14%	15%	20%
1	1.07	1.08	1.09	1.10	1.11	1.12	1.13	1.14	1.15	1.20
2	1.14	1.16	1.18	1.20	1.22	1.24	1.26	1.28	1.30	1.40
3	1.21	1.24	1.27	1.30	1.33	1.36	1.39	1.42	1.45	1.60
4	1.28	1.32	1.36	1.40	1.44	1.48	1.52	1.56	1.60	1.80
5	1.35	1.40	1.45	1.50	1.55	1.60	1.65	1.70	1.75	2.00
6	1.42	1.48	1.54	1.60	1.66	1.72	1.78	1.84	1.90	2.20
7	1.49	1.56	1.63	1.70	1.77	1.84	1.91	1.98	2.05	2.40
8	1.56	1.64	1.72	1.80	1.88	1.96	2.04	2.12	2.20	2.60
9	1.63	1.72	1.81	1.90	1.99	2.08	2.17	2.26	2.35	2.80
10	1.70	1.80	1.90	2.00	2.10	2.20	2.30	2.40	2.50	3.00
11	1.77	1.88	1.99	2.10	2.21	2.32	2.43	2.54	2.65	3.20
12	1.84	1.96	2.08	2.20	2.32	2.44	2.56	2.68	2.80	3.40
13	1.91	2.04	2.17	2.30	2.43	2.56	2.69	2.82	2.95	3.60
14	1.98	2.12	2.26	2.40	2.54	2.68	2.82	2.96	3.10	3.80
15	2.05	2.20	2.35	2.50	2.65	2.80	2.95	3.10	3.25	4.00
16	2.12	2.28	2.44	2.60	2.76	2.92	3.08	3.24	3.40	4.20
17	2.19	2.36	2.53	2.70	2.87	3.04	3.21	3.38	3.55	4.40
18	2.26	2.44	2.62	2.80	2.98	3.16	3.34	3.52	3.70	4.60
19	2.33	2.52	2.71	2.90	3.09	3.28	3.47	3.66	3.85	4.80
20	2.40	2.60	2.80	3.00	3.20	3.40	3.60	3.80	4.00	5.00
21	2.47	2.68	2.89	3.10	3.31	3.52	3.73	3.94	4.15	5.20
22	2.54	2.76	2.98	3.20	3.42	3.64	3.86	4.08	4.30	5.40
23	2.61	2.84	3.07	3.30	3.53	3.76	3.99	4.22	4.45	5.60
24	2.68	2.92	3.16	3.40	3.64	3.88	4.12	4.36	4.60	5.80
25	2.75	3.00	3.25	3.50	3.75	4.00	4.25	4.50	4.75	6.00
26	2.82	3.08	3.34	3.60	3.86	4.12	4.38	4.64	4.90	6.20
27	2.89	3.16	3.43	3.70	3.97	4.24	4.51	4.78	5.05	6.40
28	2.96	3.24	3.52	3.80	4.08	4.36	4.64	4.92	5.20	6.60
29	3.03	3.32	3.61	3.90	4.19	4.48	4.77	5.06	5.35	6.80
30	3.10	3.40	3.70	4.00	4.30	4.60	4.90	5.20	5.50	7.00
31	3.17	3.48	3.79	4.10	4.41	4.72	5.03	5.34	5.65	7.20
32	3.24	3.56	3.88	4.20	4.52	4.84	5.16	5.48	5.80	7.40
33	3.31	3.64	3.97	4.30	4.63	4.96	5.29	5.62	5.95	7.60
34	3.38	3.72	4.06	4.40	4.74	5.08	5.42	5.76	6.10	7.80
35	3.45	3.80	4.15	4.50	4.85	5.20	5.55	5.90	6.25	8.00
36	3.52	3.88	4.24	4.60	4.96	5.32	5.68	6.04	6.40	8.20
37	3.59	3.96	4.33	4.70	5.07	5.44	5.81	6.18	6.55	8.40
38	3.66	4.04	4.42	4.80	5.18	5.56	5.94	6.32	6.70	8.60
39	3.73	4.12	4.51	4.90	5.29	5.68	6.07	6.46	6.85	8.80
40	3.80	4.20	4.60	5.00	5.40	5.80	6.20	6.60	7.00	9.00

JOBSITE SAFETY REVIEW CHECKLIST

Periodically review the jobsite, considering how each of the items below has been accommodated. If treatment for any item is inadequate, notify the responsible party and ensure its immediate correction.

Condition	Date Completed	Condition	Date Completed

NOTIFICATION
1. Safety signs in place _____
2. Emergency phone numbers posted _____
3. Safety meetings held _____
4. Fire extinguisher signs posted _____
5. Job safety representative designated _____
6. Fire alarm signs posted _____
7. All exits clearly marked _____
8. "No Smoking" signs posted _____
9. Evacuation plan posted _____
10. Hot work permits secured _____
11. All personnel and pedestrians notified of loud construction noises _____
12. Warnings and instructions to the public posted _____

SAFETY EQUIPMENT AND CLOTHING ON HAND
1. Fire extinguishers (correct quantity/type) _____
2. First-aid kit (filled and supplied) _____
3. Stretcher _____
4. Temporary fire alarm operating _____
5. First-aid room designated _____
6. Safety harnesses, ropes, slings (inspected) _____
7. Safety nets (inspected) _____
8. Hard hats, eye protection, gloves, safety shoes _____
9. No loose clothing or jewelry _____

JOB SITE AND PERSONNEL SAFETY/SECURITY
1. All construction vehicles properly identified _____
2. No privately owned/operated vehicles on site _____
3. Fuel tanks and combustibles stored properly _____
4. Good housekeeping (no trash accumulation) _____
5. No unauthorized fires, burning, welding, etc. _____
6. Smoking prohibited in sensitive areas _____
7. Fire extinguishers and protection equipment present in hot work areas _____

TEMPORARY POWER, LIGHTING, AND SMALL TOOLS
1. All temporary electric systems properly grounded _____
2. All extension cords of three-wire type _____
3. All tools and equipment insulated and/or grounded _____
4. All hand tools in good repair _____
5. All extension cords in good condition _____
6. All work areas properly lit _____
7. All electric panels and exposed wiring inaccessible to unauthorized personnel _____
8. All extension cords and temporary power receptacles using ground fault circuit interrupters _____
9. All grounding conductors tested for continuity _____
10. Temporary power constructions closed to weather _____

EXCAVATIONS
1. All shoring and earth retention systems properly designed and in place _____
2. Excavations properly dewatered _____
3. Has condition of excavations open for an extended period of time changed at all (erosion, water content)? _____
4. Are all excavations large enough to complete work without unreasonable restriction?
5. Excavations ventilated and free of flammable and/or toxic gasses _____

PERSONNEL PROTECTION
1. Building perimeter protected at each floor per OSHA for the respective conditions _____
2. All floor openings protected or closed off _____
3. Ladders properly set and secured _____
4. Temporary bridges supported and with rails _____
5. All traffic areas free of materials and debris _____
6. All flammable debris removed daily _____
7. Adequate temporary lighting in all areas _____
8. Temporary heaters properly located _____
9. All materials and debris away from temp heaters _____
10. Oxygen, acetylene, and other fuel tanks properly stored and secured _____
11. Confined spaces properly ventilated _____
12. All drinking water potable _____
13. All work areas sanitary _____

PEDESTRIAN/PUBLIC PROTECTION
1. Entire site protected from unauthorized entry _____
2. Dangerous areas within the site restricted from nonconstruction personnel _____
3. All sidewalk sheds, barricades, overhead protection, and warning lights in place _____
4. Temporary pedestrian traffic areas:
    a. Properly illuminated _____
    b. Free of trip hazards, debris, materials, sharp objects _____
5. All construction noises held to reasonable levels _____
6. Work performed in areas occupied by the public properly authorized _____
7. Appropriate warnings and instructions posted

LIABILITY
1. All release forms executed and delivered for trades to use staging, hoists, elevators, and equipment _____
2. Arrange for OSHA safety inspection to advise of additional recommended precautions. _____
3. Arrange for job site inspection by liability insurance carrier. Either secure a favorable written report, or immediately make all recommended corrections and reinspect. _____

WINTER CONDITIONS CHECKLIST

PROJECT STATUS	YES	NO
1. Building portions satisfactorily closed to the weather:		
a. Roof and flashings	___	___
b. Doors and windows	___	___
c. Building skin	___	___
d. _____	___	___
2. Permanent building systems usable for temporary heat:		
a. Electrical	___	___
b. HVAC	___	___
3. All open excavations closed prior to freezing conditions	___	___
4. Permanent sources of power and fuel available	___	___
5. Temporary power provisions necessary	___	___
6. Temporary fuel provisions necessary	___	___

CONTRACT

	YES	NO
1. Who is responsible for temporary heat and protection:		
a. The owner	___	___
b. Prime contractor or construction manager	___	___
c. Sub or trade contractor	___	___
2. Temporary heat required between:		
_____ and _____		
(date) (date)		
3. Temporary heat and protection now required because of a delay	___	___
4. If (3) is yes, who is responsible?		
a. The owner	___	___
b. Owner's agents	___	___
c. Prime contractor or construction manager	___	___
d. Sub or trade contractor		
(Name) _____	___	___
5. Party named in (4) notified in writing	___	___
6. Party named in (4) accepted responsibility	___	___
7. If (6) is no, backcharge procedure has begun	___	___
8. Estimated cost of temporary		
a. Protection $_____		
b. Heat $_____		
c. Light and power $_____		

JOB PRECAUTIONS	YES	NO
1. Arrangements have been made to secure:		
a. Temporary protection materials	___	___
b. Temporary enclosure materials	___	___
c. Temporary heaters	___	___
d. Continuous fuel supply	___	___
2. Temporary heaters are:		
a. Of adequate size and type	___	___
b. Fully operational and maintained	___	___
c. Of type allowed by codes	___	___
d. Situated in a safe manner relative to personnel, pedestrians, traffic, building materials, and ventilation	___	___
e. On a service/maintenance schedule	___	___
3. Temporary fuel is:		
a. On hand in adequate supply	___	___
b. Properly and safely stored	___	___
c. On a set refueling schedule	___	___
4. All water pockets have been eliminated:		
a. Roof areas	___	___
b. Pavement and graded areas	___	___
c. Sleeves, inserts, chases, and openings	___	___
e. Other _____	___	___
5. Arrangements have been made for:		
a. Snow plowing and removal	___	___
b. Equipment cold weather protection	___	___
c. Vehicle maintenance	___	___
6. Precautions have been taken to protect exposed work:		
a. Exposed piping protected, drained or heat traced	___	___
b. Recently placed work (concrete, formwork, reinforcing steel, masonry, etc.)	___	___
7. All project areas have been adequately marked to avoid damaged during snow removal:		
a. Parking areas	___	___
b. Entrances, exits, gates, passageways	___	___
c. Pedestrian traffic areas	___	___
d. Material and fuel storage areas	___	___
8. Any necessary photographs of all pre-winter jobsite conditions have been taken for a record	___	___
HAS THIS CHECKLIST BEEN SENT TO ALL JOB SITES?	___	___

TIME MANAGEMENT TIPS

Time management is two things. First is increasing efficiency; refining your own management techniques to increase output for a given period of time. Second is learning to work smarter. Allow time for other activities that you enjoy doing. This reduces stress on your system and, in turn, improves your operating efficiency.

1. Develop observation skills. Observe intently what is going on around you. Improving ability to get clear, accurate impressions increases the odds of correct initial responses.

2. Improve capacity for observation and quick decision making by increasing alertness, energy level, knowledge base, and experience.

3. Increase your alertness by

   ■ Overcoming natural tendencies to become preoccupied.
   ■ Changing routines.
   ■ Practicing daily a relevant skill that interests you.
   ■ Cultivating interests centering on observation.

4. Improve energy levels by

   ■ Eliminating personal criticisms, defensiveness, and other negative effects that drain energy and attention.
   ■ Becoming aware of those times that you lose energy by establishing times during the day to check on your activities on all levels.
   ■ Establishing and maintaining an exercise program to improve levels of overall physical fitness.
   ■ Using the creative power of sleep. The more demands you make on yourself, the more sleep you will need.

5. Give attention every day to expanding your knowledge and experience, and increasing your managerial skills.

6. When you can't find an answer, stop. Let the problem cool. Save time by restating the problem and observing it from a different angle.

7. Talking is more than transmitting words. You speak with your whole organism. Hearing your own words as you explain your problem to another often leads you to flow directly toward the answer.

8. Use language with precision. Avoid the possibility of confusion resulting from extraneous details.

9. Be sure that you understand statements by others by restating the concept in your own words to get a "yes" response.

10. Take the responsibility to be sure that others completely understand you before proceeding.

11. Draw diagrams to get more understanding and agreement in less time.

12. Remember that one appropriate analogy is often worth more than hours of discussion.

13. It is not as important to be able to read rapidly as it is to be able to decide what not to read.

14. Set priorities. Decide what are the most important activities and arrange your efforts specifically around them.

15. Organize your day. Have a definite game plan based upon your priorities. Control interruptions. Don't let the "immediate" demands interfere with your plan.

16. Become "now" oriented. Once you decide on an activity, *focus* your energy on it until it is completed or filed for future reference.

17. Delegate. Develop the skills to train others, then depend on them. Delegate as much as you possibly can.

18. Start with the tough jobs. Do the most important work early, when your energy levels are at their highest. Save busy work and errands for later, lower energy periods.

19. Reduce meetings. Resolve as much as you can by phone. Send subordinates wherever possible. Schedule meetings to run up against the noon hour or day's end to cut ramblings.

20. Avoid procrastination. The pressure of deadlines creates inefficiency, ineffectiveness, and rework.

TRADE CONTRACT/SUBCONTRACT CHECKLIST

The following checklist is to be used as a guide in the preparation or finalization of a trade contract or subcontract. It is important to understand that laws vary across state lines, and trade practices may differ depending upon the geographic location of your business and/or the jobsite. Accordingly, before your specific contract form, procedure, etc. is determined, the advice of a competent attorney should be sought.

These items are not intended as definitive solutions. Rather, they identify certain key issues that can be addressed and resolved at the time the contract is prepared—rather than after a related problem arises.

A. PROJECT/BID IDENTIFICATION

■ 1. Project identification: Name _____
Address _____
Job # _____

■ 2. Bid package: No _____ Description _____

■ 3. Invitation to bid required: Yes _____ Date _____
No _____

■ 4. Pre-bid conference required: Yes ___ Date ___ Time ___
No ___

■ 5. Specific proposal form required: Yes ___ Ready by ___
No ___

■ 6. Bid due date: _____

B. TRADE/SUBCONTRACT

■ 1. Project identification:
Name _____
Location _____
Job # _____

■ 2. Owner _____

■ 3. Architect _____

■ 4. General contractor/construction manager _____

■ 5. Trade/subcontractor: Name _____
Address _____
_____

■ 6. Scope-of-Work: Yes No
a. Labor & Material   ___ ___
b. Labor only   ___ ___
c. Decision-build responsibility   ___ ___
d. Per plans & specifications   ___ ___
e. Equipment, scaffolding, hoisting   ___ ___
f. Storage, protection   ___ ___
g. Receipt/storage/distribution of items
purchased by others   ___ ___

■ 7. Shop drawings or other submittals required: Yes ___ No ___

■ 8. Contract price:
a. Lump sum _____
b. Unit price _____
c. Combination _____

■ 9. Alternate prices _____
_____
_____

■ 10. Billings and payments: Yes No
a. Deposits required   ___ ___
b. Schedule of values required   ___ ___
c. Requisition submissive dates, schedule required ___ ___
d. Retainage (_____%) Required   ___ ___

■ 11. Schedule:
a. Will give notice to proceed   Yes _____ No _____
b. Who provides schedule/update info. _____
c. Milestone schedule dates:
Start _____
Complete _____
Other _____

■ 12. Insurance:
a. Workman's comp.: Yes ___ Amount ___
No ___
b. General liability: Yes ___ Amount ___
No ___
c. Special
requirements: Yes ___ Description ___ Amount ___
No ___

■ 13. Standards of work:
a. Industry practice   ___
b. Applicable building codes   ___
c. OSHA   ___
d. Government/quasi-government requirements   ___

■ 14. Taxes, fringe benefits:
a. Responsibility _____

■ 15. Minimum wage standards: Yes _____
No _____

■ 16. Changes:
a. Requirements for written change orders Yes ___ No ___
b. Who authorizes damages? _____

■ 17. Cleanup:
a. Responsibility to remove debris to dumpster/central
location _____
b. Responsibility to remove debris
from jobsite _____

■ 18. Permits/fees/deposits:
a. Responsibility _____

■ 19. Equal opportunity:
a. Mandatory contract clause? _____

■ 20. Lien waivers & certifications of payment:
a. Required   Yes ___ Each payment ___
Final payment ___
No ___

■ 21. Indemnification:
a. Required   Yes ___   No ___

■ 22. Termination:
a. Breach due clause? Yes ___   No ___
b. Required notice?   Yes ___   No ___

■ 23. Breach:
a. Definition _____

■ 24. Assignment:
a. Assignable   Yes ___   No ___

■ 25. Dispute Resolution:
a. Arbitration   Yes _____ Rules _____
No _____

■ 26. Authorized contract execution
a. Identification required   Yes ___ No ___
b. Power-of-attorney   Yes ___ No ___

JOB START-UP CHECKLIST

Use this checklist to arrange for all services, supplies, and facilities necessary for a smooth and complete transition into your project's construction phase.

CONTRACT

1. Type (GC, CM, CM w/GMP, etc.) _____
2. Contract signed (date) _____
3. Start date _____
4. Completion date _____
5. Number of working days _____
6. Liquidated damages: Yes: $_____/Day
                      No: _____
7. Unusual restrictions: _____
   _____
8. Other _____

CONTRACT EXECUTION

1. Permits obtained:

Item	Who Pays	Received
a. General building permit	_____	____
b. Plumbing	_____	____
c. HVAC	_____	____
d. Fire protection	_____	____
e. Electrical	_____	____
f. Other:	_____	____

2. Billing procedure:
   a. Date subcontractor requisitions due: _____
   b. Date general requisition to owner due: _____
   c. Schedule of values prepared/approved _____
   d. Remarks _____
3. Change order procedure:
   a. Change clause present: Section _____
   b. Forms required: _____
   c. Remarks: _____
4. EEO Requirements:
   a. Mandatory _____ b. Good faith _____
5. Independent testing laboratories:
   a. Areas required: _____
   b. Payment responsibility: _____
6. Baselines and benchmark:
   Responsibility: _____
7. Job meeting schedule: _____
8. Dispute resolution:
   a. Dispute clause present: Section _____
   b. Arbitration provision: Section _____
   c. Notice requirements: _____

CONTRACT DOCUMENTS

1. Jobsite copies of:
   a. Contract ____
   b. General, special, and supplementary conditions ____
   c. Technical specifications ____
   d. Plans ____
   e. Project manual/procedures ____

COST AND PRODUCTION CONTROL

1. Documents on file:
   a. Budget ____
   b. Resource estimates: labor ____
                      materials ____
   c. Job cost report ____
   d. Other _____

SITE AND SERVICES

1. Temporary fences, protection (see safety checklist) ____
2. Guard service ____
3. Temporary electric ____
4. Temporary water ____
5. Dumpster, disposal arrangements ____
6. Progress photograph service ____
7. Testing laboratories
   a. Soils ____
   b. Concrete ____
   c. Steel and welding ____
   d. Other _____ ____
8. Weather information phone numbers ____

ADMINISTRATION

1. Supply of job forms:
   a. Field reports ____
   b. Change order forms ____
   c. Change order summary logs ____
   d. Quotation and telephone quotation forms ____
   e. Payroll forms ____
   f. Time and material tickets ____
   g. Subcontract adjustment forms ____
   h. Job meeting forms ____
   i. Memos ____
   j. Schedule status report forms ____
   k. Cost report forms ____
   l. Photograph record forms ____
   m. Other _____ ____
   n. Other _____ ____
2. Start-up submissions on file:
   a. Subcontractor payment and performance bonds ____
   b. Subcontractor insurance certificates ____
   c. Equipment use releases ____
   d. Shop drawing submission schedule ____
   e. Other _____ ____
3. Project files
   a. Contract and correspondence files ____
   b. Submittal files ____
   c. Special files ____

FIELD OFFICE AND OFFICE EQUIPMENT

1. Trailer(s) ____
2. Retail space ____
3. Temporary facilities
   a. Heat ____
   b. Lighting and power ____
   c. Telephone(s) and mobile phones ____
   d. Site radios ____
   e. Lavatories ____
   f. Water ____
4. Office furniture
   a. Desks ____
   b. Conference table(s) ____
   c. Plan table(s) ____
   d. Swivel chairs, folding chairs, stools ____
   e. File cabinets, fireproof file cabinet ____
   f. Plan rack(s), plan edge reinforcing machine ____
   g. Bookcases, tack boards ____
5. Job directory
   a. Owner representative(s) ____
   b. Design professionals ____
   c. Government and approving authorities ____
   d. Police, fire, hospital, security ____
   e. Jobsite personnel home numbers ____
   f. Subcontractors and suppliers ____
6. Fire and intrusion alarm systems ____
7. Safety equipment
   a. Fire extinguishers ____
   b. Hard hats ____
   c. First-aid kit and supplies ____
   d. Emergency phone numbers ____
   e. Stretcher ____
8. Office equipment and supplies
   a. Copier, supplies and maintenance arrangements ____
   b. Blueprint arrangements ____
   c. Computer(s), printer(s), plotter(s), software ____
   d. Telecopier ____
   e. Refrigerator, coffee machine, supplies ____
   f. Bottled water ____

PROJECT CLOSEOUT CHECKLIST

SUBCONTRACTOR SUBMITTALS
1. Each subcontractor has delivered as required: _____
   a. As-built drawings _____
   b. Guarantees and warrantees _____
   c. Inspection certificates _____
   d. Material/installation certifications _____
   e. Operating and maintenance manuals _____
   f. Operating instruction to owner personnel performed _____
   g. General releases _____
   h. Lien waivers _____
   i. Other _____ _____

   j. Other _____ _____

FINAL SUBMITTALS TO THE OWNER
1. As-built plans and specifications _____
2. Guarantee(s), transfer of subcontractors' guarantees _____
3. Transfer of all certifications, releases, lien waivers, operating and maintenance manuals _____
4. Other _____ _____

5. Other _____ _____

FINAL COMPLETION OF THE WORK
1. Certificate(s) of occupancy received _____
2. Punch list confirmed to be complete _____
3. Final/finish cleanup performed _____
4. Demobilization of all field facilities and equipment complete _____
6. Termination of temporary services complete:
   a. Heat, light, power, and telephone _____
   b. Fire, police, guard service _____
   c. Insurance _____
   d. Office equipment and furnishings _____
7. Owner/architect certificates of completion received _____
8. Other _____ _____

9. Other _____ _____

BILLINGS, CHARGES, AND PAYMENTS
1. All owner-acknowledged change orders submitted and approved _____
2. All subcontractor changes and adjustments processed _____
3. Steps taken toward resolution of outstanding subcontractor claims _____
4. Steps taken toward resolution of outstanding claims to the owner _____
5. All subcontractor backcharges finalized _____
6. Final billings received from all subcontractors and suppliers in acceptable form _____
7. Final billing including retainage release submitted _____

REVIEW THE CONTRACT, SUBCONTRACT OR PURCHASE ORDER, SPECIFICATIONS, AND COMPANY PROCEDURE TO
DETERMINE ANY ADDITIONAL REQUIREMENTS. LIST BELOW:
1. _____ _____
2. _____ _____
3. _____ _____
4. _____ _____
5. _____ _____

SUBCONTRACTOR/SUPPLIER PROGRESS PAYMENT CHECKLIST

REQUIRED SUBMISSIONS
1. Contract or purchase order executed and on file _____
2. Payment and performance bond received _____
3. Insurance certificate with adequate levels of coverage received _____
4. Lien waivers received _____
5. Material certifications received _____
6. "Passing" inspection reports received _____
7. Equipment, scaffolding, or elevator use release forms received _____

8. Other _____ _____

PAYMENT CONDITIONS
1. All material billed properly approved _____
2. All material requisitioned for on-site _____
3. If material billed for is off-site:
   a. Does the contract allow for payment? _____
   b. If so, are all required insurances, title transfers, and other requirements complete? _____
   c. Does the material require inspection? _____
   d. Will the party pay for the inspection? _____

THE REQUISITIONS FOR PAYMENT
1. Submitted on time _____
2. Each line item approved by the proper authority:
   a. Contract work _____
   b. Change order work _____
3. All supporting documentation verified _____
4. All supporting time and material tickets approved _____
5. Proper retainage percentages deducted _____
6. Payment *for this work* received from the owner _____
7. If (6) is no, can full or partial payment still be released? _____

REVIEW THE CONTRACT, SUBCONTRACT OR PURCHASE ORDER, SPECIFICATIONS, AND COMPANY PROCEDURE TO DETERMINE ANY ADDITIONAL REQUIREMENTS. LIST BELOW:

1. _____

2. _____

3. _____

SUBCONTRACTOR/SUPPLIER FINAL PAYMENT CHECKLIST

THE WORK
1. Punch list complete _____
2. *Written* acceptances for all work received from:
   a. The owner _____
   b. The design professionals _____
   c. Our company _____
3. Demobilization complete _____
4. All temporary construction and facilities removed _____

5. Other _____ _____

FINAL DOCUMENT SUBMISSIONS
1. As-built drawings _____
2. Guarantees and warrantees _____
3. Operating and maintenance manuals _____
4. Operating and maintenance instruction performed _____
5. Material certifications received _____
6. "Passing" testing and inspection reports received _____
7. Lien waivers received _____

8. Other _____ _____

FINAL PAYMENT
1. All material billed for properly submitted/approved _____
2. Each requisition line item approved _____
3. All supporting documentation verified _____
4. All supporting time and material tickets approved _____
5. All charge orders approved in the submitted amounts _____
6. All back charges resolved to your satisfaction _____
7. Outstanding claims by
   a. The subcontractor _____
   b. The owner _____
   c. Our company _____
8. Final payment including retainage received from the owner _____

REVIEW THE CONTRACT, SUBCONTRACT OR PURCHASE ORDER, SPECIFICATIONS, AND COMPANY PROCEDURE TO DETERMINE ANY ADDITIONAL REQUIREMENTS. LIST BELOW:

1. _____

2. _____

3. _____

JOB MEETING GUIDELINES

Use these guidelines as an aid to prepare and follow through on all project meetings.

GENERAL
1. Job meetings and their minutes are critically important to job coordination, documentation, and protection of your interests. If properly completed, the job meeting minutes will:
   a. Record history of all significant (or potentially significant) events.
   b. Keep open items on the front burner until they are finally resolved or filed for future reference.
   c. Force action.
   d. Clarify accountability.
   e. Provide a basis to identify required expedited action.
   f. Support interpretations and serious actions.
   g. Facilitate fast, efficient research, both soon and long after the occurrence of an event.

MEETING PREPARATION
1. Schedule morning meetings if possible.
2. Always start the meetings precisely *on time*, regardless of who may be absent.
3. Make meeting attendance *mandatory*. Absence is no excuse. All parties are responsible for information contained in the meeting.
4. Confirm attendance by all those required to attend *prior* to the meeting.
5. Notify absent parties *immediately after the meeting* of decisions, consequences, and so on that affect them.

MEETING MINUTES GUIDELINES
1. Use outline format.
   a. Consecutively number meetings.
   b. Separate "Old" and "New" business.
   c. Number each successive item for easy reference.
2. Use a title for each item.
   a. Summary description of the issue.
   b. Use exactly the same title wording at each meeting.
3. Include all appropriate file references in an item title.
   a. Change order number.
   b. Estimate number.
   c. Architect's bulletin number.
4. Name names. Pin down direct responsibility.
5. Use *short* but specific statements.
6. Read back noted language to confirm agreement on its accuracy.
7. Require definite action. Do not leave an item without determining:
   a. The next step
   b. Who is to perform it
   c. The precise date action is required by.
8. Notify all meeting recipients to immediately notify the writer of any errors or omissions in the representations.

CHANGE ORDER RESEARCH CHECKLIST

The Change Order Research Checklist forces a thorough contemplation of change order sources. Use it as an exercise in a thought process to pattern your research into an almost routine procedure. The checklist format permits completion of the process with clear thinking and a minimum of time.

CONTRACT

	YES	NO
1. Form of Contract:		
a. Adhesion	___	___
b. Negotiated	___	___
2. Is the subcontract scope of work:		
a. Owner defined?	___	___
b. Contractor-defined?	___	___
3. Does contract language exist defining the situation?	___	___
4. If 3 is yes, can it be opposed with contract law?	___	___
5. Can Trade Practice be used by you or the owner to stretch an interpretation?	___	___
6. Are rules of precedence clearly stated in the General Conditions?	___	___

SPECIFICATIONS

	YES	NO
1. Does a specification section exist?	___	___
2. If 1 is yes:		
a. Is it complete?	___	___
b. Is it subject to more than one reasonable interpretation?	___	___
c. Can it be deemed to fall into any "per plans and specs" trade or subcontract?	___	___
d. Can the work be done precisely as specified?	___	___
3. If 1 is no, does General Conditions boilerplate exist that:		
a. Clearly describes the work?	___	___
b. Might be used by your opponent to strain an interpretation?	___	___
4. Does more than one specification exist?	___	___
5. If 4 is yes:		
a. Are they included in different sections?	___	___
b. Do conflicts exist between the requirements of each?	___	___
c. Does one make any more sense than the other?	___	___
6. Are there references to industry standard specs?	___	___
7. If 6 is yes:		
a. Do they contain precise material descriptions (as opposed to simply design criteria)?	___	___
b. Do they conflict in any way with other stated (specified) requirements?	___	___

PLANS

	YES	NO
1. Do any specific notes exist related to the work?	___	___
2. Do general notes exist that might be used to strain an interpretation (boilerplate)?	___	___
3. If 2 or 3 is yes, do they conflict with the requirements included in the respective specifications section?	___	___
4. Are specific details included?	___	___
5. If 4 is yes:		
a. Have you checked *all* cuts and references to details, elevations, plans, specs, etc.?	___	___
b. Is all relevant information included?	___	___
c. Do conflicts exist between any items of 5.a?	___	___
d. Are they subject to more than one reasonable interpretation?	___	___
6. Have shop drawing been approved that differ from specified requirements?	___	___
7. If 6 is yes:		
a. Were the differences clearly highlighted and understood at the time of approval?	___	___
b. Are the differences subject to more than one reasonable interpretation?	___	___
c. Are errors or omissions evident?	___	___
d. Have they been properly coordinated with all other parts of the work?	___	___
e. Have all "by others" and "not by ___" notes been addressed?	___	___
7. Has the job been fast-tracked?	___	___
8. If 7 is yes, do the dates on the current documents match those originally included in the contract?	___	___
9. If 8 is no, are there significant differences?	___	___

SITE

	YES	NO
1. Should the work have been apparent in a pre-bid site investigation?	___	___
2. Are the changed conditions the result of owner or architect nondisclosure?	___	___
3. Are the conditions the result of some previously undetectable latent (hidden) condition(s)?	___	___
4. Is the site information given in the plans		
a. Accurate?	___	___
b. Complete?	___	___
5. Are any site conditions different now from those at the time of bid?	___	___

SUPPORTING DOCUMENTS

	YES	NO
1. Is the changed work included in the Schedule of Values?	___	___
2. If 1 is yes, did whoever prepared the schedule have a justification for it?	___	___
3. If 2 is yes, can it be credably dismissed in any way?	___	___
4. Are there any prior discussions, meeting minutes, letters, quotes, etc. that confirmed that extra cost will or will not be applicable?	___	___

ADMINISTRATION

1. Date of discovery .... ____/ ____/
2. Company and person responsible for first identification .... _____

3. Persons Notified: _____ Date: ___/___/
                     _____ Date: ___/___/
                     _____ Date: ___/___/

	YES	NO
4. Have all circumstances of discovery been recorded?	___	___
5. Has all relevant documentation been assembled?		
a. Field Reports	___	___
b. Letters and transmittals	___	___
c. Telephone logs and misc. notes	___	___
d. Material invoices and payroll records	___	___
e. Meeting minutes	___	___
6. Are before-during-after photographs necessary? If so, have they been arranged?	___	___
7. Have all relevant plans, sketches, surveys, diagrams, etc. been assembled?	___	___
8. Has the schedule impact been analyzed?	___	___

8. a. Has interface occurred? Date: ___/
  b. If not, what is the date of anticipated interference .... ___/ ___/
  c. How many extra days can be assigned to the change? ___
9. What is the date that change order approval is required before the schedule is affected? ___/ ___/

	YES	NO
10. Have all trade contractors and suppliers even remotely affected been advised of the change?	___	___
11. If 10 is yes, have all cost changes (adds and deducts) been assembled?	___	___
12. If 11 is yes:		
a. Does each positively indicate that the schedule is or is not affected (and by how much)?	___	___
b. Is each properly broken down to allow meaningful evaluation?	___	___
c. Does each have all substantiating documents attached?	___	___

CHANGE ORDER DISCOVERY CHECKLIST

The Change Order Discovery Checklist catalogs the most common sources of changes that occur in the various stages of every construction project. It is a convenient mechanism that allows clear consideration of all potential effects.

Performing the analysis at the earliest possible time will expose all real and potential interferences *before* they get an opportunity to do their worst damage. Completing the detailed checklist will help you contemplate change considerations without the risk of oversight.

PRE-DESIGN YES NO

1. Adjacent Properties
   a. Have all properties adjacent to the site perimeter been reviewed in detail? ___ ___
   b. Are there
      - Seasonal watercourses? ___ ___
      - Heavy traffic patterns? ___ ___
      - Other independent construction activities? ___ ___
      - Other: _____ ___ ___
      - Other: _____ ___ ___
2. Boring (Subsurface) Data
   a. Are boring depths inconsistent? ___ ___
   b. Are boring locations erratic or unusual? ___ ___
   c. Are boring locations relevant to construction:
      - Are borings provided outside the area? ___ ___
      - Are gaps left within the building area? ___ ___
   d. What time of year were the borings taken? ___
3. Building Code Compliance
   a. Have any violations of the building codes been observed by any building official when the building permit was applied for? ___ ___
   b. Do any portions of the design appear out of the ordinary?
      - Headroom? ___ ___
      - Entrances/Exits? ___ ___
      - Handicap provisions? ___ ___
      - Fire separations? ___ ___
      - Lighting? ___ ___
      - Ventilation? ___ ___
      - Other: _____ ___ ___
      - Other: _____ ___ ___
4. Easements/Rights of Way
   a. Are there designated easements? ___ ___
   b. If so, will they adversely affect your operation? ___ ___
   c. Do local traffic patterns restrict access? ___ ___
   d. Are there parking areas, traffic patterns, business, etc. at the contract limit line that will restrict operations in any way? ___ ___
   e. If 4.a is yes, do you know all conditions? ___ ___
   f. If a restriction to your operation is evident, has your estimate accommodated it in some way? ___ ___
   g. If 4.f is no, should a reasonable pre-bid site investigation disclose the condition? ___ ___
5. Inland Wetland Approvals
   a. Does any portion of the site encroach on Inland Wetlands? ___ ___
   b. If so, are all appropriate approvals in place? ___ ___
   c. If required approvals are not apparent, have you requested the confirming information from the owner? ___ ___
6. Interference of Utilities Not Properly Shown
   a. Have the characteristics of all existing utilities been verified with each respective company? ___ ___
   b. Has each company representative reviewed the details with you at the site? ___ ___
   c. Is anything different from that represented on the plans? ___ ___
   d. Are the current utility charges for the various tie-ins the same as those given at the time of bid? ___ ___
7. Plan Approvals (Building Permit)
   a. Has the building permit been applied for at the earliest possible time? ___ ___
   b. Were there *any* problems? ___ ___
   c. Were any notes or corrections made on the plans? ___ ___
   d. Has the permit been delayed in any way? ___ ___
   e. Is a permit required (and a Certificate of Occupancy necessary) for temporary field offices? ___ ___

PRE-DESIGN (continued) YES NO

8. Temporary Utilities—Availability Within Contract Limit Lines
   a. Have you confirmed the anticipated conditions at the time of bid? ___ ___
   b. Are conditions adequate? ___ ___
   c. Are site conditions now different? ___ ___
      - Are additional telephone/power poles needed? ___ ___
      - Is power available at all (without generating equipment)? ___ ___
      - Is previously anticipated use of existing facilities now prevented? ___ ___
      - Is temporary heat and protection now required due to owner-caused delay? ___ ___
      - Is water available in sufficient amounts for construction? ___ ___

THE CONTRACT AND BID DOCUMENTS

1. Award Date
   a. Has an extension in the contract award date been requested? ___ ___
   b. If so, is there any basis upon which to ask for an increase in the contract sum?
      - Will acceleration be necessary? ___ ___
      - Will a portion of the project now be placed into winter conditions as a result of the start up delay? ___ ___
   c. Do you have the strength to now require more favorable contract terms:
      - Is your bid substantially lower than the next bidder's? ___ ___
      - Can you complete the facility in less time than your competitors? ___ ___
      - Were you involved in design development? ___ ___
      - Is the owner tied to you in any way? ___ ___
2. Named Subcontracts
   a. Are there owner-selected subcontracts on the project? ___ ___
   b. Does any disclaimer exist that limits the owner's liability for subcontractor selection? ___ ___
   c. Are the subcontract agreements themselves owner-defined? ___ ___
   d. Is any specific procedure in place to resolve disputes between two owner-defined subcontracts? ___ ___
   e. Will the owner in fact make decisions (or will there be constant attempts to drop the responsibility on the general contractor)? ___ ___
3. (Price/Bid) Allowances
   a. Are there allowances anywhere in the contract? ___ ___
   b. If so, have all allowance items been bid or re-bid yet? ___ ___
   c. Have or will all allowance items been awarded in time to prevent schedule interruption? ___ ___
4. (Contract) Time
   a. Did the first schedule draft drastically exceed the allowed contract time? ___ ___
   b. Did subsequent schedule drafts incorporate unusual or excessive compressions and accelerations? ___ ___
   c. Have any long lead time purchases dramatically exceeded the originally anticipated deliveries? ___ ___
   d. If so, were they for specified items? ___ ___
   e. Had the contract award date been extended? ___ ___
   f. Had the site start date been extended for an owner-caused reason? ___ ___
   g. If either 4.d or 4.e is yes, was the schedule logic affected? ___ ___
   h. Did extra work result? ___ ___
   i. Can clear cause-effect relationships be demonstrated to justify more contract time? ___ ___

PLANS AND SPECIFICATIONS	YES	NO

PLANS AND SPECIFICATIONS

1. "As Indicated"
   a. Are notes without specific references common (such as "As Indicated," "See Spec," "See Plans," and so on)?
   b. Have you taken the time to research each one to confirm that completing details do in fact exist?
   c. If so, have you discovered incomplete, conflicting, or missing references?
   d. If so, have you cataloged each instance for individual consideration?
2. Ceiling Space (Conflicts)
   a. Is there a contract clause clearly noting the sub or trade contractor to be responsible for coordination of their work?
   b. Have all areas of potential conflict in the ceilings been properly coordinated:
      - Is there enough room to pitch all pipe?
      - Do pitched lines miss all steel and concrete beams?
      - Can all ducts pass below beams at all locations shown?
      - Do too many items occupy the same space in any area?
      - If so, can enough space be made, or can anything be moved?
      - Are there large ducts shown to cross large beams and/or other significant obstructions?
      - Will all light fixtures fit in the remaining spaces
        Height?
        Plan?
      - Are there elaborate architectural, structural, or special shapes continuing into the ceiling?
      - If so, do other building systems or equipment penetrate any part of them?
      - If so, have you confirmed the *actual* size of everything?
4. Changed Existing Conditions
   a. Has the estimate been reviewed for:
      - All sitework considerations?
      - Any interferences with existing structures?
      - Any noted conditions of existing structures?
      - Locations, extent, makeup, and conditions of existing utilities?
      - Traffic patterns and site access?
      - Anticipated storage and staging areas?
      - Parking and security arrangements?
   b. Have the estimators involved met with you at the site to review all items in (a)?
   c. Have any changes between conditions existing now and those existing at the time of the bid become apparent?
5. Column and Beam Locations
   a. Have the structural drawings been reviewed in detail:
      - Are column layouts erratic or unusual?
      - Are there any unusually long spans requiring relatively large structural members?
      - Are there unusual shapes, angles, slopes, or connections?
      - Are elevation changes strained or confusing?
      - Are beam sizes all different (with different ceiling spaces below them)?
      - Have the locations of all large beams been reviewed?
      - Are there unusual designs?
      - If so, is enough information included for proper shop drawing preparation the first time around?

PLANS AND SPECIFICATIONS (continued)

   b. After reviewing the architectural, plumbing, H.V.A.C., and electrical plans:
      - Are listed column line dimensions between all designs consistent?
      - Are there large ducts shown crossing large beams?
      - Are there light fixtures in the areas of large ducts?
      - Does the sprinkler main cross large beams, ducts, or light fixtures?
      - Do random spot checks of architectural dimension strings reveal any discrepancies?
6. Design Change Telltales
   a. Are there a large number of apparent last-minute design changes? Are there
      - Different styles of type or handwriting in the specifications?
      - Incomplete erasures?
      - Out-of-sequence reference marks or inserted pages in the specifications?
      - Different handwriting on the plans?
      - Different use of language for the same or similar remarks?
7. Design Discipline Interfaces
   a. Has any review to this point revealed any problems at the points where design disciplines cross each other?
8. Duplications of Design
   a. Have any duplications been observed?
   b. If so:
      - Is each description complete?
      - Are the descriptions in different specification sections with different contractors involved?
      - Are the duplications included in the same specification?
      - Is the same work specified twice?
      - Is different work specified for the same function?
      - Is any of the available options preferred?
   c. In a review of relevant contracts, plans, and specifications:
      - Are any or all contracts of an adhesion format?
      - Are any subcontractors owner-selected?
      - Are the affected subcontracts "per plans and specs"?
      - Are there modifications to any contract?
      - Are the rules of precedence outlined in the specification?
      - Are all affected plans noted to be the responsibility of the affected subcontractor(s)?
      - Do the descriptions of work included in the affected and related specification sections help your case?
   d. Objectively analyze each duplication:
      - Have all the reasons why each subcontractor should and should not have carried the work in their bids been considered?
      - Should any contractor aware of the work have reasonably construed it to be included by another trade?
      - Did anyone request clarification from the owner prior to bid?
      - If so, is the request and/or response documented?
      - Is each duplication clear and complete in itself?

e. Is there a preferred solution:
- Does any solution involve your own time or money? ____ ____
- Are the dollar estimates of each solution a consideration? ____ ____
- Is the timing of any solution particularly good or bad? ____ ____
- Is any potentially affected contractor more inclined to accept the extra work? ____ ____
- Does any solution make more sense? ____ ____

f. Do grounds exist to convince the owner that duplicated work is in fact not included anywhere? ____ ____

9. "Fat" Specifications

a. Does a review of the documents reveal:
- An unusually fat "front end?" ____ ____
- Extensive duplication in the general provisions? ____ ____
- Long and/or labored descriptions and instructions? ____ ____
- Catchall phases and boilerplate not specifically applying to project conditions? ____ ____

10. Finish Schedule vs. Specification Index

a. In a comparison of the Finish Schedule to the Specification Index:
- Is each item accounted for? ____ ____
- Is each item included only once? ____ ____

11. Inadequate Level of Detail/Missing Details

a. If enough design information has not been originally provided:
- Will the architect respond now with the complete information? ____ ____
- Is it confirmed in writing? ____ ____
- Are there any additional cost implications? ____ ____

12. Light Fixture Locations

a. In overlaying the lighting plans on the reflected ceiling plans, are there conflicts in:
- Ceiling light fixtures? ____ ____
- Emergency lights? ____ ____
- Soffit lights? ____ ____
- Exit lights? ____ ____
- Undercabinet lights? ____ ____

b. In overlaying the architectural plans, are there conflicts in walls, soffits, or cabinets? ____ ____

c. In overlaying the H.V.A.C. plans:
- Are there conflicts in register, grille, and diffuser locations? ____ ____
- Are equipment actual sizes accommodated? ____ ____
- Does everything miss the lights? ____ ____

d. In overlaying the sprinkler plans:
- Do the heads miss the lights? ____ ____
- Do the heads fall in the center or quarter center of the ceiling tile? ____ ____
- Is there an architectural pattern in the ceiling tile that will change location preference? ____ ____

e. In overlaying the electrical plans:
- Do the smoke detectors miss the lights (and everything else)? ____ ____

13. Match Lines and Plan Orientations

a. Are match lines present? ____ ____

b. If so:
- Are they necessary? ____ ____
- Are they in the same location *every* time? ____ ____
- Do they include the same information? ____ ____
- Is anything missing? ____ ____
- Are they complete and to the same extent on every plan? ____ ____

c. Is the north arrow in the same place on each drawing? ____ ____

d. Are the orientations the same for each plan? ____ ____

14. Mechanical, Electrical, and N.I.C. Equipment.

a. Are differences highlighted in *all* approval submissions? ____ ____

15. Numerous Details and Dimension Strings

a. Have repeated designs been observed? ____ ____

b. Are there many instances of multiple dimension strings? ____ ____

c. If so, have spot checks uncovered errors? ____ ____

16. Performance vs. Procedure Specifications

a. Are there any instances in which both performance *and* procedure specifications occur for the same item? ____ ____

b. If so:
- Are they mutually exclusive? ____ ____
- Can they be made to be compatible? ____ ____
- Is one or the other more expensive? ____ ____
- Is one preferred over the other? ____ ____
- Has one been included in the Schedule of Values? ____ ____
- Is it cost-prohibitive to accomplish both? ____ ____
- Is time or material availability a factor? ____ ____
- Is one more complete or otherwise more appropriate? ____ ____

c. Is one preferred over the other? ____ ____

d. Have all the details and arguments supporting your position been assembled? ____ ____

17. Proprietary Restrictions (Public)

a. Does the specification being considered:
- Name fewer than three acceptable suppliers? ____ ____
- Include the words "Or Equal"? ____ ____

b. Do you intend to use an "equal" product? ____ ____

c. If so, does the owner want a credit change order? ____ ____

d. Has the Owner Rejected your "Equal" submission? ____ ____

18. Specification Section "Scopes"

a. Does the design coordination process appear to have been done correctly? ____ ____

b. Are specific cross references included? ____ ____

c. Does the scope section appear to be complete? ____ ____

SITE

1. Grades, Elevations, and Contours

a. Has the entire site been photographed *before* any work has begun? ____ ____

b. Have the existing grades been spot-checked for accuracy? ____ ____

c. If so, have any discrepancies been discovered? ____ ____

d. If so, has a detailed check been arranged? ____ ____

e. Have the locations of existing telephone, water, sewer, fuel tanks and lines, and gas lines been verified? ____ ____

f. Have the manholes been opened to spot check actual pipe invert elevations? ____ ____

g. Have the locations of telephone poles, street signs, pole guys, and any other constructions been checked to avoid interference with site improvements? ____ ____

h. Have the actual horizontal distances between telephone poles, light poles, manholes, drainage structures, etc. been checked for accuracy? ____ ____

i. Have any discrepancies discovered been documented in the most accurate and unquestionable manner available? ____ ____

SHOP DRAWING SUBMITTAL CHECKLIST

This checklist will help to make certain that all submissions for approval meet requirements, are acted upon properly by the design professionals, and are coordinated in a timely manner with those who need the information.

SUBMISSION REQUIREMENTS

1. All approval submissions contain:
   a. Project title and job number _____
   b. Contract identification _____
   c. Date of submission, including dates of all previous submissions and revisions _____
   d. Names of the contractor, supplier, and/or manufacturer _____
   e. Identification of all products, with specification identification numbers _____
   f. Field dimensions, clearly identified as such _____
   g. Relation to adjacent and/or critical features of the work or materials _____
   h. References to applicable standard specifications _____
   i. *Clear* identifications of deviations from the contract documents _____
   j. All other pertinent information as may be required by the specifications or our company, such as
      ■ Model numbers _____
      ■ Performance characteristics _____
      ■ Dimensions and clearances _____
      ■ Wiring or piping diagrams and controls _____
   k. Manufacturer's standard or schematic drawings or diagrams include:
      ■ Modifications to delete information not applicable _____
      ■ Supplemental information specifically applicable _____
   l. Check the specifications for additional requirements:
      ■ _____ _____
      ■ _____ _____

SUBMITTAL REVIEW PROCEDURE

1. Ensure that subcontractors and suppliers submit all materials promptly. _____
2. Determine and verify:
   a. That the sub has incorporated and will guarantee all field dimensions _____
   b. All field conditions and construction criteria have been accommodated _____
   c. That the product either complies with the specifications requirements in every respect, or that any deviations have been properly identified, and include their respective explanations _____
3. Coordinate each submittal with both the field and the contract document requirements of the work. _____
4. Research and confirm all "justifications" for any deviations from the contract requirements. Do this *before* submitting the documents to the architect for approval. _____
5. Determine if a credit or addition to the contract is in order, based on any changes incorporated into the submission. _____
6. Determine if back charges to any other subcontractors are in order as a result of changes brought about by them. _____
7. Determine that the submission is timely, and that the material conforms to the confirmed delivery times as currently required. _____
8. Positively identify the responsibility for all "Not by Subcontractor" or "By Others" kinds of notations. Correct as necessary *before* submission to the architect for approval. _____
9. Compare all resubmissions with the file copy of the previous submissions. Confirm that all required corrections have been made. _____

Note: It is helpful to the shop drawing review process if by prior arrangement you and the design professionals consistently use different color markers throughout the review process. This makes it easy at a later date to determine who originated a particular remark.

DISTRIBUTION

1. Upon receipt of submittals bearing the stamp indicating architect action, distribute copies to:
   a. Job site file ("For Construction" documents only) _____
   b. Record documents file _____
   c. Other affected subs and suppliers _____
   d. The supplier or fabricator _____
   e. The erector or installer _____
   f. Anyone else who may need the information to coordinate work properly _____

FOLLOW-UP

1. Monitor the time it takes for the approval process.
   a. Be sure that the architect is giving proper, timely attention. _____
   b. Be sure that all delays and other inappropriate actions are duly noted in the correspondence. _____
2. Be certain that the design professionals:
   a. Include all information required of them by way of questions in the submittals _____
   b. Do not overstep their authority _____
   c. Do not overstep their professional capacities or their licenses _____
   d. Do not add work without regard to the established change order procedure _____
   e. Include only meaningful action that will allow proper completion of the submittal _____
   f. Affix the *accepted* stamp and initial/sign it _____
   g. Clearly indicate any requirements for resubmittal, or approval of the submittal _____
3. Upon distribution of the submittal back to its originator:
   a. Reconfirm the delivery schedule(s) _____
   b. Confirm that the submission is being returned in good time for the subcontractor or supplier to meet its own requirements _____
   c. Note any significant information for the next construction schedule update _____
   d. Begin any actions that may be necessary to resolve problems that have been exposed by the review process _____

EQUIPMENT SAFETY, PRESTART, AND MAINTENANCE CHECKLIST

Equipment safety, reliability, and operating efficiency are no accident. Developing good habits of following simple rules of observation and reasonable care will pay back thousands of dollars in reduced equipment down time, increased operating efficiency, and operator well being. Follow this simple checklist* and begin saving real dollars now.

GENERAL SAFETY RULES
1. Only qualified people should operate the equipment.
2. Learn the location and purpose of all controls, instruments, indicator lights, and labels.
3. Fasten a first-aid kit to all major equipment.
4. Keep a fully charged fire extinguisher mounted conveniently. Learn to use it correctly.
5. Wear fairly tight clothing and safety equipment.
6. Avoid high pressure fluids that can penetrate skin and cause injury.
   a. Relieve pressure before disconnecting hydraulic or other lines.
   b. Tighten all connections before applying pressure.
   c. Keep hands and body away from pinholes and nozzles that eject fluids under high pressure.
   d. Use a piece of cardboard to search for leaks. Do not use your hand.
   e. If ANY fluid is injected into the skin, it must be surgically removed within a few hours by a doctor familiar with this type of injury, or gangrene may result.
7. Wear suitable hearing protective device such as earmuffs or earplugs to protect against loud noise.
8. Start engine only from operator's seat; avoid possible injury or death from machine runaway.

OPERATION SAFETY RULES
1. Use hand rails and steps to enter or leave the operator's station. Do not use the steering wheel.
2. Keep hand rails, steps, floor, and controls free of water, grease, and dirt.
3. Do not operate any equipment in unsafe condition. Put a tag on the steering wheel.
4. Before you start or operate the equipment:
   a. Check the condition of the equipment (see pre-start inspection, below)
   b. Be sure there is enough ventilation.
   c. Know the correct starting and stopping procedure.
   d. Sit in the operator's seat.
   e. Clear the work area of people and obstacles.
   f. Check service brakes and parking brake.
5. Be sure engine is running and foot brakes are operating before releasing parking brake.
6. Do not allow riders on the equipment.
7. Drive slowly in congested areas, over rough ground, and on slopes and curves.
8. Do not drive near the edge of ditch or excavation.
9. Keep loading areas smooth.
10. Check locations of utilities, cables, gas lines, water mains, etc. before digging.
11. Keep away from power lines at all costs. Do not touch power lines with any part of the equipment.
12. Carry buckets and loads as low as possible for better stability and visibility.
13. Keep equipment in gear when going down steep grades.

OPERATION SAFETY RULES (continued)
14. Before you dismount:
   a. Engage parking brake.
   b. Lower all equipment to the ground.
   c. Stop engine.
   d. Release hydraulic pressure: turn steering wheel back and forth, move hydraulic control levers until equipment does not move.
15. Use accessory lights and devices to warn operators of other vehicles.
16. Position backhoe booms on uphill side when driving across hillsides.
17. Set stabilizers before operating any backhoe equipment.
18. Use care when raising stabilizers; they may be the only restraint preventing the equipment from rolling into an excavation.
19. Don't dig under stabilizers.
20. Avoid swinging any backhoe bucket in the downhill direction. Always dump on uphill side, if possible.

PRE-START INSPECTION
Follow the checks below to inspect all equipment before you start it each day that it is used:
1. Vandalism. Check to see that:
   a. Smokestacks and exhaust pipes are clear of debris and obstructions.
   b. Fuel, water, gas, and oil filters have not been tampered with.
   c. Lights and glass are not broken or loosened.
   d. Gauges are not damaged.
   e. Wires have not been cut.
   f. The equipment looks in overall good condition.
2. Tires and Wheels
   a. Inspect for loose or missing bolts.
   b. Check tire pressure.
3. Operator's Station
   a. Be sure it's clean.
   b. Check pedals for freedom of movement.
4. Hydraulic System—check:
   a. Oil level.
   b. For leaks, kinked lines, and lines or hoses that rub against each other or other parts.
5. Engine Compartment—check:
   a. Engine oil level.
   b. Transmission oil level.
   c. Fuel filter for sediments.
   d. Air cleaner.
   e. Radiator coolant level and clean radiator.
6. Lubrication—check:
   a. Lubrication points shown in the respective equipment service manual.
7. Electrical system—check:
   a. For worn or frayed wires and loose connections.
8. Protective Devices—check:
   a. Guards, canopy, shields, seat belt.
9. Booms, buckets, structural components—check:
   a. For bent, broken or missing parts.

SERVICE SAFETY RULES
1. Put a support under all raised equipment.
2. Before beginning service:
   a. Review requirements for hard hat, safety shoes, safety glasses or goggles, gloves, reflective vest, ear protectors, or respirator.
   b. Be sure service is approved.

SERVICE SAFETY RULES (continued)
   c. Understand the procedure.
   d. Stop all equipment.
   e. Stop the engine (unless necessary for service).
3. Before welding or working on the engine or electrical system, disconnect battery ground wires.
4. Before working on hydraulic system:
   a. Release all pressure.
   b. Loosen fittings slowly.
5. Do not smoke:
   a. When you fill the fuel tank.
   b. When you work on the fuel system.
   c. When you handle fuels or lubricants.
6. Do not fill fuel tank when the engine is running.
7. Guard against eye injury when hammering connecting pins in or out.
8. Do not lubricate or work on equipment when it is in motion.
9. Avoid high pressure fluids:
   a. Relieve pressure before disconnecting hydraulic or other lines.
   b. Tighten all connections before applying pressure.
   c. Keep hands and body away from pinholes and nozzles that eject fluids under high pressure.
   d. Use a piece of cardboard to search for leaks. Do not use your hand.
10. Only add coolant to radiator when engine is stopped or running at slow idle. Do not remove cap unless engine is cool. Release all pressure before removing cap, and loosen slowly.
11. Do not attempt to mount tires without the proper equipment and experience to perform the job safely. Failure to follow proper procedure can produce an explosion which may result in serious bodily injury.
12. Be sure all tire rim parts are correctly assembled and interlocking before inflating tires. Use an inflation cage, safety cables, or some such protective device during inflation.

FIRE PREVENTION MAINTENANCE
1. Daily Pre-Start Maintenance
   a. Check fire extinguisher for correct charge.
   b. Open all access hoods and shields. Remove all trash from all areas inside these compartments from
      ■ Exhaust manifold, turbocharger, and muffler
      ■ Bottom guards and under engine
      ■ Sides of engine
      ■ Radiator and oil cooler
      ■ Batteries
      ■ Hydraulic lines
      ■ Fuel tank
   c. Check for leaking fuel lines, hydraulic lines, or fittings. Tighten loose fittings. Replace bent or kinked lines.
   d. Clean trash from grilles.
   e. Clean trash from cab areas.
   f. Be sure all doors and grilles are in place.
2. Shut-Down
   a. Temperature in engine compartment may go up immediately after stopping the engine. Be on guard for fires, especially when refueling.
   b. Wait until the engine has cooled before filling the fuel tank.
   c. Do not smoke while refueling.

*Most source information by Deere and Company, Moline, IL.

NOTIFICATION CHECKLIST PRIOR TO PROPOSED EXCAVATION

OPERATOR	PHONE	PERSON'S NAME	TIME NOTIFIED	NOTIFIED
Gas–Local				
Gas–Transmission				
Electric				
Telephone–Local				
Telephone–L.D.				
State Maintenance				
County Maint.				
Local Water Dept.				
Local Sewer Dept.				
Local Highway D.				
Local Police Dept.				
Local Fire Dept.				

IF ONE CALL SYSTEM IN EFFECT, CALL: _____

INFORMATION TO BE TRANSMITTED TO ABOVE OPERATORS

Company Name _____   Co. Field Rep. _____

Co. Address _____   Co. Field Add. _____

Co. Telephone _____   Co. Field Phone _____

Project Owner _____   Contract No. _____

Plans Available at _____

Location of Work: County _____   Street _____

City _____   State _____

Purpose of Excavation _____

Method of Excavation _____

Dates Work is to be done _____

Special Requirements/Notes _____

CHECK LIST PREPARED BY: _____

CONSTRUCTION CLAIMS CHECKLIST

People necessary for information and/or testimony:

Key project people: _____
_____

Subcontractors involved: _____
_____
_____
_____

Project executive: _____

Project engineer: _____

Project superintendent: _____

Scheduler: _____

Architect: _____

Engineers: _____
_____
_____

Experts/consultants: _____
_____

Lawyers: _____

Accountants: _____

Other: _____
_____

Key documents (originals)

Plans, specifications, addenda . . . . _____

Related files . . . . _____

Notice date establishment . . . . _____

Pass-through reference . . . . _____

Change clause . . . . _____

Dispute clause . . . . _____

Arbitration clause (agreement to arbitrate) . . . . . . _____

Other: _____ _____
_____ _____
_____ _____

Project records

Contract/subcontract/P.O. . . . . _____

Files: _____ _____

Subfiles: _____ _____

Change order files: _____ _____

Change order summary log . . . . _____

Daily field reports . . . . . From: _____ To: _____

Schedule: Baseline (target) . . . . _____

Updates . . . . _____

Projections/analysis . . . . _____

Narratives . . . . _____

Job cost records . . . . _____

Shop drawings and transmittals . . . . _____

Shop drawing log . . . . _____

Other: _____ _____
_____ _____
_____ _____
_____ _____

CHANGE ORDER GENERAL CONDITIONS CHECKLIST AND ESTIMATE SHEET

Project _____ # _____ Change Estimate No. _____

Owner Bulletin No. _____

	Material	Labor	Total
1. Supervision			
a. Project manager			
b. Superintendent(s)			
c. Project and office engineer(s)			
d. Field engineer(s)			
e. Additional foremen			
f. Accountant/time keeping/material check			
g. Home office supervision			
h. _____			
2. Temporary Facilities			
a. Field office(s)			
b. Material trailers/sheds			
c. Temporary toilets			
d. Temporary roads			
e. Safety protection/equipment			
f. _____			
3. Field Support			
a. Office/first-aid supplies			
b. Blueprinting/copying/photos			
c. Telephone			
d. Fire/theft alarm			
e. Insurances			
f. Home office expense			
g. _____			
4. Temporary Utilities			
a. Heat			
b. Light and power			
c. Water			
d. Elevators/lifting/moving			
e. Tests/inspections			
f. _____			
5. Construction Equipment			
a. Small tools (expendables)			
b. Trash removal/light trucking			
c. _____			
6. Special Conditions			
a. Winter conditions			
b. Snow removal			
c. Cutting and patching			
d. Final cleanup			
e. _____			

Total change order general conditions $_____

PROJECT SAFETY MEETING OUTLINE

Project Safety responsibilities include:

a. Ensuring that all operations are performed safely.
b. Preparing reports outlining violations observed.
c. Conducting "Tailgate" Safety Meetings.
d. Administering First Aid.
e. Maintaining appropriate and adequate First Aid materials.
f. Being sure that Safety Rules are posted in a prominent place.
g. Making sure that the Safety Rules are observed.

Safety starts with each individual using common sense to perform his task, realizing that common sense is an integral part of any construction activity.

A meeting called specifically to present safety policies and procedures should be arranged early, during the project start-up period. The suggested outlines and topics listed below are not intended to be comprehensive. Other topics are encouraged, and may provide a counterpoint that may ease communication gaps, and motivate all meeting participants to think SAFETY.

SAFETY MEETING OUTLINE

1. Emergency care and procedures to follow to obtain aid.
   a. Treatment
      — Control/Restore breathing.
      — Aid a choking victim.
      — Aid a burned victim.
      — Aid a poisoned victim.
      — Aid a shocked victim.
      — Aid a victim with a broken bone.
   b. Who is qualified to administer First Aid?
   c. Posted emergency numbers to call.
2. Fire Regulations at the work site.
   a. Smoking/Non-Smoking areas.
   b. Location and use of fire fighting equipment.
   c. Periodic check of extinguisher "charges".
   d. Storage and use of combustible materials.
3. On-Site Accidents (see "Treatment", above)
   a. Cave-ins.
   b. Falls—Causes and prevention.
   c. Are accidents caused?
   d. Jewelry—Rings, chains, etc.
4. Off-Site Accidents.
5. How to manually lift loads safely.
6. Chains and Slings—Care and proper use.
7. Personnel safety rules and equipment.
   a. Hard hat.
   b. Safety shoes.
   c. Safety glasses.
   d. Gloves.
   e. Proper use of safety belts and nets.
8. Safety equipment policy.
   a. The first item listed in (7) above is given to each employee and goes on his personal record. If lost, it is immediately replaced, and the cost of the replacement is deducted from his pay.
9. Safety Rules for Power Tools.
10. Erecting and Working on Scaffolding.
11. Ladders—Types and Uses.
12. Piling and Storing Materials.
13. Welding Operations.
    a. Proper cylinder storage.
    b. Safety procedures.
    c. Types of eye and face protectors.
    d. Fireproof clothing.
14. Good Housekeeping.
    a. The date, time, persons attending, and any significant proceedings are to be headed and noted as such on the DAILY FIELD REPORT.
    b. If periodic meeting minutes are normally being taken and distributed by _____ Company for the particular project, minutes of the Safety Meeting should also be included (see PROJECT MEETINGS).
    c. "Tailgate" Safety Meetings.
       — At an early, convenient moment, the designated Safety Officer is to advise any and all new workers of the policies and procedures outlined above. It is the Safety Officer's continuing responsibility to be sure that all new employees are so informed.
       — The date, time, people involved, and any significant proceedings of the "Safety Meeting" are to be noted on the DAILY FIELD REPORT.
    d. Field Accident Report (see SAMPLE attached).
       — Is to be completed by the designated Safety Officer.
       — Records the information necessary to report an accident to the Central Office, and to the insurance carrier.
       — ALL accidents (personal injury/vehicles) are to be reported—no matter how insignificant.
       — The "Action Taken" Section of the Report refers to:
         • How the accident was handled
         • What steps were taken to ensure that the accident will not happen again
       — If photographs can be taken at the time of an accident, do so. They may refute later claims that arise.
    e. The Employer's First Report of Injury (see SAMPLE attached).
       — This form is completed at the Central Office with the information given on the Field Accident Report. It is then forwarded to the appropriate insurance carrier by the Administrative assistant, for final processing.
    f. FOR EMERGENCY SERVICE, CONTACT:

NAME (Doctor) _____ PHONE _____

ADDRESS _____

NAME (Hospital Emergency Room) _____

ADDRESS _____ PHONE _____

NAME (Hospital Emergency Room) _____

ADDRESS _____ PHONE _____

HOW TO USE THE FORMS IN THIS SECTION

The reproducible forms included here are designed for your ready use. Each form's effectiveness is proven. Even so, before you have them reproduced, review them carefully. Determine if there may be some small modification that may make a form even more meaningful, given the way you conduct your own business.

TELEPHONE QUOTATION FORM

Use the Telephone Quotation Form to expedite subcontractor and supplier proposals to you for both contract bid items and for change orders. The form will prompt you to get the facts on every real and potentially critical issue involving price, time, and coordination that will or may have an effect on the total scope of work. Using the checklist format guarantees that every important item will be given direct consideration in every pricing situation, thereby eliminating possible oversight.

SUBCONTRACTOR/SUPPLIER REFERENCE FORM

The subcontractor/supplier reference form is to be sent to each company on or about the date of the respective subcontract or purchase order. It is to be completed and returned immediately, in order to have all information on file that will speed all communications.

FIELD ACCIDENT REPORT

The Field Accident Report is a sample of a form intended to be completed by the jobsite Safety Officer immediately upon the discovery of an injury—after immediate care has been administered. The superintendent or other responsible person can complete the form if that person is the designated Safety Officer. Check with your insurance company to see if they can suggest improvement in the form, or if they have a form of their own.

DAILY FIELD REPORT (Long and Short Forms)

The categories on the Daily Field Report form are for the most part self-explanatory. The most important idea is to understand that "daily" means *daily*. The field staff must complete the report on jobsite activities each day to ensure that the information is as accurate (and believable) as it can be. Have the form printed on two-part NCR paper to make it easy to send a copy *each day* to the home office. Make this a policy requirement and enforce it. The information can be used to check the validity to subcontractor, architect, or owner claims. It can help you to quickly reconstruct history and evaluate production. It will strongly support your own change order proposals, evaluations of job impacts, and claims—but only if the information is kept complete, accurate, and in usable form. Keep notations on the form brief but precise. Make summary descriptions that positively identify constructors (use names) and locations (column line designations, elevation references, and so forth). Take the time as the work progresses, and it will pay large dividends later. The short form is included as an option. It maximizes efficient use of paper, but it becomes more important to be sure that all relevant pieces of information are included each day.

FIELD PAYROLL REPORT FORM

The Field Payroll Report Form can be used for manual time reporting systems, but is designed to accomodate computer reporting by activity as well. Appropriate areas on the form are completed each day by the on-site field superintendent. Each worker's day is reported by major activities performed. There is no need for a work description beyond type of work performed, because the Daily Field Report includes these details. Of concern here are acitivities that will be compared against those budgeted. Combined with the Daily Field Report, the result is a total recording system that provides critical information required for timely management action. Alternate forms for employees with single or multi-project responsibilities are included.

JOB MEETING MINUTES FORM

Fill out all information as indicated at the top of page one of the form. Keep notes in outline form, if possible. Use the identical heading for the same issue if it continues through multiple meetings. Include file cross references in the issue heading to simplify research. *Never* leave any issue at a meeting without definitely assigning and agreeing on responsibility for the next step, and the date by which action is required. Before proceeding with a new meeting, confirm acceptance by all of the minutes of the previous meeting. Indicate this acceptance in the *first* item of the new meeting minutes. Finally, be sure the minutes are written and distributed promptly.

CHANGE ORDER SUMMARY LOG

Use the Change Order Summary Log to keep track easily of an otherwise complicated process—maintaining control over contract modifications. Establish a change order file for each issue that has the *potential* to become a contract change. Include those dates and references that will establish origins of actions and information. This will be the key to calculating the effect on a job resulting from a delay in a change order resolution. Insert the dates and amounts of each change order proposal. Include approved amounts, key remarks, and cross references. Reviewing the summary information at any point will reveal unsubmitted or unprocessed proposals, or trends such as unacceptable approval times, unfortunate price "negotiations," or other effects adversely affecting the job that might otherwise go undetected.

SHOP DRAWING SUBMITTAL SUMMARY RECORD FORM

Use a separate form for each subcontractor and supplier or for each specification section, whichever makes the most sense, given the way you structure your job files. Immediately after the subcontract or purchase order has been prepared, review the appropriate specification sections and itemize each required submittal on the left side of the form. As each submittal is received, processed, and transmitted to the party next in the approval chain, record the date and action information in the appropriate box. Doing this at the same time that the transmittal is being prepared will ensure the most accurate and timely information possible.

The log is most useful in policing the submission and approval of all items required by the contract, and evaluating performance relative to that required by the construction schedule.

BAR CHART

Bar charts are fundamental to planning and executing production for contractors and construction managers of every size, because of their speed, ease of use, low cost, and visibility. Place the total job duration across the top of the form by listing the appropriate time periods (months, weeks, days). List the major project activities along the left side. Indicate their corresponding dollar amounts and the percentage of the total job that each represents. Display each activity's relationship to time with a line drawn through the appropriate time slot under the periods noted across the top. Continuing this process for each activity will complete the schedule for the job.

To create a job cost projection (S-Curve), begin by prorating the cost of each activity across its respective duration (the activity bars drawn through the time periods). Total all costs falling within each payment period, and list the sums across the bottom of the form. Using the % scale or $ scale on the right, plot the *cumulative* percentages or dollar amounts on the form. Connecting the cumulative plots will most often result in an "S" shaped curve. This will become an important cost projection against which to compare actual data that become available as the work progresses.

TELEPHONE QUOTATION FORM

Date: _____ 19 _____   Firm: _____

                                            _____

Project: _____   _____

   no.: _____   By: _____

Change no.: _____   Phone: (_____) _____

Documents Included:

Description	Date/Rev.	Description	Date/Rev.
_____	_____	_____	_____
_____	_____	_____	_____
_____	_____	_____	_____
_____	_____	_____	_____

_____ Price increase: $_____   Sales tax included? _____

_____ Price decrease: $_____   Bonds supplied? _____

_____ No change

Material/equipment delivery lead times after C.O. approval: _____

Time required to complete the work (separate the major items): _____

_____

Work of any other trade affected: _____

_____

Special conditions required to perform the work: _____

_____

Significant weather, site, or other constraints: _____

_____

Other applicable information: _____

_____

Alternates, qualifications, exclusions: _____

_____

Taken by: _____

SUBCONTRACTOR / SUPPLIER REFERENCE FORM

PROJECT_____ SECTION(S) _____

OWNER NO. _____ _____

(_____) NO. _____ _____

Please complete all applicable items below, and return this form to _____ Company in order to facilitate
correspondence between our offices. Should you desire similar information from our company, please do not hesitate to ask.

Your correct mailing address is: NAME _____

STREET_____ CITY_____ STATE _____ ZIP_____

Your Order No. _____ ____ Subcontractor   ____ Supplier (Check one)

Office correspondent responsible for PROJECT COORDINATION

Name _____

Title _____

Phone: Business _(_____)_____

Home _(_____)_____

Correspondent responsible for Shop Dwg submission: DRAFTSMAN

Name _____

Phone: Business _(_____)_____

Home _(_____)_____

FIELD SUPERINTENDENT

Name _____

Phone: Business _(_____)_____

Home _(_____)_____

PRESIDENT_____

VICE PRES. _____

VICE PRES. _____

SALES MANAGER

Name _____

Phone: Business _(_____)_____

Home _(_____)_____

PRODUCTION MANAGER

Name _____

Phone: Business _(_____)_____

Home _(_____)_____

CREDIT MANAGER

Name _____

Phone: Business _(_____)_____

Home _(_____)_____

Correspondent responsible for REQUISITION SUBMISSIONS

Name _____

Phone: Business _(_____)_____

Home _(_____)_____

YOUR subcontractors, and YOUR material and equipment suppliers are:

ITEM _____

CO. Name _____

Street _____

City _____ State_____ Zip_____

Phone _(_____)_____

ITEM _____

CO. Name _____

Street _____

City _____ State_____ Zip_____

Phone _(_____)_____

ITEM _____

CO. Name _____

Street _____

City _____ State_____ Zip_____

Phone _(_____)_____

ITEM _____

CO. Name _____

Street _____

City _____ State_____ Zip_____

Phone _(_____)_____

FIELD ACCIDENT REPORT

This Report is to be filled out by the designated Safety Officer after EVERY accident, and forwarded to the Central Office for processing.

PROJECT NAME _____ PROJ. NUMBER _____

Date of Accident _____ Reported by _____

Type of Accident (Check One):

( ) Vehicular   ( ) Personal   ( ) Other

Name of Injured _____ Date of Birth or Age _____

How Long Employed _____

Names of Witnesses _____

_____

Did the Injured Lose any Time? _____ How Much (Days/Hours)? _____

Was Safety Equipment in use at the time of the Accident (Hard Hat, Safety Glasses, Gloves, Safety Shoes, etc.)? _____

_____

(If not, it is the EMPLOYEE'S sole responsibility to process his/her claim through his/her Health and Welfare Fund.)

DESCRIPTION OF THE ACCIDENT _____

_____

_____

_____

ACTION TAKEN _____

_____

_____

INDICATE STREET NAMES, DESCRIPTION OF VEHICLES, AND NORTH ARROW

Company Driver/Operator _____

Insurance Carrier_____

Driver Name _____

Address _____

_____

Operator License No. _____

Vehicle License No. _____

Owner Name _____

Other Driver/Operator _____

Insurance Carrier_____

Driver Name _____

Address _____

_____

Operator License No. _____

Vehicle License No. _____

Owner Name _____

DAILY FIELD REPORT

Project:_____No:_____ Date:_____
Location:_____ Weather:_____
Superintendent:_____ Temp: 8AM_____1PM_____4PM_____

Staff

Name	Classification	Name	Classification
_____	_____	_____	_____
_____	_____	_____	_____
_____	_____	_____	_____
_____	_____	_____	_____

EQUIPMENT

Quant	Type/Size	Work/Idle	Work performed	Arrival	Departure
____	_____	___/___	_____	____	____
____	_____	___/___	_____	____	____
____	_____	___/___	_____	____	____
____	_____	___/___	_____	____	____
____	_____	___/___	_____	____	____
____	_____	___/___	_____	____	____
____	_____	___/___	_____	____	____
____	_____	___/___	_____	____	____
____	_____	___/___	_____	____	____
____	_____	___/___	_____	____	____

VISITORS / CONVERSATIONS / MEETINGS

REQUIRED MATERIALS / INFORMATION

Item	Requested form	Company	Promised by
_____	_____	_____	_____
_____	_____	_____	_____
_____	_____	_____	_____
_____	_____	_____	_____
_____	_____	_____	_____

_____   _____
Project   Manager   (Signature)   Superintendent   (Signature)

FIELD WORK REPORT

Quant	Classification	Sub	Description and Location of Work	CO #
	TOTAL			

DAILY FIELD REPORT
(Short Form)

Project:_____ No:_____   Date:_____   Page____of____
Location:_____   Weather:_____
Superintendent:_____   Temp: 8AM_____1 PM_____4 PM_____

Quant	Classification	Sub	Description and Location of Work	CO #
	TOTAL			

FIELD PAYROLL REPORT FORM
(For Employees with *Single Project* Responsibility)

Project: _____ No. _____ Week Ending: ____ / ____ / ____

EMPLOYEE	SUN		MON		TUE		WED		THUR		FRI		SAT		TOTAL HOURS
	Act. No.	Hrs	Act. No.	Hrs	Act. No.	Hrs	Act. No.	Hrs	Act. No.	Hrs	Act. No.	Hrs	Act. No.	Hrs	
No. _____ Name: _____															
Total															
No. _____ Name: _____															
Total															
No. _____ Name: _____															
Total															
No. _____ Name: _____															
Total															
No. _____ Name: _____															
Total															

FIELD PAYROLL REPORT FORM
(For Employees with *Multi-Project* Responsibilities)

Employee: _____ No. _____ Week Ending: ___/___/___

PROJECT	SUN Act. No.	SUN Hrs	MON Act. No.	MON Hrs	TUE Act. No.	TUE Hrs	WED Act. No.	WED Hrs	THUR Act. No.	THUR Hrs	FRI Act. No.	FRI Hrs	SAT Act. No.	SAT Hrs	TOTAL HOURS
No. _____ Name: _____															
	Total		Total		Total		Total		Total		Total		Total		
No. _____ Name: _____															
	Total		Total		Total		Total		Total		Total		Total		
No. _____ Name: _____															
	Total		Total		Total		Total		Total		Total		Total		
No. _____ Name: _____															
	Total		Total		Total		Total		Total		Total		Total		
No. _____ Name: _____															
	Total		Total		Total		Total		Total		Total		Total		

JOB MEETING MINUTES

Job Meeting No. _____   Page 1 of __
Date: **Project No.:**
Location:

PRESENT		DISTRIBUTION	
Name	**Company**	**Name**	**Company**
		Attendees,	

NOTICE to attendees and minutes recipients:

    If any of the following items are incomplete or incorrect in any way, please notify the writer. Failure to advise of such corrections by or before the next job meeting constitutes acceptance of all information contained therein as it is represented.

SUBJECT	ACTION REQUIRED	
	By	**Date**
A. <u>OLD BUSINESS</u>		

JOB MEETING MINUTES

Job Meeting No. _____

Date:

Location:

Project No.:

SUBJECT	ACTION REQUIRED	
	By	Date

CHANGE ORDER SUMMARY LOG

Rac <	> C.O.	Description	Date Discovered	Date Design Finalized	Date Proposal Requested	1st Proposal Submission		2nd Proposal Submission		Approved		Projected Impact/ Remarks
						Date	Amount	Date	Amount	Date	Amount	

SAMPLE SUBMITTAL SUMMARY RECORD FORM

Project _____ Sub. _____ Sect _____

Owner No. _____ Phone _____

Co. No. _____ Persons _____

page _____ of _____

ACTION CODE:
- A   Approved
- AN   Approved As Noted
- ANR   App. As Ntd; Rev. & Resub.
- NA   Not Approved
- FU   For Your Use

Description	Company	Sub Dwg. No.	Dwg. No.	First Submission	Returned From Arch.	Action	Second Submission	Returned From Arch.	Action	File Copy	Job Copy	Copy	Copy	Copy	Copy	Copies

JOB SCHEDULE (BAR CHART)

PROJECT _____ NO. _____

REVISION NUMBER _____
PREPARED BY: _____

ACTIVITY	NO.	VALUE	% OF TOTAL

% 100 90 80 70 60 50 40 30 20 10 0

Estimated Amount

Estimated % Complete

Actual Amount

Actual % Complete

RHODE ISLAND BLUEPRINT N 501 91

TIME ZONES AND PHONE AREA CODES

ALASKA TIME	PACIFIC TIME	MOUNTAIN TIME	CENTRAL TIME	EASTERN TIME	ATLANTIC TIME
7:00 am	9:00 am	10:00 am	11:00 am	12:00 noon	1:00 pm

709 New Foundland

902 Prince Edward Island

506 New Brunswick

902 Nova Scotia
207 Maine
603 New Hampshire
802 Vermont
413 Mass.
617
401 Rhode Island
203 Conn.
516
914
718

212 New York
201 New Jersey
609
302 Delaware
301 Maryland
202 Wash. D.C.

809 Puerto Rico,
Virgin Islands,
Bermuda and
other islands of
the Caribbean

Quebec
418
514
819

Ontario
807

705

906

514
613
416
315
613
613
519
517
313

518
New York
716 607
716
Penn. 717
814
412
216 Ohio
419 513 614 W. Va.
812 606
502 Kentucky
901

804
Virginia
304
703
919
North
Carolina
803 704
South
Carolina
912
Georgia
404
Alabama
205
Tenn.
615
Miss.
601

Florida
813 305

Yukon &
N.W. Territory
403

British Columbia
604

206 509
Washington

Oregon
503

Idaho
208

Nevada
702

916
707
415
408
209
California
818
213
805
714
619

Alberta
403

Montana
406

Wyoming
307

Utah
801
802

Arizona
602

Saskatchewan
306

N. Dakota
701

S. Dakota
605

Nebraska
308

Colorado
303

New Mexico
505

Manitoba
204

Minnesota
218

612

Iowa
515
507

712
Kansas
913
316
Oklahoma
405
806
817
Texas
915

913
402

Wisconsin
715
414
608
Illinois
815
309
217
314
618
Missouri
816
417
Arkansas
501
918
214
409
713
512

La.
318
504

Mexico
903

Alaska
907

HAWAII TIME
7:00 am

Hawaiian Islands
808

Ind.
219
317
812
Michigan

432

ROAD MILEAGE CHART BETWEEN U.S. CITIES

	Atlanta	Baltimore	Birmingham	Boston	Buffalo	Chicago	Cincinnati	Cleveland	Dallas	Denver	Des Moines	Detroit	Houston	Indianapolis	Kansas City, Mo.	Los Angeles	Memphis	Milwaukee	Minneapolis	Nashville	New Orleans	New York City	Philadelphia	Phoenix	Pittsburgh	St. Louis	Salt Lake City	San Francisco	Seattle	Washington, D.C.
Atlanta	—	669	152	1071	877	695	461	686	805	1401	894	726	814	508	810	2197	366	784	1105	256	493	855	766	1810	697	558	1900	2523	2756	630
Baltimore	669	—	787	399	345	687	494	351	1458	1701	1025	511	1449	580	1099	2695	947	776	1097	725	1138	187	97	2325	230	817	2118	2876	2748	39
Birmingham	152	787	—	1185	902	636	476	716	653	1282	808	741	662	480	706	2056	247	745	1066	205	351	974	884	1658	742	476	1781	2393	2575	748
Boston	1071	399	1185	—	449	975	876	632	1819	1989	1311	699	1916	941	1456	3052	1355	1064	1385	1165	1536	216	304	2682	598	1178	2405	3163	3036	437
Buffalo	877	345	902	449	—	536	435	186	1387	1404	878	252	1529	515	1003	2535	902	586	917	728	1341	372	365	2190	217	724	1920	2734	2580	386
Chicago	695	687	636	975	536	—	295	343	936	1016	338	275	1085	187	499	2095	544	91	412	451	929	843	762	1722	461	291	1431	2189	2063	695
Cincinnati	461	494	476	876	435	295	—	244	943	1169	571	265	1040	108	590	2186	479	384	705	290	820	659	578	1816	284	338	1644	2402	2356	492
Cleveland	686	351	716	632	186	343	244	—	1187	1357	679	167	1284	309	824	2420	723	432	753	533	1063	507	426	2050	125	546	1772	2530	2404	351
Dallas	805	1458	653	1819	1387	936	943	1187	—	784	704	1188	242	882	499	1403	464	1015	956	686	498	1607	1526	1005	1232	645	1241	1806	2112	1372
Denver	1401	1701	1282	1989	1404	1016	1169	1357	784	—	679	1284	1026	1061	604	1134	1035	1040	841	1158	1282	1851	1770	818	1482	856	512	1270	1347	1696
Detroit	726	511	741	699	252	275	265	167	1188	1284	606	—	1337	277	821	2347	713	370	685	555	1085	667	586	1977	285	543	1700	2458	2336	511
Houston	814	1449	662	1916	1529	1085	1040	1284	242	1026	946	1337	—	997	737	1553	561	1174	1198	783	359	1636	1546	1155	1319	794	1431	1955	2302	1410
Indianapolis	508	580	480	941	515	187	108	309	882	1061	483	277	997	—	484	2080	436	276	597	294	805	729	648	1983	354	237	1536	2294	2245	564
Jacksonville	314	793	426	1191	1067	1009	775	952	994	1708	1208	996	911	822	1123	2397	673	1098	1419	570	572	980	890	1999	865	872	2207	2799	3070	754
Los Angeles	2197	2695	2056	3052	2535	2095	2186	2420	1403	1134	1801	2347	1553	2080	1596	—	1831	2176	1940	2017	1901	2915	2721	398	2533	1848	734	403	1145	2644
Memphis	366	947	247	1355	902	544	479	723	464	1035	664	713	561	436	451	1831	—	624	840	222	401	1100	1057	1466	758	294	1534	2157	2331	908
Mexico City	1800	2435	1648	3052	2451	2071	2026	2270	1309	1754	1852	2337	986	1983	1647	1831	1547	2164	2104	1769	1345	2622	2532	1648	2533	1848	2086	2557	2948	2396
Miami	665	1144	765	1542	1418	1360	1126	1303	1309	2046	1559	1347	1216	1173	1470	2712	1011	1449	1770	921	875	1330	1241	2314	1216	1223	2545	3075	3421	1105
Minneapolis	1105	1097	1066	1385	917	412	705	753	956	841	252	685	1198	597	437	1940	840	326	—	861	1241	1253	1172	1630	871	546	1239	1997	1641	1097
Nashville	256	725	205	1165	728	451	290	533	686	1158	758	555	783	294	530	2017	222	540	861	—	530	949	868	1725	559	302	1670	2410	2512	686
New Orleans	493	1138	351	1536	1341	929	820	1063	498	1282	989	1085	359	805	821	1901	401	1013	1241	530	—	1325	1235	1503	1093	695	1739	2303	2610	1099
New York City	855	187	974	216	372	843	659	507	1607	1851	1173	667	1636	729	1198	2915	1100	900	1253	949	1325	—	92	2459	386	966	2267	3025	2904	225
Omaha	1012	1163	911	1449	1003	476	691	817	656	540	139	744	898	583	205	1662	664	500	358	756	1026	1312	1230	1335	942	454	955	1713	1667	1156
Philadelphia	766	97	884	304	365	762	578	426	1526	1770	1092	586	1546	648	1150	2721	1057	851	1172	868	1235	92	—	2464	305	885	2186	2944	2823	136
Phoenix	1810	2325	1658	2682	2190	1722	1816	2050	1005	818	1430	1977	1155	1983	1213	398	1466	1757	1630	1725	1503	2459	2464	—	2163	1478	653	800	1541	2274
Pittsburgh	697	230	742	598	217	461	284	125	1232	1482	804	285	1319	354	821	2533	758	540	871	559	1093	386	305	2163	—	591	1890	2648	2522	230
St. Louis	558	817	476	1178	724	291	338	546	645	856	336	543	794	237	256	1848	294	365	546	302	695	966	885	1478	591	—	1368	2126	2109	801
Salt Lake City	1900	2118	1781	2405	1920	1431	1644	1772	1241	512	1094	1700	1431	1536	1116	734	1534	1430	1239	1670	1739	2267	2186	653	1890	1368	—	759	871	2111
San Francisco	2523	2876	2393	3163	2734	2189	2402	2530	1806	1270	1852	2458	1955	2294	1874	403	2157	2177	1997	2410	2303	3025	2944	800	2648	2126	759	—	827	2869
Seattle	2756	2748	2575	3036	2580	2063	2356	2404	2112	1347	1773	2336	2302	2245	1872	1145	2331	2010	1641	2512	2610	2904	2823	1541	2522	2109	871	827	—	2748
Washington, D.C.	630	39	748	437	386	695	492	351	1372	1696	1018	511	1410	564	1048	2644	908	776	1097	686	1099	225	136	2274	230	801	2111	2869	2748	—

WEATHER INFORMATION NUMBERS

Alabama
Birmingham 205-322-9222
Montgomery 205-269-0555

Alaska
Anchorage 907-936-2525, 2526,
2527 or 2528

California
Fresno 209-442-1212
Los Angeles 213-554-1212
Oakland 415-936-1212
San Diego 714-289-1212
San Francisco 415-936-1212

District of Columbia
Washington 202-936-1212

Connecticut
All Cities 203-936-1212

Florida
Orlando 305-422-1611
West Palm Beach 305-675-1212
Winter Park 305-646-3131

Georgia
Albany 912-883-4610
Atlanta 404-871-1212
Rome 404-295-1212

Illinois
Bloomington 309-827-7111
Chicago 312-936-1212
El Paso 309-527-4554
Highland 618-654-8711
Hoopeston 217-283-2345
Jacksonville 217-243-0111
Joliet 815-722-3456
Quincy 217-223-7750
Toledo 217-849-2424

Indiana
Indianapolis 317-222-2362
Kokomo 317-457-9211
Princeton 812-385-4801

Iowa
Des Moines 515-244-4500

Kentucky
Lexington 606-293-1616
Louisville 502-482-1212
Owensboro 502-926-8121

Louisiana
Houma 504-868-6670
Minden 318-371-1776
La Rose 504-693-8463

Maryland
Baltimore 301-936-1212

Massachusetts
Boston 617-936-1212

Michigan
Detroit 313-932-1212
Muskegon 616-726-1212

Mississippi
Meridian 601-693-5311

Missouri
Columbia 314-442-5171
St. Louis 314-936-1212

Montana
Kalispell 406-755-2345

Nebraska
Lincoln 402-432-9211

New Jersey
Northern Cities 201-936-1212
Southern Cities 609-936-1212

New York
Buffalo 716-643-1234
Long Island 516-936-1212
New York 212-936-1212
Westchester 914-936-1212

North Carolina
Raleigh 919-829-1111

Ohio
Cleveland 216-931-1212
Columbus 614-231-5212
Toledo 219-931-1212

Pennsylvania
Philadelphia 215-936-1212
Pittsburgh 412-936-1212

South Carolina
Beaufort 803-524-3333
Columbia 803-355-1212

Tennessee
Athens 615-745-0250
Jackson 901-423-4600
Memphis 901-521-1500

Virginia
Hampton 804-936-1212
Norfolk 804-936-1212

Washington
Seattle 206-662-1111

Wisconsin
Milwaukee 414-936-1212
Rhinelander 715-369-1010

TOLL-FREE HOTEL NUMBERS

Several major hotel chains now have toll-free 800 phone numbers for easy access:

AMFAC 800-227-4700	HOWARD JOHNSON'S 800-654-2000	RAMADA 800-228-2828
BEST WESTERN 800-528-1234	HYATT 800-228-9000	REGENT 800-545-4000
EMBASSY (including GRANADA) 800-EMBASSY	INTER-CONTINENTAL 800-327-0200	RITZ-CARLTON 800-241-3333
FAIRMOUNT 800-527-4727	LOEWS 800-223-0888	SHERATON 800-325-3535
FOUR SEASONS 800-268-6282	MARRIOTT 800-228-9290	SONESTA 800-343-7170
GUEST QUARTERS 800-424-2900	MERIDIEN 800-223-9918	STOUFFER 800-325-5000
HILTON (Worldwide) 800-HILTONS	OMNI (including DUNFEY) 800-228-2121	TRUSTHOUSE FORTE 800-223-5672
HOLIDAY (including CROWNE PLAZAS) 800-HOLIDAY	PREFERRED 800-323-7500	WESTIN 800-228-3000
	RADISSON 800-228-9822	

If you need to make a last-minute deposit with a hotel to ensure your reservation, 5,000 hotels now accept CARDeposits. You simply charge to your American Express credit card.

TEMPORARY HELP AND PLACEMENT FIRMS

Adia Personnel Services
64 Willow Place
Menlo Park, CA 94025
415-324-0696

Kelly Services
P.O. Box 1179
Detroit, MI 48266
313-362-4444

Norrell Corporation
3092 Piedmont Road, N.E.
Atlanta, GA 30305
404-262-2100

Tops Temporarys
4155 E. Jewell
Suite 1018
Denver, CO 80222
303-758-8677

DIRECTORY OF CONSTRUCTION ASSOCIATIONS
Classified in accordance with the Uniform Construction Index

Division 1—General Requirements
American Arbitration Association
140 W. 51st St., New York, NY 10020

American Institute of Architects
1735 New York Ave., NW, Washington, DC 20006

American Society for Testing and Materials
1916 Race St., Philadelphia, PA 19103

Associated Builders and Constructors, Inc.
444 N. Capitol St., NW, Suite 409, Washington, DC 20001

Associated General Contractors of America
1957 E St., NW, Washington, DC 20006

Environmental Protection Agency
401 M St., SW, Washington, DC 20460

National Association of Home Builders of the United States
15th and M Streets, NW, Washington, DC 20005

Underwriters Laboratories, Inc.
333 Pfingsten Rd., Northbrook, IL 60062

Division 2—Site Work
American Society of Landscape Architects, Inc.
1900 M St., NW, Washington, DC 20036

Associated Landscape Contractors of America
1750 Old Meadow Rd., McLean, VA 22101

National Asphalt Pavement Association
6811 Kenilworth Ave., Suite 620, Riverdale, MD 20737

National Landscape Association, Inc.
230 Southern Bldg., Washington, DC 20005

Division 3—Concrete
American Concrete Institute
P.O. Box 19150, Detroit, MI 48219

American Society for Concrete Construction
World Concrete Center, 426 S. West Gate, Addison, IL 60101

National Association of Reinforcing Steel Contractors
Box 225, Fairfax, VA 22030

Prestressed Concrete Institute
201 North Wells St., Chicago, IL 60606

Division 4—Masonry
International Masonry Institute
823 15th St., NW, Suite 1001, Washington, DC 20005

Mason Contractors Association of America
17 West 601-14th Street, Oakbrook Terrace, IL 60181

Masonry Institute of America
2550 Beverly Blvd., Los Angeles, CA 90057

National Concrete Masonry Association
2302 Horse Pen Rd., Box 781, Herndon, VA 22070

Division 5—Metals
American Institute of Steel Construction, Inc.
400 N. Michigan Ave., Chicago, IL 60611

American Iron and Steel Institute
1000 16th Street NW, Washington, DC 20036

American Society for Metals
Metal Park, OH 44073

American Welding Society
P.O. Box 351040, Miami, FL 33135

Division 6—Wood and Plastics
American Wood Council
1619 Massachusetts Ave., NW, Washington, DC 20036

Architectural Woodwork Institute
2310 S. Walter Reed Drive, Arlington, VA 22206

National Forest Products Association
1619 Massachusetts Ave., NW, Washington, DC 20036

National Hardwood Lumber Association
332 S. Michigan Ave., Chicago, IL 60604

Division 7—Thermal and Moisture Protection
Asphalt Roofing Manufacturers Association
1800 Massachusetts Ave., NW, Suite 702, Washington, DC 20036

Building Waterproofer's Association
60 E. 42nd St., New York, NY 10017

National Roofing Contractors Association, Inc.
1515 N. Harlem Ave., Oak Park, IL 60302

Sealant & Waterproofers Institute
1800 Pickwick Ave., Glenview, IL 60025

Division 8—Doors and Windows
Acoustical Door Institute
9820 S. Dorchester Ave., Chicago, IL 60628

American Society of Architectural Hardware Consultants
77 Mark Drive, P.O. Box 3476, San Rafael, CA 94902

Builders Hardware Manufacturers' Association
60 E. 42nd St., New York, NY 10017

Door & Hardware Institute
1815 N. Ft. Myer Drive, Suite 412, Arlington, VA 22209

Division 9—Finishes
National Association of Decorative Architectural Finishes
112 N. Alfred St., Alexandria, VA 22314

National Paint and Coatings Association
1500 Rhode Island Ave., NW, Washington, DC 20005

Painting and Decorating Contractors of America
7223 Lee Highway, Falls Church, VA 22046

Tile Contractors Association of America
112 N. Alfred St., Alexandria, VA 22314

Division 10—Specialties
Instrument Society of America
67 Alexander Drive, Research Triangle Park, NC 27709

National Association of Glue Manufacturers, Inc.
663 Fifth Ave., New York, NY 10022

National Association of Mirror Manufacturers
5101 Wisconsin Ave., Suite 504, Washington, DC 20016

The Refractories Institute
3760 One Oliver Plaza, Pittsburgh, PA 15206

Division 11—Equipment
Gas Appliance Manufacturers Association, Inc.
1901 N. Fort Myer Drive, Arlington, VA 22209

National Kitchen Cabinet Association
136 St. Matthew Ave., Louisville, KY 40207

Division 12—Furnishings
American Canvas Institute
1918 N. Parkway, Memphis, TN 38112

Furniture Manufacturers Association
220 Lyons St., NW, Grand Rapids, MI 49502

Division 13—Special Construction
Association of Energy Engineers
4025 Pleasantdale Road, Suite 304, Atlanta, GA 30340

Manufactured Housing Institute
2000 K St., NW, Washington, DC 20006

Metal Building Manufacturers Association
1230 Keith Bldg., Cleveland, OH 44115

Solar Energy Industries Association
1001 Connecticut Ave., NW, Suite 800, Washington, DC 20036

Division 14—Conveying Systems
Material Handling Institute, Inc., The
1326 Freeport Rd., Pittsburgh, PA 15238

National Association of Elevator Contractors
2864 Peachtree Rd., NW, Suite 635, Atlanta, GA 30305

National Elevator Industry, Inc.
600 Third Ave., New York, NY 10016

Division 15—Mechanical
American Society of Heating, Refrigerating, and Air Conditioning Engineers, Inc. (ASHRAE)
1791 Tullie Circle, NE, Atlanta, GA 30324

American Society of Mechanical Engineers
345 E. 47th St., New York, NY 10017

Mechanical Contractors Association of America, Inc.
5530 Wisconsin Ave., NW, Suite 750, Washington, DC 20015

Plumbing-Heating-Cooling Information Bureau
35 E. Wacker Drive, Chicago, IL 60601

Sheet Metal and Air Conditioning National Association, Inc.
8224 Old Courthouse Rd., Tysons Corner, Vienna, VA 22180

Division 16—Electrical
Electronic Industries Association
2001 Eye St., NW, Washington, DC 20006

Institute of Electrical & Electronic Engineers, Inc.
345 East 47th St., New York, NY 10017

National Electrical Contractors Association
7315 Wisconsin Ave., Bethesda, MD 20814

National Electrical Manufacturers Association
2101 L St., NW, Washington, DC 20037

PERSONAL DIRECTORY

Name	Telephone	Name	Telephone

GENERAL BUSINESS DIRECTORY

Name	Telephone	Name	Telephone

PROJECT DIRECTORY

Project Name: _____   Project No.: _____

Name	Telephone	Name	Telephone

PROJECT DIRECTORY

Project Name: _____   **Project No.:** _____

Name	Telephone	Name	Telephone

PROJECT DIRECTORY

Project Name: _____   **Project No.:** _____

Name	Telephone	Name	Telephone